CREATING
THE REVOLUTIONARY ARTIST

CREATING
THE REVOLUTIONARY ARTIST

Entrepreneurship for the 21st-Century Musician

MARK RABIDEAU

Foreword by Tayloe Harding

ROWMAN & LITTLEFIELD
Lanham • Boulder • New York • London

Published by Rowman & Littlefield
An imprint of The Rowman & Littlefield Publishing Group, Inc.
4501 Forbes Boulevard, Suite 200, Lanham, Maryland 20706
www.rowman.com

Unit A, Whitacre Mews, 26-34 Stannary Street, London SE11 4AB

Copyright © 2018 by Mark Rabideau

All rights reserved. No part of this book may be reproduced in any form or by any electronic or mechanical means, including information storage and retrieval systems, without written permission from the publisher, except by a reviewer who may quote passages in a review.

British Library Cataloguing in Publication Information Available

Library of Congress Cataloging-in-Publication Data
Names: Rabideau, Mark, 1956–author.
Title: Creating the revolutionary artist : entrepreneurship for the 21st-century musician / Mark Rabideau ; foreword by Tayloe Harding.
Description: Lanham : Rowman & Littlefield, 2018. | Includes bibliographical references and index.
Identifiers: LCCN 2018007746 (print) | LCCN 2018008026 (ebook) | ISBN 9781538109939 (ebook) | ISBN 9781538109915 (cloth : alk. paper) | ISBN 9781538109922 (pbk. : alk. paper)
Subjects: LCSH: Music entrepreneurship.
Classification: LCC ML3795 (ebook) | LCC ML3795 .R3 2018 (print) | DDC 780.23—dc23
LC record available at https://lccn.loc.gov/2018007746

∞™ The paper used in this publication meets the minimum requirements of American National Standard for Information Sciences—Permanence of Paper for Printed Library Materials, ANSI/NISO Z39.48-1992.

Printed in the United States of America

This book is dedicated to my wife, Laura, for her unceasing love and support. The one person who always sees me. My happily-ever-after. And to my three beautifully talented children, Mary Pauline, Luke, and Aidan, who show me every day that our shared future is in good hands. I love you every day and always.

CONTENTS

Acknowledgments	ix
Foreword	xi
How to Use This Book	xiii
Background	xv

1	Being a 21st-Century Musician	1
2	Exploring Curiosity: Finding Opportunities to Make a Community Impact	17
3	Assessing Your Strengths: Tenacity and the Superpowers	31
4	Thinking about Creativity: Fueling the Imagination	43
5	Building a Team: Collaboration and Networking	57
6	Problem-Solving: Developing Solutions That Work for You	65
7	Diversity and Inclusivity: Abandoning Bias and Listening to Voices Unlike Our Own	73
8	The Business Side: Laying the Groundwork for a Successful Project	85
9	From Inspiration to Action: Your Project Takes Flight	101
10	Getting the Word Out: Storytelling, Marketing, and Communications Strategy	115
11	Finding the Funds: Donations, Grants, and Finance Management	133

Epilogue: From Single Project to Rewarding Career: Continuing the Revolution	147
Toolkit	
Goals and Objectives How-To	153
Organizational Chart How-To	155
Operating Budget How-To	157
Action Plan How-To	159

Event Planning How-To	161
Volunteer Recruitment How-To	163
Follow-up How-To	165
Income/Expense How-To	167
Evaluation How-To	169
Final Report How-To	171
Press Release How-To	173
Elevator Pitch How-To	176
Postcard/Flyer How-To	178
Data/Infographic How-To	180
Prezi How-To	182
Social Media Campaign How-To	184
Video Profile How-To	186
Website/Blog How-To	188
Sponsorship How-To	190
Fundraising Goal How-To	192
Environmental Scan How-To	194
Case for Support How-To	196
Crowdfunding How-To	198
Digital Appeal How-To	199
Direct Mail How-To	201
Peer-to-Peer Fundraising How-To	203
Individual Prospect Research How-To	205
Institutional Prospect Research How-To	207
Matching Gifts How-To	209
Grant Stewardship How-To	210
Grant Writing How-To	212
Return on Investment How-To	214
Thanking Donors How-To	216
Notes	219
Index	225
About the Author	235

ACKNOWLEDGMENTS

This course, based on the 21CM initiative at DePauw University, is part of a broader effort to transform the ways in which we prepare 21st-century musicians by cultivating the creative and imaginative powers that reside at the heart of the artist-entrepreneur. Leading a national dialogue about the future of music, 21CM was conceived of by Mark McCoy, then dean (now president) of the School of Music at DePauw; Judson Green, past president/CEO of NAVTEQ; and world-renowned cellist Yo-Yo Ma. Guided by a prestigious Board of Advisory, 21CM takes aim at reimagining the future of music, developing best practices in preparing emerging musicians, and exploring meaningful ways of engaging communities.

My name is Mark Rabideau, and I find the joy of my professional life in the efforts of fostering curiosity, creativity, and collaboration within a generation of artist-entrepreneurs. Or, as my friend Larry Livingston likes to say, "forming an army of ninja warriors" to leverage their creative energies in order to usher beauty into the world and strengthen the cultural fabric of their communities. To have the opportunity to partner in this effort, even if only as a Diaghilev alongside the beautifully creative company of Ballets Russes, has been a gift.

Creating the Revolutionary Artist: Entrepreneurship for the 21st-Century Musician is the collective inspiration of countless emerging musicians, the vision of valued collaborators, and a Sisyphean effort of a team of remarkable colleagues.

To relay this effort, I turn to a quote from a true artist-revolutionary, David Taylor, sharing the parallels between achievement in the practice room and in life: "You know the story of Sisyphus? He's condemned to an eternity of repeating the same meaningless and impossible task: to push a boulder to the top of a peak, only to see it roll down again. Every day I strive to perfect this instrument even though I know it is impossible. So why do I do it? Because in the unceasing task of striving for mastery, I have found meaning in embracing the joy of the struggle."

I would like to recognize my mentor, David Sporny, who showed me the importance of "embracing the joy of the struggle" when following my own passion for making music. Thank you for a lifetime of friendship and leadership.

This book will impact emerging musicians across the globe only because of the enduring trust and remarkable generosity of Joyce and Judson Green and the unstoppable leadership of Mark McCoy.

Gretchen McIntosh, as curriculum architect of this project, maps complexity in a way that is rare and beautiful. Thank you for succeeding in bringing this effort to fruition amid the impossible job of keeping me focused and on task.

Matthew Champagne produced the audio elements referenced within this text, a Herculean effort, vastly done in the confines and solitude of his studio, and one for which I cannot repay him beyond simply sharing my gratitude and a cold, hoppy beverage.

Thank you to my editor, Elizabeth Hinckley, whose expertise in editing words is exceeded only by her brilliance in expanding upon ideas. And Natalie Mandziuk and the team at Rowman & Littlefield for their guidance and professionalism.

And who could have imagined that ink on a page could come to life in such colorful and rich ways as this book (and the related articles shared on 21CM.org) has under the artistic direction of Jenn Logan and her team at Studio Fuse? Thank you. All introductory chapter imagery has been provided by Studio Fuse, Inc., and is used with permission.

Lastly, my sincere gratitude to each of the remarkable thinkers and doers who contributed their ideas, wisdom, and experience as shared through their writings:

- Alain Barker, Indiana University
- Astrid Baumgardner, Yale University
- Gary Beckman, North Carolina State University
- Mark Clague, University of Michigan
- David Cutler, author of *The Savvy Musician*
- James Doser, Eastman School
- Tayloe Harding, University of South Carolina
- Mary Javian, Curtis Institute
- Deanna Kennett, Ensemble Connect
- Jonathan Kuuskoski, University of Michigan
- Steven Linville, DePauw University
- Jeffrey Nytch, University of Colorado
- Laura Hlavacek Rabideau, human resources executive
- Mary Pauline Sheridan-Rabideau, Furman University
- Jenny Thompson, Dunch Arts
- Stanford L. Thompson, Play On, Philly!

FOREWORD
by Tayloe Harding

It has, gratefully, become widely accepted across the landscape of higher education that the preparation of tomorrow's professional in music must include exposure to and instruction in how one thinks more broadly about one's musical offerings to the world and to the center of one's own livelihood. As we hear often nowadays, "It's not just about being a good singer or player or composer or teacher anymore."

Though this relatively new acceptance comprises many different insights and representations—from audience-building skills to ideas for new community engagements that benefit whole populations and for opportunities to demonstrate leadership that will help musical agencies impact more and more deeply—it is also coming to be understood in our college music schools that creative action is at the heart of this broader approach to education. Into this emerging and evolving context steps expert Mark Rabideau with this new course material.

Mark's *Creating the Revolutionary Artist: Entrepreneurship for the 21st-Century Musician* is a distinctive and powerful new effort to realize, in both practical and ideal ways, a methodology to help professional music students imagine and behave more entrepreneurially in their musical lives. Through solid logic, informed intuition, and examples of numerous experienced professionals themselves, this book creates roads for music students and emerging professionals to create sustainable careers. The book also advances in unique instructional ways how such approaches benefit the wider community, a goal we all strive to achieve in the experiences we create.

Creating the Revolutionary Artist manifests important and unique ways of approaching creative behavior. As a result, we are not only delighted to include this book in our music entrepreneurship coursework at the University of South Carolina School of Music but also eager to watch how this approach revolutionizes how we deliver an experience with entrepreneurship to music students and faculty, on our campus and beyond.

I am honored to offer the foreword to this wonderful work, and I look forward not only to the book holding a special place in my personal library but also to it helping students and emerging musicians change their futures and the world around them through music as a result. This is a special book, written by this special educator, Mark Rabideau.

Tayloe Harding
Dean, School of Music
University of South Carolina
Columbia, South Carolina

HOW TO USE THIS BOOK

Creating the Revolutionary Artist: Entrepreneurship for the 21st-Century Musician is a self-directed course of study that explores the mindsets of the artist-entrepreneur and develops the skill sets to move your ideas into action. The goal of the book is to open the reader's imagination about what is possible within a 21st-century music career and how engaging communities in meaningful projects can help build sustainable careers and lifelong partnerships.

Here is what you should expect from the book:

- Chapters that challenge you to think differently about your own entrepreneurial spirit
- Leadership advice from some of the most influential thinkers within the field of music entrepreneurship
- Activities to develop creative problem-solving strategies
- A Toolkit of how-to worksheets and examples
- Case studies of revolutionary artists in today's world
- Related articles and interviews found on 21CM.org, a resource for 21st-century musicians

BACKGROUND

Driven by the shared belief that education is a lifelong process of learning how to make the world a better place, *Creating the Revolutionary Artist* has unfolded out of a sense of urgency to equip the next generation of arts leaders to build a more promising future; a conviction that the arts must play a central role in a society that is more hopeful and open; a dedication to help prepare emerging musicians to thrive within the profession; a deep belief that experiential learning is of particular value, especially when student opportunities to succeed are prized and when student opportunities to fail are present; and a commitment to the notion that career success is defined in three parts: a life of means (the ability to care for those you love most), a life of meaning (to do good work that creates lasting impact), and the chance to give back, with special attention to those at the margins.

This model embraces the civic-mindedness of community engagement, the high intellectual and performance standards of the academic community, and the open-ended creative energy of the entrepreneur and artist.

Creating the Revolutionary Artist is a response to a contemporary paradox: Music is embraced throughout every culture without boundaries. An increasingly connected world offers influence and inspiration for opening our imaginations, as technology provides unprecedented access to global audiences. Communities gather around music to mourn collective hardships and celebrate shared moments, and every parent understands that music enhances their child's chances to succeed in life. Yet it has never been more of a struggle for musicians to make a living at their art—at least when following traditional paths.

Although traditional career paths for professional musicians have become more and more difficult, 21st-century musicians leverage their creative energies toward forging new paths, engaging broader audiences, and collaborating across cultural boundaries. Beyond simply being talented, 21st-century musicians must become more adaptable, creative, and entrepreneurial.

VISION AND MISSION

Our shared vision and mission will serve as our uniting compass, pointing us toward that which we aspire to and do.

Judson Green, one of the key founders of the 21CM initiative at DePauw University, sent me these definitions by e-mail: "A vision statement is a statement of aspiration (or inspiration); it's something that the organization always strives for but it's just out of reach. A mission statement is a statement of what the organization does (without amplification of any kind). A vision is about 'to be,' and mission is about 'to do.'"

Our vision: Revolutionizing the ways people engage through music, we envision a world connected, enriched, and transformed by musical experiences.

Our mission: *Creating the Revolutionary Artist* unleashes the creative energies of the 21st-century musician toward making the world a better place when forging new paths, engaging broader audiences, collaborating across cultural boundaries, and playing in the messy, fertile space of the artist-entrepreneur.

THE 21CM DIFFERENCE

What is different about our approach when comparing it to other arts entrepreneurship models?

- We recognize and harness that which resides at the intersection of the artist and entrepreneur—curiosity, creativity, collaboration, and tenacity.
- The work is truly interdisciplinary, drawing from the arts, social and cultural entrepreneurship, business, rhetorical theory, the social sciences, organizational theory, design thinking, and beyond.
- The work is collaboratively authored, bringing together in one space some of the most compelling thinkers, educators, leaders, and musicians of our day.
- We challenge readers to be outcome focused, building on theory and policy concerns to move to practice. This resource facilitates the doing by straddling both outcome- and process-oriented pedagogies. It recognizes the knowledge of systems required but with the intent of changing behaviors, attitudes, and assumptions regarding the implementation of projects and programs to impact a community.
- The model has been crowdsourced by tapping the field's leading arts entrepreneurship scholars/teachers and entrepreneurial musicians.

Developed through extensive research of best practices across disciplines and analysis of case studies of remarkable successes and difficult failures within universities and the profession, the arts entrepreneurial framework—the Way Forward—will guide you through the process of paying attention to the world around you; identifying a need, gap, or opportunity you hope to address; and launching a project of your ideas into action.

CHAPTER 1

BEING A 21ST-CENTURY MUSICIAN

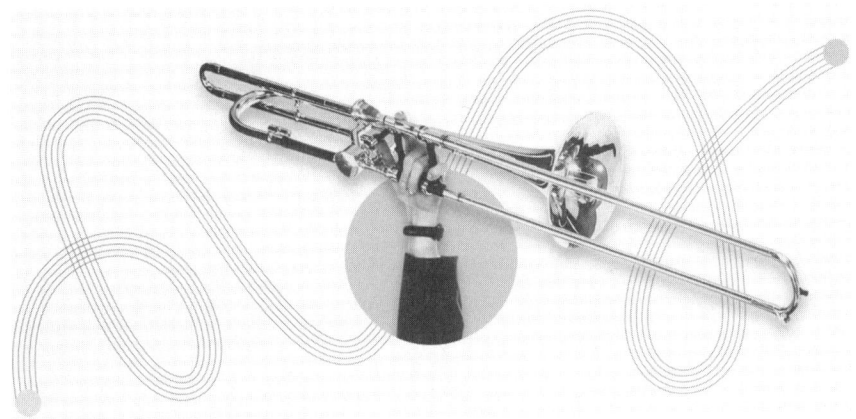

THERE ARE ENDLESS OPPORTUNITIES to thrive as a musician in the shifting cultural landscape of the contemporary moment. This chapter features exemplars within the field and emphasizes the entrepreneurial mindset as a way forward.

In 2015, I was inspired to write an article entitled "Entrepreneurship and the Artist-Revolutionary" for two reasons: to celebrate some of the most innovative, moving, and courageous musicians I know, artists who are teaching the rest of us what is possible, and to reclaim the word *entrepreneurship*. I wanted to move the focus away from monetary gain and make it more about the act of invention, believing musicians could connect to this perspective.

The article received some highly impassioned responses from the music community when it first came out—particularly regarding my assertion that artists are insatiably curious, creative, and collaborative.

Michael Drapkin, a dear friend and fierce defender of the truth about the state of music in America, commented, "Seriously? Artists, and in particular musicians, are one of the most conservative groups I have ever met. They seek to distinguish themselves by being better at 'sameness' than the other guy, and live in fear of being truly different or innovative. It sounds good, but as they say in Texas, 'That dawg don't hunt.' I'm still waiting for the revolution to begin."

Michael's comments still resonate with me on a deep level. But I have to disagree with him. Or, at least, I disagree with the schools of music and conservatories across the nation that have placed creativity off to the side in favor of exclusively training excellence. This focus has enforced a narrow definition of what it means to be a musician.

If we are to prepare emerging musicians to thrive and truly be "revolutionary artists," a term we will use quite a bit here, creativity must become central and integral within the academy and within practicing musicians' ways of thinking. It is no longer possible to bury oneself in the practice room, graduate from a top conservatory, and take a paper credential to a symphony or opera company with the hopes of launching a career. This is not the way the world works now. It probably never did.

We must think like a 21st-century musician.

• • • •

Entrepreneurship and the Artist-Revolutionary[1]

The term *arts entrepreneurship* seems to have flummoxed the music profession, with half believing it's a merger of B-school and conservatory practices and the rest decrying *l'art pour l'art*. While, at first glance, the artist and the entrepreneur may seem worlds apart, in fact they are remarkably similar. Artists, by definition, exude curiosity about the world we live in and help us see opportunities and ideas from a rare vantage point. Through creativity, they find new ways to usher beauty into the world and challenge popular assumptions. And who is more collaborative than members of a string quartet or a jazz trio or more tenacious than a musician who has faced difficulty or failure in the practice room or concert stage but pushed through anyway, striving for the unattainable?

> *What artists and entrepreneurs share is the ability to address complexity and thrive while playing in the messy, fertile space of uncertainty, ambiguity, and promise.*

By that same token, entrepreneurs begin by "problem-finding." They want to both identify the issues and opportunities that they are best equipped to address and then solve them with innovative solutions. They are driven by the question "What can be?" rather than "What is?" These pioneers understand that succeeding where others have failed is their defining task. Then they build collaborative teams to usher in new ways of conducting the world's business.

What artists and entrepreneurs share is the ability to address complexity and thrive while playing in the messy, fertile space of uncertainty, ambiguity, and promise. Arts entrepreneurship embodies this ethos of creativity and risk taking and has gained a footing in university curricula and summer workshops. Institutions like the Eastman School's Arts Leadership Program, University of South Carolina's Spark Laboratory, and DePauw's 21st-Century Musician initiative are paving the way for a new model of learning that helps emerging musicians envision themselves as creative agents of change. Organizations like fresh inc,[2] created by Fifth House Ensemble's Melissa Snoza, provide continuing education for musicians who have an entrepreneurial idea or initiative, offering workshops that live up to the company's tagline, "equal parts new music and new ideas."

Promising young artist ensembles that are emerging from organizations like the ACJW fellowship program[3] are being trained to create a unique identity rooted in artistic vision, built upon collective skill sets, and fueled by a shared passion to make a difference. Decoda[4] is one such ensemble. Their Performance + Community programs engage meaningfully with the homeless and hospitalized, the incarcerated, and, through their guerrilla-style Street Studio workshops, the innocent bystanders who find themselves pulled into impromptu moments of joyful music-making.

Decoda violist and founder of Musicambia,[5] Nathan Schram, recently spoke at DePauw University about his organization's commitment to developing conservatories in the prison system, suggesting that inmates are in the perfect position to harness the full potential of an artistic journey. "How many of you would say that music has been life changing?" he asked. "And if we believe this to be true, then who more than those incarcerated in our prison systems are poised to take advantage of an opportunity to engage in the life-changing experience of making music?"

Our shared challenge is to build synergy across a unique set of local conditions and take on the ideas we are best equipped to address.

It is easy to discount our own ability, or even feel overwhelmed by the suggestion that we too must run out and launch a program similar to Musicambia. Even if that were possible, it would be a fundamental misunderstanding of the very essence and strength of the entrepreneurial mindset—the ability to look at a local problem, where many of these opportunities reside, and invent a unique solution that draws upon one's skills, knowledge, passions, and resources. Our shared challenge is to build synergy across a unique set of local conditions and take on the ideas we are best equipped to address.

Musicians, by design, are built to be creative agents of change, yet somehow we have fallen victim to a narrowly defined set of professional standards focused on memorizing and mastering set repertoire and a list of career options that hasn't expanded much since the Middle Ages, particularly if you are a classical musician. Not only does this not align with the opportunities that exist in today's marketplace, it does not align with what most people, especially today's under-30 generation, want out of a career—a life of means, the ability to provide for those whom they love most; a life of meaning, doing good work and making an impact within their community; and a chance to give back. Rather than fearing the trends of shrinking traditional career paths, we must embrace a willingness to invent our own most promising futures and craft an excitedly uncertain future for our music.

Whether you are talking to Peter Seymour, the innovative bassist and founder of Project Trio; self-proclaimed banjoist-instigator Jayme Stone of the Lomax Project; or academics studying the field of arts entrepreneurship, they all seem to agree that meaningful change begins by feeding your curiosity about the world around you and asking yourself what impact you hope to make.

To position ourselves as change agents, we must continue to foster our own creativity, build collaborative teams of like-minded artists who have a shared vision for what the future might hold, and turn our imaginations toward establishing new connections—between the power of music and our desire to deepen our relationships with the communities we hope to impact.

> **Musicians of the golden age of music were composers, performers, improvisers, and connectors. In a word: they were creatives.**

In Schram's remarks, he also said, "So many musicians fear we are living at a time when music is dying. But for me, we are living in the second golden age of music where anything is possible, everything is possible. Just by staying true to your art, your vision, you can create something that did not exist otherwise, something beautiful, joyful, powerful, and draped in meaning."

Musicians of the golden age of music were composers, performers, improvisers, and connectors. In a word: they were creatives. This is precisely what characterizes the most impactful musicians of our day: they understand the power of music to do good in a world full of need.

Perhaps the second golden age of music is upon us, one that prepares a generation of artist-revolutionaries. I think of cellist Yo-Yo Ma, arguably the most beloved and respected artist of the 21st century, as a great example of the artist-revolutionary. Ma could have continued to play Bach Cello Suites for the remainder of his career and would have done just fine. But instead, we see a revolutionary spirit, in both performance and pedagogy, expanding the boundaries of classical music by embracing world influences (Silk Road Ensemble) and cross-genre exploration (Goat Rodeo Sessions and his recent appearance with ballerina Misty Copeland) as well as his work with emerging musicians through Silk Road's Global Musician Workshop[6] and his launch of the Citizen Musician Initiative with the Chicago Symphony Orchestra Association. And he's not alone. From Gustavo Dudamel to pretty much every artist and organization on 21CM.org's POP list,[7] there is proof that something very special is happening.

So why not an artist revolution? Artists want more than a life chained to the same chair. Music is embraced throughout every culture without boundaries. An increasingly connected world provides influence and inspiration for opening our imagination to a world of music waiting to be created. Technology provides viral access to a global audience. And the entrepreneurial mindset being explored throughout the profession has unleashed the curious, creative, and collaborative energy of the artist-entrepreneur.

Some will say leave art for art's sake. I say, let the revolution begin.

• • • •

Greg Sandow, many would agree, is among the most profound thinkers on the topic of the contemporary moment in classical music and a sought-after consultant. I have referred to him as "the Voice of the Revolution," a title well earned. 21CM.org asked him what distinguishes a 21st-century musician, and here's what he had to say.

What Is a 21st-Century Musician?[8]
by Greg Sandow

There are many ways to define a 21st-century classical musician, which makes sense, because as the century evolves, so does the idea of what it means to play classical music. Many people reading this—especially younger ones—are forging that definition right now.

But here are some things I think these artists might be.

- They go their own way.
- They perform or compose the music they like, in the way they like. And that music isn't always classical.
- They make their own opportunities. They shape their careers like entrepreneurs and might produce their own performances.

This contrasts with the way things used to be. Under the old rules, if you played the clarinet, the music you played was the clarinet repertoire. Your musical life was defined by that music. Your role was to serve the composers who wrote it, and your own identity mattered much less.

You didn't control your performances. Others—whoever booked you to perform—would decide how your performance would look and what the program notes would say. Your audience would be their audience. You wouldn't have one of your own. But times have changed. Here are musicians who play by new rules.

ANDERSON & ROE: ENTREPRENEURIAL WIZARDS

Elizabeth Roe and Greg Anderson. *Courtesy of the artist.*

They're duo pianists, Greg Anderson and Elizabeth Roe (www.andersonroe.com). They have, in their own words, "a nonstop touring schedule" and a diverse repertoire.

The key to their diversity? They don't just play music written for two pianos. They'll arrange anything they want to play, whether it's a Michael Jackson song or the first-act finale from Mozart's opera *Così fan tutte* (which they feature on the third of their three albums, *An Amadeus Affair*).

And they do all this with fabulous visual flair, as you can see on a page of their website devoted to their many videos. Here are links to two of them, which also show their musical range:

- "Der Erlkönig" https://www.andersonroe.com/mv-der-erlknig
- One of Schubert's most famous songs, now transformed into a musical/video production so dramatic, so intense, that Roe is literally swept off her piano bench.
- "A Rain of Tears" https://www.andersonroe.com/mv-a-rain-of-tears
- An aria from a Vivaldi opera becomes a quiet soundtrack for images of rain and melancholy.

Now, extending their success, they're selling scores of their transcriptions. And coming soon: Anderson & Roe merchandise.

STEWART GOODYEAR: FOLLOW YOUR DREAM

Stewart Goodyear. *Courtesy of the artist.*

Stewart Goodyear (https://www.stewartgoodyearpiano.com) is a pianist, born in Canada, who studied at the Royal Conservatory in Toronto, at Curtis, and at Juilliard. Has played with many leading orchestras.

Many would be satisfied with such success. But Goodyear had a crazy dream—to play all the Beethoven sonatas in a single-day marathon, for which, he said, he'd have to train like an athlete.

And he did it. Every year, he plays his marathon at major venues: the big opera house in Dallas; the Mondavi Center in Davis, California; Toronto's Luminato Festival.

He also composes—most recently a piano concerto, which he premiered at the Peninsula Music Festival, and *Count Up*, a fanfare, written for the Cincinnati Symphony.

He's made recordings. Beethoven, of course—all the sonatas. And, just released, the Tchaikovsky and Grieg concertos with the Czech Philharmonic Orchestra. Who writes the liner notes? These are *his* performances played his way, so he writes the notes himself.

JAMES ROSS: EMPOWERING HIS STUDENTS

James Ross performs. *Courtesy of the artist.*

From 2001 to 2017, James Ross taught conducting and conducted the orchestra at the University of Maryland School of Music.[9] Two of his conducting projects went viral—performances of "Prelude to the Afternoon of a Faun"[10] and *Appalachian Spring*,[11] in which the students played the music from memory and danced it while they played. This empowered them, bringing out a creative force they may not have known they had.

Another empowering project: a performance of *Petrushka*, with the musicians doubling as actors. This was so impressive that the New York Philharmonic did it, too, empowering its own musicians.

Ross also empowered the students in his Maryland orchestra to help create a new kind of concert dress—informal black, with an accent color picked for each performance and applied (or not!) in creative ways by the musicians.

Ross has also run the National Orchestral Institute, a summer program for young professionals, where he gave musicians power to produce concerts on their own. Their programs featured classical performances alongside rock arrangements and improvisations.

MASON BATES: FUSION OF OPPOSITES?

Mason Bates. *Courtesy of the artist.*

Not so. No opposites here. Yes, Mason Bates (www.masonbates.com) is a classical composer and a dance DJ. But in the 21st century, why should these things be opposites?

Here's proof of that. Who likes what Bates does? No less a maestro than Riccardo Muti, who personally picked him—along with Anna Clyne (www.annaclyne.com), whose work also isn't in a normal concert style—to be composer in residence with the Chicago Symphony.

Bates also does projects with his hometown band, the San Francisco Symphony—and with many other orchestras, including the YouTube Symphony, with which he performed in 2009 and 2011 as electronica soloist, as he often does, in symphonic pieces that he wrote.[12] You'll find an outline of his thriving classical career, along with details of his DJ work, on his website.

And, proving that all of this has an audience, he and Clyne exploded the Chicago Symphony's new music series, MusicNOW,[13] into something that attracts huge young crowds.

LARA DOWNES: DOING IT HER WAY

Lara Downes. *Courtesy of the artist.*

Lara Downes (www.laradownes.com), a pianist, has recorded multiple albums that are not standard classical releases. On 2014's *Some Other Time*, she and cellist Zuill Bailey play American music: Barber, Copland, Bernstein, Lukas Foss. But with a twist. Yes, they play Barber's Cello Sonata, a formidable work written for their instruments. But they also play music they've arranged from songs by Barber, Bernstein, and Copland, including two from Bernstein's musicals. They play the music that they like.

In San Francisco, where she lives, Downes founded what she calls an "alt-classical" concert series called the Artist Sessions, which is hosted in clubs and performance spaces for people who never go to classical events.[14] Downes has written about how hard she works to attract these people[15] and to make the concerts memorable.[16]

Other recordings? Highly varied. *13 Ways of Looking at the Goldberg*: thirteen composers write their own takes on you know which Bach piece.[17] *Exiles' Café*: poignant works by composers living in exile.[18] And Downes's "But Beautiful,"[19] is a heartfelt tribute to the greatest of jazz singers, Billie Holiday, featuring arrangements that evoke not just her songs but her singing.[20]

If you follow the links, you'll see that Downes promotes these highly individual releases with video trailers.

● ● ● ●

CREATING THE REVOLUTIONARY ARTIST

We entered the music field because of our deep commitment to the art form, our refusal to go forward without music in our lives, and the belief that our art has a place in the world.

This book is built upon the premise that the arts possess a transformative power to uplift those in need, spark curiosity and innovation, and build healthy communities. This is your guide to forge your own path so that your music is heard, your passions are fulfilled, and your impact is felt. Of course, music entrepreneurship is not a shortcut for the 10,000 practice hours that writer Malcolm Gladwell argues are required to develop into a world-class artist. Each artist we explore within this text is at the top of his or her game technically and artistically.

• • • •

James Doser is the director of the Institute for Music Leadership at the Eastman School of Music, among the nation's leading entities for preparing future generations for "creating, sharing, supporting and implementing innovative ideas and programs to ensure the relevance of music in today's world."

Artistry at the Core
by James Doser

As entrepreneurial musicians, let's remember that we are not required to produce the next musical widget (nothing wrong with that, of course), but rather, our mission is to add value to the lives of others through artistry.

Though it may not be possible to define artistry, I am confident that these characteristics apply:

- Artistry is characterized by honesty, integrity, and the intent to move people in profound ways.
- Artistry is present in all cultures, genders, ages, races, and economic strata.
- Artistry may include, but is not defined by, technical mastery, advanced degrees, or critical/popular acclaim.

If we remove artistry from the foundation of our entrepreneurial projects, then let's not call ourselves artists who are entrepreneurial thinkers, but rather entrepreneurs who use musical tools in our work.

As entrepreneurial artists we accept the responsibility that comes with the potential to connect people in profound ways. We utilize our artistic core to bring value to others; we search for ways to solve problems and meet needs; we facilitate connections where they did not exist previously.

We do so with artistry as our foundation, with a commitment to apply it honestly and with integrity, and with the intent to contribute to people, society, and our art. We use entrepreneurial thinking as a strategy to make our world a better place through our artistry.

And there is nothing wrong at all with using our artistry to facilitate a rewarding career, produce a stable income, and sell some widgets along the way....

• • • •

Think of your life's work the way composers go about their artistic process. They see the big picture first—the scope of the work, the instrumentation as it impacts orchestration, moments of arrival, and transitions that lead us on a hero's journey or glide us across a dance floor, four feet scrambling to find three beats.

The thought that a composer begins a masterpiece in measure one and never lifts her pen from the page until the final note of the coda is absurd. Neither art nor life unfolds in linear fashion. Nor will your career or the project you choose within this course.

So what if you were to think of your life's work as your masterpiece? What do the big moments look like? How do the transitions unfold? Who will be in your ensemble? And who will be your audience? How will you orchestrate the composition of your first arts entrepreneurial effort?

The revolutionary artist takes authority over his artistry and path. On this shared journey, you won't find a map. Which is exciting, because this tells you that you are not being asked to complete a set of tasks or assignments but rather are being challenged to shape your own future as a musician of the 21st century; one in which your music will make a difference.

You will not take this journey alone. Know, musicians everywhere are busy reimagining how they can shape their own careers. Look around and you will find inspiration abounds. And although I am rooting that you do not fail, I also know from personal and professional experience that the only way to ensure success is by repeating the ordinary.

So do something extraordinary. And risk
- being curious
- being creative
- being collaborative
- bringing your vision to fruition

Make your life a work of art.

THE WAY FORWARD

When you launch your first entrepreneurial project, you will have something tangible that reflects your unique path in music, to date. I have witnessed first efforts that have resulted in live radio shows from New York City's Upper West Side that aired to more than 250,000 weekly listeners, not-for-profit organizations that thrived for more than a decade, and art healing projects that impacted ailing children.

Creating the Revolutionary Artist is directed enough to keep you from wandering astray, but open-ended enough to allow you to breathe life into your own creative, out-of-the-box solutions. We are guided by a framework made up of five mindsets and three core career skills we believe are critical to your success as an entrepreneurial artist. They are:

Mindsets
- **Unquenchable Curiosity.** When we focus our minds outside of ourselves and become curious about our purpose and how we can directly impact our world, we see endless intersections between the issues that most matter to us, our art form, and meaningful change.
- **Purposeful Creativity.** When we (again) give ourselves license to think creatively, opening our eyes to unique perspectives, we begin to think like an inventor who identifies the problems he is best equipped to address. Or the entrepreneur who sees needs, gaps, and opportunities in everyday challenges. Fostering our creativity is essential in both developing our artistry and creating a life as a citizen-musician, shaping our own most promising future and impacting our community through our music.
- **Strategic Collaboration.** No man is an island. We all need the support of those whose skill sets complement our own. When we learn to identify the "strengths in the room" and strategically leverage these talents for better results, we accomplish more and enjoy the journey.
- **Passionate Persistence.** Your tenacity and grit learned in the practice room will be your greatest asset as you grapple with the complexity of the world you will soon inherit, a world that is most often won by those who prize persistence, resilience, and perseverance.
- **Critical Optimism.** Mapping a more promising future prepares us to play what rhetorical theorist Peter Elbow calls the believing game, rather than the doubting game. The believing game challenges us to think optimistically when seeing ourselves as agents for change, but critically when taking feasible action toward making meaningful impact.

Skill Sets
- **Telling Idea-Driven Stories.** Communicating in an authentic, real way that captures the audience's attention and keeps them captivated is an essential skill.
- **Funding Priceless Ideas.** Financing opportunities to create, share, teach, and explore the boundaries of art music must be pursued through earned revenue, donor relations, crowdfunding, and grant-writing skills.
- **Moving Ideas to Action.** How can you move your meaningful ideas from vision to fruition? Assessment is no longer identified by our ability to fill in the bubble completely with a #2 pencil but rather by generating projects that advance the art form, connect with new audiences, and strengthen existing ones. It's also about impacting those at the margins while grappling with real-world problems of overcoming obstacles, facing adversity, and even enduring failure.

We all share a path. We all have our journey. I wonder if yours will be like mine.

At a Crossroads

When I was completing my undergraduate studies in music performance, I found myself at a crossroads: should I consider applying for high-school band director positions or continue pursuing my aspirations to become a professional orchestral musician (with a "fallback" plan of becoming a college professor)?

For me this meant, "Should I take the safe path or the one less traveled?"

What happened next is impossible to describe in brief, but it goes something like this.

I wanted to play in the Chicago Symphony. So I went to graduate school, studied with Frank Crisafulli (trombonist with the CSO for 50 years!) and practiced (a lot).

When Frank retired, I auditioned for his chair. I did not win. Some young guy with an Australian accent did. He is likely to play with the CSO for the next 50 years. I needed a new plan.

So I went on my version of "professional autopilot." I graduated with my master's. Took a sabbatical replacement. Taught trombone, jazz, marching band, pop music, and more. I got a doctorate and won a professorship and earned tenure. Life is good, right? Then things got interesting and a little more creative.

I accepted a two-year postdoc in a "Center for Creativity," started a not-for-profit arts organization, hosted a live jazz radio show from NYC, and produced a ballet. Most radical of all, I started asking questions.

> ***What if, in the real-life game of musical chairs,***
> ***there is a seat for everyone?***

FOUR KEYS TO CREATING A CAREER YOU LOVE

What I have discovered since leaving school is that a map does not guide life's adventure. Instead, something vastly more exciting and promising does.

Life is more like a scavenger hunt: each person's path and prizes are different from the next, so the question becomes, What will guide you on your personal "scavenger hunt" to create your perfect career?

Curiosity is what led you to the arts in the first place. Artists by definition see the world from a unique perspective and help audiences understand something about the world around us. Be curious about all the possibilities that the future holds.

Creativity is what the artist, inventor, and entrepreneur share. You will invent your own future, whether you know it or not. And like the entrepreneur who sees needs, gaps, and opportunities and creates innovative solutions for financial gain, arts entrepreneurs build rich cultural entities and diverse, thriving careers.

Collaboration is how you will accomplish your goals. Who is more prepared to work collaboratively than a musician?

Tenacity is learned. All musicians are inevitably faced with failure while pursuing their desire to usher beauty into the world. David Taylor calls this "embracing the joy of the struggle."[21] It is learned in the practice room.

Your grit is among the greatest attributes acquired through an education in the arts. What you have learned and will continue to learn through your studies is more than music performance. You have sparked curiosity, fostered creativity, harnessed collaboration, and endured in the face of adversity. These skills will serve you well as you invent your own future career as a professional musician.

HOW MANY OPPORTUNITIES DO YOU SEE?

I recently spoke with David Cutler, a friend and truly one of the most coherent thinkers about creating opportunity within our profession.

David, in speaking about the need to explore career paths innovatively and strategically, said this: "There are people who see one or two opportunities, or zero. And then there are people who see 1,000 opportunities. I have never met someone who sees five opportunities."[22]

So our shared challenge is to foster divergent thinking about the infinite number of unique possibilities to usher new models of connecting artists and audiences, amid the sea of sameness currently flooding our profession.

Our challenge is to develop convergent thinking to hone in on the ideas that will best advance our life's work. Inspiration is everywhere.

• • • •

SUMMARY

Chapter 1 posed the question, "What is a 21st-century musician?" It introduced us to artists who are leveraging their art form toward goals as diverse as impacting those at the margins, engaging new audiences, and creating new educational models. Yet, we instinctively know that our chosen paths will draw upon our own passions, talents, and personal and professional attributes. Understanding these musicians' mindsets and attributes opens the possibility of identifying our own entrepreneurial capacities. Ultimately, this is in preparation for the most important question: How will you take up the mindset and attributes of the 21st-century musician?

CHAPTER 2

EXPLORING CURIOSITY: FINDING OPPORTUNITIES TO MAKE A COMMUNITY IMPACT

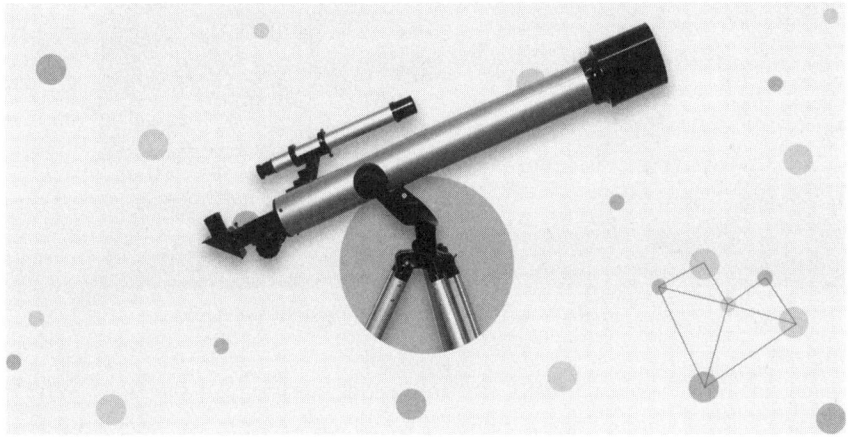

AN UNQUENCHABLE CURIOSITY IS what guides artists in their exploration to share something about the world around them. In this chapter, we highlight musicians and artists who use curiosity to look for answers to previously unanswered questions, expand boundaries of the art form, and solve societal issues. We also consider the importance of the question "Why?" in looking for meaning and purpose.

THE CURIOUS ARTIST

The impressionist painter Edgar Degas once said, "Art is not what you see, but what you make others see." Art, after all, is about challenging the intellect, spirit, and emotions. But before an artist can challenge others to see something new, he must challenge himself first. And that pretty much always begins with curiosity. An artist probably starts with curiosity about what she can do on her instrument, which leads to how she can share a more compelling musical story. This exploration next expands to the world around her and how to make sense of it, and finally a consideration of how she can help others see that world from her unique perspective.

JOHN CAGE

The "As Slow as Possible" organ playing John Cage in Halberstadt, Germany.

When we think about curiosity and influential musicians of the 20th century, composer John Cage comes to mind. If we were to sum up his life's work in a few simple words, we might say he challenged our assumptions about the world around us.

Remember Cage's 1952 three-movement composition *4'33"*? Even today it feels groundbreaking. In this work, Cage breaks down the fourth wall. He shifts those in the audience away from their traditionally tacit role sitting in the theater and places them center stage in the spotlight, as the pianist sits in silence. The sonic emphasis becomes everyday sounds generated by the attentive, and often increasingly fidgety, "listeners."

Less familiar to some is his composition *Organ²/ASLSP* (1987). Striving to live up to the composer's instruction of "as slowly as possible," the work is currently in progress in Halberstadt, Germany, being played over the course of 639 years. Again, Cage redefines the parameters in which we work and move by challenging the very definition of "the audience." (And although most readers of this book are significantly younger than the authors, it is unlikely any of us will be around to hear the end of the performance in 2640!)

Cage is an artist who reminds us that our world is highly constructed and that there are many ways to make sense of some of the most basic assumptions that impact us every day. As revolutionary artists, we need to think outside of constructions, outside of our assumptions, and outside of ourselves.

EXPLORING CURIOSITY • 19

VINCENT LAFORET

Adventure by Vincent Laforet. *Courtesy of the artist.*

Lake Powell Aerial 02 by Vincent Laforet. *Courtesy of the artist.*

For many, seeing is believing. Through his aerial photography, Pulitzer Prize–winning photographer Vincent Laforet (laforetvisuals.com) illustrates the artist's ability to examine the world from a rare vantage point. Sharing his artistic view of a world too vast to comprehend from the ground, Laforet captures the undeniable impact of global climate change (in his Exploring the West series), the excitement of life devoted to exploration (Adventure series), and the human experience (Life series). In some cases, the action literally unfolds frame by frame so that we can grasp how everyday life unfolds moment by moment. This is the artist's gift—to help us make sense of the human condition.

What Cage and Laforet both teach us is that it is within the inseparable relationship of the art, artist, and audience that the true artistic experience resides. This ephemeral, never-to-be-replicated moment opens our eyes to broader perspectives based on a shared willingness to risk letting go of our current understanding in favor of expanding our worldview of what is possible.

If an unquenchable curiosity is at the heart of what an artist is, then we need to talk more about curiosity: how it works; how we can flex it, expand upon it, leverage it; and how we can imitate today's most profoundly curious, innovative, and influential musical artists.

What is an artistic moment you have experienced that changed your perspective on the role art plays in the world?

TODAY'S REVOLUTIONARIES

21CM.org regularly highlights artists we consider revolutionary in the field. We sat down with a few to learn how they leverage their work toward a purpose that is dear to their belief system—whether that is impacting community, pushing the boundaries of possibility, or sharing their music with those most in need. These folks were once in your shoes, exactly in the moment you are in now: entering the profession, on the verge of being a pro, no longer a kid.

Peter Seymour of PROJECT Trio[1] aims to strengthen the cultural fabric of communities. Like other 21CM artists, he defines himself, rather than letting others define him. Entrepreneurially minded, Peter shapes his career by producing his own performances, leveraging social media, and developing educational programming.

Prior to PROJECT Trio, Peter performed with some pretty traditional musical organizations, including the Cleveland Orchestra. Today he performs exclusively with the trio, earning a living through performance, teaching, composing, and arranging; YouTube royalties; producing his own music; and connecting to new audiences across the globe. PROJECT Trio plays everything from baroque to nu-metal and is committed to sharing music with children through public school workshops.

> **IN CONVERSATION WITH PETER SEYMOUR**
>
> "I can't imagine not having playing for young people as part of my musical career, and we always say that if an ensemble or soloist wants to get great, then they need to be out there in the schools and experiencing what it's like to play for that audience. There's nothing like a student audience for getting the kind of instant feedback that you just don't get from adult audiences. Adult audiences will clap and even stand up and clap no matter what the show is on stage, but I tell you this, you stand in front of a thousand junior high kids in an auditorium and you're going to get some legit feedback that's instantaneous! So I say, get out there in the schools and start developing new music and start developing also your voice—how you talk to audiences and how you address audiences. There's nothing like being in the schools."

What drives your passion for building new audiences of the future? How does your work strengthen the cultural fabric of communities you engage?

Revolutionary artist collectives like Fifth House Ensemble[2] reside at the intersection of the artist and the entrepreneur. They exude curiosity, expanding the boundaries of the art form when collaborating with artists from various genres and fusing music with other art forms.

It is nearly impossible to share here all that Fifth House Ensemble executes within an average week. They perform, teach, consult, commission, and collaborate. They serve on the faculty of a leading arts entrepreneurship workshop, fresh inc; create original community-based projects like Harvest,[3] done within the Greencastle, Indiana, community; and collaborate across cultural boundaries, including a profoundly interesting work with Baladino.[4] And as if jetting across traditional musical boundaries were still too limiting, they have created recent projects that celebrate storytelling, poetry, and video game music.

Decoda[5] uplifts those at the margins through the healing powers of the arts. Since the chamber ensemble's launch in 2011, Decoda's projects have reached audiences in schools, hospitals, homeless shelters, and prisons as well as in prominent concert halls from Abu Dhabi to Iceland, Hong Kong to Denmark, and in every major city across the United States.

Describing Decoda's impact on inmates within a maximum-security prison, the *Washington Post* wrote, "If you doubt that within every person resides a divine spark, listening to prisoners express their joys and sorrows—ever-luminous even in this dark place—may cause you to reconsider."[6]

To expand the boundaries of their artistic output, Decoda collaborates with artists from vastly different backgrounds to create unique projects of their own invention. One such collaboration has been forged with Red Tail Ring. And although Decoda is a classical chamber ensemble and Red Tail Ring is a folk duo, Decoda's double bassist, Evan, claims that he shares a musical language with Red Tail Ring's Laurel "more than anyone else that [he] knows." Why? Their last names are both Premo; brother and sister, they grew up together in Michigan surrounded by the same mixture of classical, American folk, and Scandinavian music.

Both Premos have found success in their preferred genres. Decoda is the first-ever Affiliate Ensemble of Carnegie Hall; its members met while in fellowship together during the Ensemble ACJW program, a joint creation by Carnegie Hall, the Juilliard School, and the Weill Music Institute. And in 2016 Red Tail Ring released the fourth of their critically praised full-length albums. The band performs and tours extensively, putting on well over 100 shows per year.

But Evan and Laurel's musical lives still intersect. Decoda has founded Beethoven and Banjos, an ongoing cross-genre collaboration wherein the ensemble works with a select folk act to specifically explore the musical heritage of Michigan's Upper Peninsula. Decoda and Red Tail Ring's joint performances—which feature songs written by Laurel and arranged by Evan—are an outgrowth of this project.

I had the opportunity to interview Evan Premo and Anna Elashvili of Decoda as well as Laurel Premo and Michael Beauchamp of Red Tail Ring during their recent joint residency at DePauw. Below are the interview highlights.

• • • •

Decoda and Red Tail Ring Interview Highlights

MARK RABIDEAU: Your music emerges from very different musical spaces, but you have shared history. So tell me about that background and how this collaboration came about.

EVAN PREMO: I've always had a passion for bringing different kinds of music together, and that came from my upbringing, playing folk music with my family. So it's really wonderful to have the opportunity to bring this group that I'm now part of, Decoda, together with [Laurel's] group, Red Tail Ring. We grew up in the same tradition, diverged, and now we're bringing our two traditions back together.

LAUREL PREMO: Both my mother and my father were great instrumentalists and singers, and got Evan and I started very, very early on whatever we could pick up. So we both had rhythm in our bones very quickly.

MARK RABIDEAU: Could you describe the nature of your collaboration?

EVAN PREMO: We started working together in the Upper Peninsula of Michigan, where Laurel and I are both from. For that concert, we wanted to celebrate some of the land in Michigan and particularly the water—so, different bodies of water that were important to us growing up. Laurel [did] a lot of the composing; I was doing a lot of the arranging with the string players.

MARK RABIDEAU: What do you take back to your own genres after your collaborations? Are there fiddle techniques that you take back to the violin?

ANNA ELASHVILI: Definitely—probably in very subtle ways—but I wanted to program [a] Bach piece specifically because I wanted to get in touch with the folk feeling of that gavotte, being able to also have a lighter touch to it, which I think very much has a fiddle-y origin. I think having the fiddling next to me—it definitely helps go there. It's funny: violins used for fiddling do have a different sound. And you look for a different sound. You want something that has a slightly more nasal quality.

LAUREL PREMO: I find that maybe you're looking for a more focused sound with classical, and I'm looking for more overtones.

MARK RABIDEAU: Are there rules to the collaborative process? What's the game plan for a successful collaboration?

MICHAEL BEAUCHAMP: I think trying is really important, because it doesn't always work. But that's the name of the game. You try it, and, at a minimum, you've got to just be open to giving it a go. Maybe it won't sound like music at all, but it's really exciting to walk in, meet someone, and 20 minutes later, you're tackling a piece.

LAUREL PREMO: The more open you are and the more willing you are, the better it is.

MICHAEL BEAUCHAMP: Yeah, the more willing you are to engage in an open conversation about the music—just thinking, what do we need to do in this part to really accentuate aspects of the music that are unique and interesting to all of us?

To dive into a deeper understanding of how Decoda has thrived when working with artists that emerge from different traditions, listen to the full interview on 21CM.org.[7]

• • • •

What cause or audience do you hope to impact through your music?

MAKE TIME FOR CURIOSITY

Among the greatest concerns, when thinking about how we prepare musicians for the challenges and opportunities of the 21st century, is the structural opposition schools of music create in providing students with time to be curious. I wonder if, as you think back on your time in school, this resonates with you.

The National Association of Schools of Music (NASM) hosts an annual conference for music school directors and deans. It is arguably one of the most important gatherings of music professionals within the academy and, equally so, among the most tedious, with hours spent discussing piano proficiency requirements, 120-credit degree caps, and outcomes assessments. In recent years, however, NASM has invited cutting-edge musicians to perform and host a talkback session about their work.

In 2015, the conference featured the innovative vocal ensemble Roomful of Teeth.[8] Roomful's Caroline Shaw[9] had won the 2013 Pulitzer Prize for *Partita for 8 Voices*, becoming the youngest-ever winner of the music prize. Roomful of Teeth had secured a Grammy for their recording of her work. After Roomful delivered a well-received performance of *Partita for 8 Voices* at the NASM conference, an attendee asked the opening question in the talkback session: "If you were to change one thing about your undergraduate education, what would that be?" Taking the mic, a member of the vocal chamber ensemble simply said, "I would give more time to explore curiosities." Wait, I am confused. No mentions of piano proficiency requirements or tallying of credit hours—simply find time to be curious? When the attendee asked if any other member of the ensemble wanted to add anything, they shared a collective "Nope, that about says it all."

As revolutionary artists, we take on the challenge of creating moments that challenge others to imagine infinite opportunities. We do this by connecting dots. Not dots as in notes on a page, but dots with bigger implications. Dots that bridge cultural differences, invite into the art form new audiences, and reignite existing fans. They also can impact learners of all ages, strengthen the cultural fabric of our communities, expand the boundaries of the art form, and collide artistic experience with issues of social justice.

But to accomplish such lofty goals requires time. Time to be curious about what can be. I asked two musicians, both members of Yo-Yo Ma's Grammy-winning Silk Road Ensemble, about their thoughts on the role curiosity plays in the life of a musician.

The first, Sandeep Das, is arguably the world's leading tabla player. When I ask him the question "Does curiosity still matter?" this was his response: "Absolutely. Oh my God, I think that's the biggest prayer I make to God is not to make me the best musician or best whatever, but not to ever close my eyes and ears to hearing and learning more. I think the curiosity of a child—again I take Yo-Yo Ma's name, he's at the top of his professional world but he's still as curious as a five-year-old boy. I think that's death, man, if your curiosity is over; you have nothing else to live for."

The second, Mike Block, founder of the Global Musician Workshop, a summer program that brings together musicians from around the world to study traditions unlike their own, had this response to the central importance of curiosity:

> Within the music world, if your goal is to play Beethoven, well, we've had two hundred years to teach you how to play Beethoven and for better or for worse, there's going to be some potentially wrong and right answers to that question. We can almost create a checklist for all the things you need to know in order to play Beethoven well. What I enjoy about a place like the Global Musician Workshop is that when we show up here on day one, we have no idea what the final concerts are going to sound like and the participants don't even necessarily have a full grasp that they're going to be collaborating with instruments that they may not have ever even seen before. So, we're starting from a point where there is no right or wrong answer, and I think that makes curiosity one of the most invaluable tools.
>
> Even for the faculty to be able to pull this together, you know, I'll observe a rehearsal and a faculty member will have to ask somebody a question about their instrument, like what are the open strings they're using. Sometimes the basic assumptions that seem so fundamental for yourself become the gateways for someone on the outside to really start to meaningfully work with you. It all starts with curiosity.

Find time to focus your curiosities about your relationship with art, artist, and audience and how you hope to make a difference.

Following your curiosities takes courage. To leap into the conversation about where your curiosities might lead you, and how to find that courage, consider some advice from the dean of the School of Music at the University of South Carolina, Tayloe Harding.

• • • •

> Tayloe Harding is one of the profession's most respected and beloved deans. He has served as president of the College Music Society, cofounded the Brevard Conference on Music Entrepreneurship, and has led the profession in developing and implementing curricular and co-curricular explorations of music advocacy, music entrepreneurship, and community engagement in an effort to formulate the 21st-Century Music School.
>
> What advice does Tayloe Harding offer on how to transition from being curious about leadership to becoming a leader?

Overcoming Fear: Turning Talk into Action
by Tayloe Harding

When envisioning ourselves as leaders, we imagine two things: (1) being in charge of something, feeling responsible for it, and taking on the weight that someone else is depending on us; (2) that leading means we must make change happen.

In accepting that it is our leadership that will compel change, it follows that to be a leader we must first understand the change we aim to bring about, and then know what that will look like on the other side.

As a young musician, you have likely noted the behaviors of leaders you have witnessed who brought about meaningful change. And as an emerging musician, through this study, you are now invested in the change you seek. The truth is, however, talking about leading change is not hard. But leading change is. Nothing inhibits our ability to turn deliberation into action more than the unknown. The unknown inspires fear, and fear is action's greatest impediment. My hope for emerging musicians is to have faith that what lies ahead is more promising and exciting than it is daunting and concerning.

Turning the talk of understanding into the action of knowing is the key to good leadership. It makes whole all of the parts of a young musician's desires, talents, and aspirations to impact the world. To thrive we must overcome fear. And taking it head-on is our only way forward.

• • • •

FIND YOUR WHY

Curiosity guides us toward a better understanding of ideas and concepts outside of ourselves. Curiosity fuels the innate desire to seek knowledge. Artists begin their work out of exploration. So do entrepreneurs. This is our shared compass as we search for the problems we hope to address in the world.

Simon Sinek, a well-regarded thinker, author, and speaker on leadership, is the architect of *Start with Why*. Sinek presses us to rethink what motivates our life's work and challenges us to home in on our purpose. Sinek argues that most organizations tell their story to others by beginning with "What" they do, then "How" they do it. But, most often, they never tell stakeholders "*Why*."

For example, start with the following information:

- *What:* play trombone
- *How:* a local jazz ensemble
- *Why:* love to be creative

Now consider which statement is more inspiring to you: "Hi, I'm Mark. I play the trombone, mostly in a local jazz ensemble. I love to feel creative." Or "I love the feeling of being creative, so I play in a local jazz ensemble as a trombonist. Hi, I'm Mark."

If you noticed, we led with our *Why* in the second example. The *Why* had energy and got your attention.

For Musicambia founder Nathan Schram, the *Why* was rooted in his belief in music as an agent of rehabilitation and social change. Not only is his project remarkable (as is Nathan), but the telling of Musicambia is powerful in this write-up by Decoda violinist Anna Elashvili.

Musicambia[10]

by Anna Elashvili

Music can bring joy, but it also can bring a sense of identity and a greater good to those seeking to better themselves. Nathan Schram, founder and director of New York–based Musicambia, understands this and believes that the rehabilitation of inmates is vital to our society's health and prosperity. His network of creative music conservatories serves prisons and jails nationwide, making a difference in the lives of incarcerated men and women. Through the discipline of learning an instrument, these inmates have an opportunity to enrich their lives and build a supportive, collaborative community while serving their time.

When you begin with your *Why*, you inspire your team and stakeholders to be more productive and creative, more motivated and joyful. The *Why* drives productivity and makes for a stronger organization.

Finding your *Why*, both within the partnerships you seek within the profession and more broadly in your life's work, will likely make the difference between following the path others have mapped out for you—the siloed perspective of the music profession everywhere—or a path as unique as your own talents, passions, and worldview.

Want to learn more? Check out Simon Sinek's TED Talk "How Great Leaders Inspire Action."[11]

LOCATE YOUR GENIUS

"Genius is seeing what everyone else sees and thinking what no one else has thought."
—Albert Szent-Györgyi, Nobel Prize–winning biochemist

This book aims to help you "locate your own particular kind of genius," as we say at 21CM, and help you show others something new.

Having taught this material through university coursework, and practiced its lessons within my own professional exploration, the very best projects I have seen and have been a part of were achieved when those engaged focused on their best, not their most; matched their internal talents with synergistic community partners; cared about people, rather than resume building; and knew why they were doing what they were setting out to do.

We have seen amazing projects like:

- Future Doors, whose founders wanted to raise awareness and funds for not-for-profits impacting those at the margins in Lexington, Kentucky. Partnering with local artists, the group created original paintings that reflected their shared values with those of community organizations like the National Alliance on Mental Illness and the Ronald McDonald House. Arts administration students turned doors-as-canvas into powerful messages that gave voice to the disenfranchised, as well as raised more than $6,000 through a silent auction, shared between artists and organizations.
- Pop-Up Philly, a series of pop-up concerts in inner-city Philadelphia organized by high school musicians who wanted to share the music that they love. Starting with the premise that classical music is not accessible to everyone and, in some cases, is unwelcoming to new listeners, students took to the streets to perform impromptu chamber music recitals.

SUMMARY

There is nothing that shakes up our view of the world more than dropping ourselves in the middle of someone else's reality. So consider volunteering within a local organization that is making a difference in ways you admire and that resonate with your own belief system. Volunteering allows for just that, shaking up our worldview. It provides us with the chance to experience someone else's life, if only for a few hours. And when we are in unfamiliar surroundings and afforded the opportunity to see the world through a life unlike our own, it leaves us vulnerable and curious. Vulnerable to knowing that our life is only that, our one experience. And curious about all that is unfamiliar. All that is uncertain. All that is possible.

Curiosity guides us toward a better understanding of ideas and concepts outside of ourselves. Curiosity fuels the innate desire to seek knowledge. Artists begin their work out of exploration. So do entrepreneurs. This is our shared compass as we search for the problems we hope to address in the world.

CHAPTER 3

ASSESSING YOUR STRENGTHS: TENACITY AND THE SUPERPOWERS

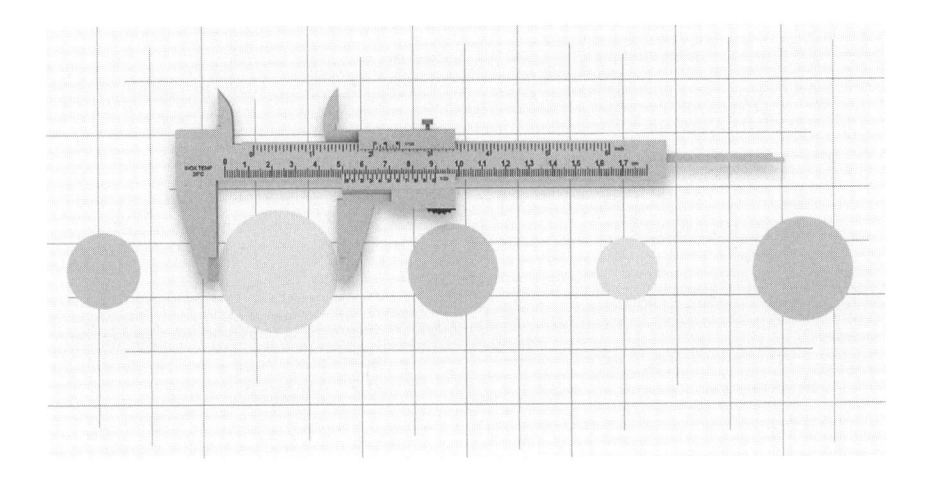

WE TOO OFTEN THINK of ourselves as trombonists, vocalists, or oboists. We are more. We are tenacious and complex and clever. We understand failure as a process, not an ending. And we are good at things like communicating with others, building relationships, solving problems, and learning from others' stories. We have superpowers that will prove invaluable as 21st-century musicians.

Chapter 3 opens the pathway for us to find our not-yet-known superpowers and to better understand how others have reframed the experience of disappointment, frustration, and failure to be understood as growth, learning, and opportunity.

THE TRUTH ABOUT TESTS

Creative ideas always work when they're just ideas rambling around in our heads. But bringing them to life is an entirely different challenge.

The truth is, getting stuff done is hard. It involves vision, organization, communication, action, stick-to-itiveness, and more. And if my educator colleagues and I are truthful, we have not prepared our graduates with the skills to be involved in the world. Yes, we have asked them to volunteer within their communities, but outside of this co-curricular resume building, we have focused our efforts on the work of teaching students how to take tests.

No matter how hard tests can be, they are predictable in a number of ways:

- *They have a start time and a stop time. And then we get to move on.*
  REALITY: Most of life does not work this way.
- *Generally, there are right and wrong answers.*
  REALITY: The real world is rich with complexity, ambiguity, and contradiction.
- *Finally, they affect only one person: you.*
  REALITY: No one lives in a bubble in the real world. Our actions always affect others.

And they don't teach us:

- *How to pose a thoughtful question.*
  We are too busy pretending to have all of the answers.
- *How to ask for and get help.*
  Almost always we take tests all by ourselves. But relying on a friend or colleague can be the second most-rewarding aspect of hard work. And having them rely on you is even more rewarding.
- *How to use failure as a means to achieving goals.*
  It is hard to believe while filling in a bubble sheet that failing can be the best test of all when preparing us for all that lies ahead.

Real tests, as you have learned since entering the world beyond university, are about overcoming obstacles to achieve your goals. Any project you engage in will have issues that must be overcome along the way. No matter the scale, what you will learn while actualizing your ideas is an inevitable consequence of the act of invention. You will also learn that tenacity and resilience are required throughout the process. And the world can be changed in ways big and small.

Through the ideas shared within this book, we are looking to impact your professional life, as well as provide you with a space that allows you to grapple with intellectual content. At the same time, we want you to actively participate in the generation of local solutions to the social problems that are already defining a future you can help shape. By embracing the creativity of both the artist and the entrepreneur, you are empowered to meet the challenges of today—and to see yourselves as players who can change the world for the better.

Stanford Thompson is founder and executive director for the El Sistema–inspired program Play On, Philly! and a 2017 TED Fellow. What excites this successful performer, teacher, administrator, and speaker? In his own words: "I believe that society thrives when artists prioritize the needs of their communities, so I create social harmony and opportunity through music."

\ˈfālyər\ in the 21st Century
by Stanford L. Thompson

The word *failure* comes from the mid-17th century and originally meant "non-occurrence" and "cessation of supply." Over time, however, *failure* has morphed into meaning "lack of success" and "an unsuccessful person, enterprise, or thing." Under this modern definition, we rightfully try to avoid failure, even questioning ourselves when we begin thinking outside the lines. Swerving to avoid the potholes on the paved path, we inevitably hit them, and it hurts, because we can easily attribute the error to a deficiency we feel we have inside ourselves.

I want to offer a different perspective, taking an off-road journey that avoids the worn, familiar terrain traveled by the cautious. To be sure, this journey has switchbacks and trip roots and will require you to be sure-footed, but it ultimately offers a view of the world that uniquely reflects your experience. And each step brings you closer to arriving at what you believe is possible.

Like Edison trying to invent the light bulb, we must be willing to try 10,000 times to achieve our dreams. The success of any long-term goal is not achieved without failure. It may be one big one. It may be a bunch of little ones. But the true definition of *failure* goes back to its roots: Failure is when you stop supplying ideas to complete the journey. Your journey will look different than mine, but each path leads to the same final destination: success.

Remember a time when you were part of an epic failure? What went wrong? And what would you do differently next time?

As an aspiring classical musician, Sarah Robinson did everything right.[1] She went to a conservatory for an orchestral studies program, she honed her technique with a "flute guru" until she was a "monster player," and she devoted all of her time and money throughout her 20s to the task of winning a full-time orchestra job. After all, you need that orchestra job to be a successful musician. At least, that's what Robinson believed, and she was working her very hardest to get it.

But what if you still don't win the job? Do you really have to forever resign yourself to the idea of being a "failure"? During the 2016 21CMposium, DePauw University welcomed performers, educators, entrepreneurs, and musicians of all kinds to reimagine the 21st-century musician. Sarah shared how she learned how to take charge of her own career: how she came to book her own shows; make her own programs; create opportunities; and, most important, how she learned to embrace music once again as something that could be not just life-affirming but also fun.

Want to learn more from Sarah? Me, too. Read highlights from her Talk21, delivered during DePauw's 2016 21CMposium, and watch the full presentation, "How I Stopped Asking Permission to Have a Career in Music," at 21CM.org.[2]

TALK21 HIGHLIGHTS

On the grueling ordeal of orchestra auditions . . .
A funny thing happened. The more auditions I took, the worse and worse I played—because I felt so much pressure. I knew there were only so many jobs available. . . . I had one really heartbreaking day as runner-up for a full-time job in Hawaii. But runner-up, final rounds—they get you nothing. You go home empty-handed, minus all the money and time you've spent. And I kept having to do this . . . failure after failure after failure. No job. I got depressed, and I felt terrible all the time. And I started to take auditions really hard. When it didn't go well, I would come home, and I wouldn't be able to get out of bed for two or three days.

On the turning point . . .
One winter evening in Cincinnati, I went into the Blue Wisp Jazz Club, and I saw the musicians of Classical Revolution Cincinnati performing there. And they were taking their music straight to their audience. . . . They booked their own clubs, they found their colleagues, [they] chose what they were going to play. And I saw creativity, joy, life, music, and this beautiful connection between audience and performers. And it was like I had spent 10 years banging my head against a door that would never open, only to look around and realize that there were no walls. I could just walk outside and create the career that I wanted.

On what performance started to mean . . .
Gradually I came to realize that I really didn't care if I had the job that would prove I was a successful musician. I was too busy being a musician. I was creating projects, collaborating, contributing to other people's projects. And I found that I wasn't a fearful performer anymore. Because performing meant getting together with a bunch of people I really liked and making something awesome.

On personal definitions of success . . .
I came to my own definition of success. And I would check my internal compass against what I was doing to see if it was successful. So [now] I ask myself: Is it interesting? Am I supporting other artists? And am I helping to make people's lives a little happier and a little bit more fulfilling? And those questions are how I decide what I do next in my career.

LOCATING YOUR NASCENT SUPERPOWERS

If you are going to succeed on your journey, you will need to do more than excel as a musician. You will need to be a superhero with the requisite superpowers.

* * * *

To share with you something about her journey and how it might inform yours, we asked Jennifer Rosenfeld, CEO of iCadenza, president of Cadenza Artists, and co-author of Awakening Your Business Brain: An iCadenza Guide to Launching Your Music Career, *about harnessing your superpowers.*

Harnessing Your Superpowers[3]
by Jennifer Rosenfeld

Eight years ago, my partner Julia and I were music majors finishing up our senior years. While our classmates practiced for their graduate school auditions, we pondered how to attract different kinds of audiences to their future concerts. Not sure the performance track was the right one for us, yet knowing nothing about the business world, we were at a crossroads.

We knew we were on to something with our audience-development ideas, so we gathered whatever how-to books we could get our hands on, created a business plan, and, on a whim, entered it into a competition. Imagine our surprise when we won second place! This victory (because that's how it felt to us) was the impetus to launch iCadenza.

That's when we entered the real world. Nothing prepares you for just how challenging it is to start a new company. The first two years were brutal! The confidence we had gained writing that business plan fell like a house of cards when it became painfully clear how little we really knew. But we had tenacity. Over time, we realized that what it takes to become a successful entrepreneur is not a PhD or a secret formula. It is simply the repetition of core behaviors that we had already developed through our years as students and musicians. By acknowledging those powerful skills and refining them, we turned them into what we like to call our "superpowers."

WHAT ARE SUPERPOWERS?

Your artistry and ideas are the substance, and "superpowers" are the vehicles for achieving your mission—the unique abilities that exist at the intersection of passion, skill, and drive. "Superpowers" are shaped by your values and beliefs as well as your professional habits. The specific powers we call on regularly in our own work include:

Wonder
Definition: curiosity mixed with a driving impulse to seek out problems worth solving
Before we ever had the idea to launch a consultancy and agency, we were curious about the challenges musicians face in the industry. Talking to many people—legends and up-and-comers—gave us a broader sense of their needs.

Imagination
Definition: devising unique solutions to observed challenges
Thinking about those conversations with the many musicians, we considered what didn't exist yet that would make a difference in their lives. How could we tackle the challenge, using our specific talents and background?

Critical Optimism
Definition: believing we can make a difference in the world, if we create a feasible plan of action
When we started iCadenza, there were lots of reasons why we were doomed to fail (as many people told us). Fortunately, Julia and I discovered that our natural optimism along with a healthy dose of pragmatism was a powerful combination. We sought out others' advice, weighed our own instincts and research, and ultimately came up with a thoughtful, well-reasoned plan of action. It's a process that continues to work well for us.

Tenacity
Definition: polite persistence in the face of challenges
We have found that tenacity shows up when optimism is put to the test. When we started out we were young and inexperienced; the industry was shrinking and closed-minded, and we were women in a male-dominated field. Yet, we were politely persistent in seeking out new inspiration, advice, and guidance. By not listening to a few naysayers or giving up, we eventually found our champions: the people who admired our stick-to-itiveness—and even offered to help.

Community
Definition: assembling the support and collaboration needed to bring an idea to fruition
Whether you are starting a business, ensemble, or movement, you can't do it alone. As best friends from high school who bonded over music, Julia and I had a history of collaborating. That laid the perfect foundation for our business partnership. We also benefited from early champions who gave us the scaffolding we needed in challenging times. Today, our community has grown to include our staff, artist clients, and the venues we service.

Communication
Definition: expressing meaningful content in a way that resonates with others
Your ability to communicate clearly and convincingly has a fundamental impact on how others perceive you. For iCadenza, we didn't initially realize that this would be one of the most important activities in running our business. We've continued to work to improve our communication skills so that we can enhance our efficacy.

Julia and I truly believe that developing these areas can help build your confidence and empower you to dream bigger. The first step is to recognize them. So, now it's your turn. We've created a Superpowers Assessment to help you identify and strengthen the six superpowers that have helped us so much.

• • • •

Spoiler alert: You have superpowers. Sometimes they are as simple as giving yourself permission to get in the game and be the superhero you know resides inside yourself. Want to find your nascent ultra-abilities? Take Jennifer's assessment on 21CM.org and find out more about how to harness your superpowers.[4]

• • • •

The ultimate musical "test" for an upstart artist with revolutionary ideas may be "imagineering" a festival. Composer Matt McBane did just that as director of the Carlsbad Music Festival. The festival was founded in 2003, about the time Matt began his professional career as a musician. He shares his experience here, to provide, as he says, either "an inspiration to younger musicians with visions of how they want to shape their musical world or a cautionary tale to those who prefer a saner life path."

A Composer's Take on Building a Festival[5]
by Matt McBane

In an issue devoted to "doing it yourself," the ultimate musical challenge may be "imagineering" a festival. Composer Matt McBane did just that as director of the Carlsbad Music Festival. The festival was founded more than 12 years ago—essentially the entirety of his professional career as a musician. He shares his experience here, either to provide, as he says, "an inspiration to younger musicians with visions of how they want to shape their musical world or a cautionary tale to those who prefer a saner life path."

GETTING IT GOING

The Carlsbad Music Festival was born out of dissatisfaction and love—dissatisfaction with the musical world that was presented to me, and love of the music I was learning about in and out of school. Living in Los Angeles after graduation, I found no existing organizations or communities interested in nurturing the work of a composer at the beginning of his career and very little opportunity to hear the work of my peers once outside academia. I also had a sense that I wanted to do something with my life that served the community in addition to following my muse as a composer. My experience at the Bang on a Can Summer Institute showed me that composers with a vision and dissatisfaction with the status quo could change the musical landscape.

I came up with the crazy idea to start a festival at age 23—with no real prior experience other than organizing a few musical concerts in college—in part out of missionary zeal to share the music I loved and in part to figure out how to have a musical life for myself in the world as a creative musician. The idea for the first year was two concerts in a weekend plus outreach events in the schools in my California hometown of Carlsbad (a beach town north of San Diego) with several friends from USC, including the Calder Quartet (which served for the first 10 years as Founding Ensemble-in-Residence). To this humble series, with the support of a risk-taking grant from the City of Carlsbad Arts Office (thanks, Colleen Finnegan!), I gave a somewhat grandiose title: the Carlsbad Music Festival.

This first year, I did literally every job that went into making the festival happen: from programming, to program layout, to writing a major new piece (my string octet "2×4"—check it out!), to writing grants to fund the event, to marketing, to setting up chairs. That first year, I worked incredibly hard, and the necessity of hard work has been one of the constants in the years since.

From this first year, the Carlsbad Music Festival has grown to become an organization with four part-time employees that puts on two major events of "adventurous music by the beach" per year: our three-day festival in August and one-day Village Walk in June. Each event includes more than 60 performances and draws on average 4,500 audience members for a total of 9,000 annually.

Son de San Diego and Wu Man at Carlsbad Music Festival. *Photo courtesy of Tommy McAdams.*

The festival has garnered widespread critical acclaim, including praise from the *Los Angeles Times*, Alex Ross of *The New Yorker*, and just about every local paper. We have presented world and national premieres by master musicians such as Wu Man, David Lang, and Steven Schick; we have championed emerging musicians such as Jennifer Bewerse, Scott Worthington, and Trouble in the Wind; we have helped bring together disparate music scenes for new collaborations; and we have built a substantial audience for adventurous music where one didn't exist before.

SHAPING THE VISION (CONTINUALLY)
From the get-go, I had a clear vision of what I wanted the festival to be. However, a key to its success, growth, and sustainability has been the continual expansion and refining of this vision. As my musical perspective broadened, the festival grew, our audience developed, and I learned how to run an organization.

The most consequential reshaping of the vision of the festival to date came in its seventh year with a move from its library auditorium home out into the streets of the historic Village neighborhood. This decision came from an openness to new ideas and a continual rigorous evaluation of the vision of the organization.

The festival started out and spent its first six years growing and refining as a handful of ticketed concerts on a weekend in an auditorium in one of the city's libraries. However, despite the library's charm, it was located in a strip mall with little character, surrounded by recently built tract homes (your typical SoCal suburbia) and was a venue that felt appropriate to only certain genres. This limited what the festival could be, the range of music it could present, and how much it could actually feel like a "festival" as opposed to a concert series.

Opus Orange performing at Carlsbad Music Festival.

In 2010 I took a leap to present our first "Village Music Walk" to kick off the fest on a Friday. Inspired by my experiences in DIY venues in Brooklyn (where I live) and by festivals that made creative use of their city, like Big Ears in Knoxville, Tennessee, the music walk took place in businesses (record store, art gallery, etc.) and public spaces (train station, parking lot, etc.) throughout the city's historic core near the beach known as the Village. This event was such a success and revelation about what the festival could be that the next year, we moved the entirety of the festival to the Village, forgoing $12,000 in funding tied to the library venue and moving from the known to the unknown (much to the consternation of our board).

In its current state, the Carlsbad Music Festival maintains its highly curated ticketed concerts but has a wide range of free concerts as well (60 per festival) in an array of venues. This allows the festival to present a huge diversity of musicians working in different forms and at different stages of their careers, all under the large umbrella of "adventurous music"—everything from contemporary classical to creative rock bands to world music to experimental instrument builders to all kinds of music that can't be categorized.

FINDING THE MISSION

Once in the Village, the true nature of what the Carlsbad Music Festival is revealed itself. Two words began to emerge as a description of its mission, musicians, and audience: *adventurous* and *community*. These two words now permeate our organization and are used as everything from marketing taglines to conceptual guides. I didn't realize when I founded the festival, but as the organization has developed, I see that these two concepts have been through lines from the get-go, and they were only allowed to fully bloom with this venue move.

In many ways, the journey of the festival has resolved several of the dissatisfactions I had with the musical world I was presented and allowed me to share a wide range of music I love with the broader public.

In imparting whatever wisdom I can, I think if you want start an organization, a crucial thing is to know clearly why you want to start it. What do you feel is lacking in your musical world that a new organization can change? What are the things you love in your musical world that a new organization can better serve?

One of the things I have seen through starting and running my own organization and through watching friends start and run their own, such as New Amsterdam Records, wild Up, and Switchboard Music, is that musical culture is not a fixed thing that has to be handed down to us from above, but is something to which we all contribute and help shape. So, think about what you're dissatisfied with and what you love, what you want to change and what you want to share. Then, if you're moved to, start your own organization. Your passion and ideas can help build the musical world you want to live in.

Also, be ready to work very hard!

CREATE YOUR FESTIVAL

Intrigued at the thought of starting your own music festival or presenting organization? Here is a list of questions (and my answers) to start off your exploration.

1. **What do you love and want to share with the world?**
   For me, I wanted to share the music of the composers I loved with the broader world. It was also critical to me to build an organization that could support the work of emerging composers and performers.

2. **On the flip side, what are you dissatisfied with and want to change in the world?**
   At the time of the Carlsbad Music Festival's conception, I felt that the existing Southern California music organizations I knew of seemed closed off to emerging composers or to composers crossing genres and working outside of academia.

3. **What kind of musical life do you want to create for yourself and how does this dream organization fit into that concept?**
   I wanted to find a community of like-minded composers and musicians. I wanted to include this sense of community in the fabric of "Carlsbad."
4. **Which artists and people do you want to work with?**
   It was important to bring in both my friends, whose music I loved, as well as some of my musical heroes like Michael Gordon, Steven Schick, Wu Man, David Lang, and Shara Worden.
5. **What are other like-minded organizations with whom you can partner?**
   Partnerships have been one of the most crucial elements to the festival's success. For instance, our long partnership with ArtPower at UCSD has resulted in six co-commissions.
6. **Who are some of your dream collaborators?**
   I still have a long and ever-expanding list of musicians I would love to bring to the festival, and each year I check a few names off that list.

• • • •

SUMMARY

Tenacity is likely the most valuable attribute you possess. It gets you through difficult practice sessions, disappointing performances, and failed auditions. But if tenacity were only a survival mechanism for life's most challenging moments, some would simply prefer to avoid failure altogether. Your tenacity is what pushes you to seek something that currently exists only at the edge of your imagination. It's a superpower. Now that you know you have superpowers, how will you harness them? We can't wait to find out!

CHAPTER 4

THINKING ABOUT CREATIVITY: FUELING THE IMAGINATION

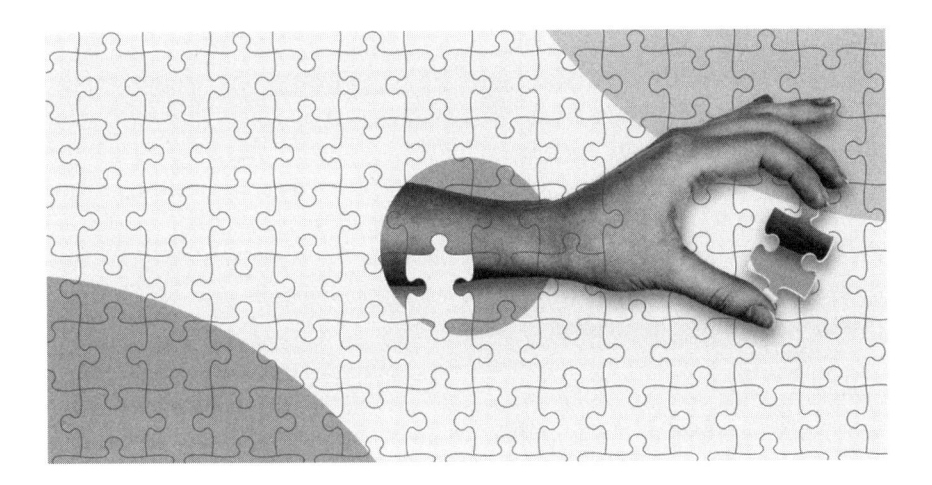

YOU ARE A CREATIVE artist. Yet in the pursuit of your career, you may have spent little time actually investigating creativity, its applications, and how to nurture and develop it toward greater artistry and invention. In this chapter, we take a deep dive into creativity with the hope of gaining a more comprehensive understanding of both its process and the foundational role it plays in our artistry and entrepreneurial thinking.

DEFINING AND FOSTERING CREATIVITY

Curiosity drives us to ask questions. Creativity helps us answer them.

As performers, this is true as we prepare for all that is required of us to make our art. Curious about what we can achieve on our instrument, we answer with creativity. Whether technically mastering complex passages through multiple approaches in practice or breathing life anew into a piece by crafting an interpretation that both embodies the history of the work and infuses our unique voice, creativity is the defining line. It is the line that distinguishes the careful from the courageous, the impressive from the impassioned, and the memorable from the indelible. Creativity is the secret sauce, or what Elizabeth Hinckley—one of the most creative thinkers I have known and my editor for this book—called "the plus factor" in her 21CM.org piece "The Art (+ Science) of 'It.'"[1]

So if creativity defines inspired performances, breathtaking moments, and plus-factor artistry, what is the field of music doing to foster it?

In higher education today, courses sprinkled across the curriculum touch on elements of creativity, frequently in very positive ways. Electives such as "Improvisation for Classical Musicians" are popping up within music schools, challenging students to move beyond the confines of their comfort zone and to see themselves as spontaneous composers.

Arrangement and composition assignments within theory sequences provide a glimpse into the composer's mind, but these opportunities are few and far between and do not truly allow students to develop the chops necessary to move beyond crafting a functional assignment, never mind affording the headroom to stretch the students' imaginations.

World music and new music ensembles provide broad exposure to diverse cultural norms, rare access to composers' intentions and thought processes, and hands-on experience with unfamiliar instruments, notational systems, and extended techniques. When grappling with foreign traditions, we learn to see through the mind's eye of the composer, expanding notational systems and the sonic palate of an otherwise familiar instrument in the process. Everything about these experiences exudes creativity, yet these ensembles are most often "in addition to" rather than the "officially approved" ensembles for credit—band, choir, orchestra. To be clear, creativity can thrive anywhere, but we have seen that experiences that push us beyond the confines of familiarity, stretch our imaginations, invite us to think outside of ourselves, and expand our creative thought must become core, not ancillary, curricular requirements.

Research aimed at unveiling the creative process is being conducted in almost every field of intellectual study, including inquiry into the many intersections of musical creativity and what we might otherwise think of as disparate fields. Book titles such as *The Improvising Mind: Cognition and Creativity in the Musical Moment* (Berkowitz); *Gender, Age, and Musical Creativity* (Haworth and Colton); *Computer Models of Musical Creativity* (Cope); and *Steal This Music: How Intellectual Property Law Affects Musical Creativity* (Demers) provide research-rich insights from such diverse perspectives as psychology, gender studies, computer science, and the law. Understanding these perspectives can help foster our creativity, detangle the creative process (or processes), and introduce many new applications of creativity for our art—at the edges of the disciplines and in our life's work.

BRUCE ADOLPHE—COMPOSER, AUTHOR, PIANIST

To ground our thinking about how embracing creative activity across diverse planes of thinking can influence our lives as revolutionary artists, I want to examine the professional life of one of our authors, Bruce Adolphe.

It is difficult to envision a career more diverse and meaningful than Bruce's. A sought-after composer, with world premieres delivered by cellist Yo-Yo Ma and violinists Itzhak Perlman and Joshua Bell, Bruce carves time out every day to keep pace with commissions contracted from across the classical music spectrum. As a leading voice on creativity, Bruce's ability to communicate complexity extends from the cerebral to the playful. He is the author of three books, and he has held faculty appointments at Juilliard, Yale, and NYU and a composer-in-residence position at the Brain and Creativity Institute in Los Angeles. He also taps into his talent for making classical music accessible to new and young audiences as the Piano Puzzler in his weekly spot on American Public Media's *Performance Today* and as founder and director of Lincoln Center's family concert series Meet the Music!

In Bruce's book *The Mind's Ear*, he unveils the hidden mechanisms of the creative process as well as provides concrete exercises to foster our own creativity, shared on the book's companion website. Recently, the 21CM.org Book Club featured *The Mind's Ear*. Readers, intrigued to expand their own creativity, posed interview questions about the psychology behind the exercises, the thought process behind the development of these ideas, and the role the exercises have played in the author's own creativity in his career as a composer, thinker, and artist. Additionally, Bruce puts listeners to the test with an exercise to push their creative boundaries. You can listen to the full interview on 21CM.org.[2]

So if creativity can be fostered, harnessed, and honed to expand our artistic perspectives, increase our ability to generate creative programming and projects, and reimagine our careers, where do we go from here?

CREATIVITY IN YOUR OWN WORDS

When I want to wrap my head around a big, new subject, I start my research by hunting for definitions from a variety of sources. I have found that this exercise helps me define parameters as well as where the subject "sits"—in the world and in my own life. In applying this exercise to "creativity," I've discovered a bonus benefit: it helps craft a vision statement for one's artistic life. Questions like these are generated: How do I move past my comfort zone? How do I embrace new approaches to performance (improvisation, global music influences, interdisciplinary collaborations)? How can I think more creatively and act innovatively, moving ideas into action? Universally, it speaks to our role in advocating for the arts as a means of fostering creativity more broadly, including ongoing arguments of STEM v. STEAM. All useful ideas to grapple with for a *revolutionary artist*.

So, with that introduction, perhaps the best place to begin an exploration of expanding our creative capacity is to define creativity in our own words.

For me, Mark Rabideau, creativity is the wondrous space between things familiar and things yet imagined.

In music, this gap lies somewhere beyond pop tunes that I can sing along with, even upon the first hearing. Right? You've never heard the song, but somehow you can already anticipate the form, harmonic structure, and melodic shape and even take a pretty good stab at the next lyric rhyme scheme. Creative? Not so much. It's predictable. On the other hand, in my experience, when something is so foreign that there is no path to follow, creativity is simply chaos.

Inarguably my definition is flawed and likely somewhat different from your concept of creativity and the words that surround your definition. For instance, those with ears bigger than my own will be able to trace the thought process driving highly complex music and deem it as creative. For them, it *falls in the gap*.

In my own efforts to solicit a definition via online and print resources like YouTube videos, TED Talks, and PBS features, among others, I found an enormous breadth of thought on what creativity means across disciplines, most expressions more eloquent than my own.

In Wikipedia, creativity is described as "a phenomenon whereby something new and somehow valuable is formed." The entry continues:

> Scholarly interest in creativity includes many definitions and concepts pertaining to a number of disciplines: engineering, psychology, cognitive science, education, philosophy (particularly philosophy of science), technology, theology, sociology, linguistics, business studies, songwriting, and economics, covering the relationship between creativity and general intelligence, mental and neurological processes, personality type and creative ability, creativity and mental health; the potential for fostering creativity through education and training, especially as augmented by technology; . . . and the application of creative resources to improve the effectiveness of teaching and learning.

It is important to note that academics have a fraught relationship with this less-than-scholarly source, but even with that said, something doesn't feel right about this. A little sterile? For sure. But as an artist, I'd like to see more mention of the arts—literature, dance, sculpture, music, film, theater.

My generation's Wikipedia was called the *New Encyclopaedia Britannica*. Here's its definition of creativity: "The ability to make or otherwise bring into existence something new, whether a new solution to a problem, a new method or device, or a new artistic object or form."

I love this definition, as it embraces such a breadth of outcomes. Although, if we were to be technical, most would agree that this more accurately defines *innovation*, as it moves the creative thought into action, with a clear outcome as a result.

In an effort to discover ever-broadening definitions of creativity, I thought to ask some of the most creative folks I know—all from very different cultural backgrounds—what their definition is for creativity.

Gamin performs on traditional Korean wind instruments in the Contemporary Gugak Orchestra.[3] The group performs at the National Gugak Center, which serves as the hub for training and preserving Korean traditional music. When we asked Gamin to help unearth the habits of the creative mind, she spoke about the need to take an "honest and very personal" approach to our own creative work, insisting that it must reflect the individual, above all.

Here's what Melissa Snoza of Fifth House Ensemble[4] had to say about individual creativity and creativity at the organizational level:

> Creativity for me is about a couple of things, and I know where I am in this. There's a person like Dan Visconti who can create something from nothing. He can sit down at a table and a piece of music flies out of his brain that's never been there before. That's a particular kind of creativity. For me, creativity is less about making something from nothing than about collage. I'm the kind of person where creativity means seeing the connections between really disparate things that other people don't see.
>
> And so, within the organization, my job is to look at a piece of music that someone really wants to play and a potential partner that came into our orbit through attending a conference (like the 21CMposium) or a problem that I see going on in the world around me or that someone has come to me with, and I find the nexus of those things that turns into a project. That's for me what creativity means in my particular world, but a project like Fifth House needs creativity of many different kinds, and that's one of the reasons that I'm so grateful to have the people in our group that we do. Every single person comes into it with a different facet in mind, with a different set of skills, and that's a beautiful thing.

What's your definition of creativity?

A CREATIVE PROCESS FRAMEWORK

You might think creativity is uncontrollable—a fleeting spark of inspiration. It's romantic to think of our favorite creatives as being inspired solely by their muses. But the truth is, the most prolific ones I know also rely on a process. And as with anything you want to get good at, the more aware you are of the steps of the creative process, the better chance you have to master them and harness them for your work.

Enter Mihaly Csikszentmihalyi. Csikszentmihalyi has written some of the seminal work in the field of creativity. His book *Creativity: Flow and the Psychology of Discovery and Invention*[5] offers the following five-step framework for the creative process.

1. Preparation
The first step, *preparation*, is the act of "becoming immersed in problematic issues that are interesting and arouse curiosity." For musicians, this is our deep dive into the practice room and rehearsal halls, what famed bass trombonist David Taylor calls "embracing the joy of the struggle."[6]

Csikszentmihalyi is clear that to truly become a creative within a "domain," one must spend at least 10 years of study within that field. Interestingly, this aligns with Malcolm Gladwell's 10,000-Hours Rule, as shared in his 2008 book *Outliers: The Story of Success*. Gladwell makes the argument that it takes 10,000 hours of practice or apprenticeship to truly obtain mastery, whether that is as a concert pianist, a professional hockey player, or a successful entrepreneur. Honing your craft brings you to the gateway of the creative process, poised to enter the longer conversation about the art form, and the endless possibilities of what can be.

As an example, when we think of jazz musicians on the front edge of the learning curve, we see that they spend their time emulating their heroes. Transcribing solos, copying inflection, and memorizing clichés (standard phrases) positions emerging jazz artists in close proximity to creative output, even if not their own at first. Although this is essential, it is by definition re-creative, not creative.

It is only as these young jazz artists begin to think about the tune in a way that no one else has thought about it and "stretch"—a term I love and one for which I desperately wish there were a classical-music parallel—that their own creativity comes to life. Stretching is when musicians go for something they have never heard, never played, in search of alternate chords over standard changes or craft their sound to make it uniquely their own. It is at those times that they begin to find their own voice and see and share their art from a rare vantage point. It is this very distinction that draws the line between true innovators of jazz—Duke Ellington,

Charlie Parker, Miles Davis, Ella Fitzgerald—and those of us still in search of our voices. Great examples include how Miles Davis transformed "Someday My Prince Will Come"[7] and John Coltrane captured "My Favorite Things."[8]

2. Incubation
When "ideas churn around below the threshold of consciousness," you are in the *incubation* stage. Here, it's important to take a moment and think. The scaffolding of our daily lives is not structured around affording us time to sit with our thoughts, imagine new projects, and envision future collaborations. Rather, we fill every moment of silence with commitments or distractions, some important, some urgent, and many neither important nor urgent. Yet they all find their ways onto our calendars. We manage work, gigs, friends and family, our real lives, and, sometimes—even more time consuming—our virtual lives.

Find time to think. Time to play in the messy, fertile spaces of our imagination where creative thought begins. Find time to be creative.

3. Insight
"The Aha! moment when the puzzle starts to fall together" is *insight*. This is the moment that many theories refer to as the muse—the inspiration brought down from the heavens by the daughter-goddesses of Zeus. More likely, this is the moment when your time logged in at your craft joyfully collides with your exploration of that wondrous space between things familiar and things yet imagined, culminating in a creative, original idea. Even if it is incomplete.

Insight is when you first get a taste of an idea, often catching you off guard. It could happen in the car or on a run. It sometimes happens in the shower or while asleep. Wherever, whenever it happens, you are aware of your thoughts.

David Cutler, truly a leader in the field of arts entrepreneurship, once asked me if I ever noticed that some folks have 1,000 ideas and some folks have one or two, but almost nobody has eight or nine ideas. Although this completely took me off guard, once I had a moment to digest it, what I thought at the time to be a radical notion made complete sense. We have the "idea people" and those who execute ideas, but it is not often that you find these to be the same folks, all bundled up in one. (Note: You met David in chapter 1, and he appears again later in this book. He is a great and rare combination of the idea guy and the guy who gets it done.)

4. Evaluation
"Deciding if the insight is valuable and worth pursuing" sums up *evaluation*. Evaluation is a great moment to bounce ideas off trusted colleagues. Something different happens when we simply share our ideas out loud with others. Even

as our own ears hear the words, we begin to process our evaluation of the idea's validity, feasibility, importance, and impact differently. This, too, is the moment that separates those who enjoy imagining creative ideas and those who are capable of moving these ideas beyond the Aha! to truly bring about meaningful change—innovators.

We introduced Peter Seymour in chapter 2 as one of today's artist-revolutionaries. When Peter talks about the earliest days of PROJECT Trio, you can almost pinpoint the moment he realized this new ensemble was worth chasing down. With endless optimism in the process, you can hear in this interview excerpt how committed he is to bringing it to life in ways not yet imagined.

IN CONVERSATION WITH PETER SEYMOUR

"When PROJECT Trio first started, we knew it could be something special because of the amazing music we were putting out. All three of us had been kind of chasing this orchestral career, and we found ourselves in our late 20s and we just weren't happy with where our musical paths had taken us. I think it was a special moment because all of us were on the verge of being out of the music business completely, so I think that when we came together and just started making music, we knew that this could be the thing that could guide the next 10 and 20 and 30 years of our careers. And we also knew that we *had* to do it, and I think that's the most special thing about it—we all came to this place where if we didn't make something happen, if we didn't create something that was our own, then we were going to get pushed out of the business. So we all just went full force into making music, producing videos, and doing all of the things that it takes to have a full-time ensemble."

5. Elaboration

"Translating the insight into its final work," or *elaboration*, is when ideas move from vision to fruition, creativity to innovation, concepts to action. Having creative thoughts and bringing your creative energy to life are very different attributes.

It is my belief that creativity is the defining line between desperation and hope. With no way of imagining a better life, we are only left with our current reality. For those living at the edge of desperation, knowing that they can reimagine their own existence and be an agent for change in their own world makes way for hope. This is why providing creative opportunities for everyone is crucial, with special attention to those at the margins.

It is important to note that, although presented here linearly, the creative process is iterative, continually circling back through each stage, allowing the ideas to toggle across the stages and mature.

What does your creative process look like?

To learn more about Csikszentmihalyi's theory of flow, watch his 2004 TED Talk "Flow: The Secret to Happiness."[9]

Creating the Revolutionary Artist is about preparing you to move your creativity into the marketplace. It is about equipping you with the entrepreneurial mindset and providing you with the skills and knowledge needed to bring your ideas to life. Hopefully, it will serve as a forum to take measured risks, leverage your greatest resources—time, money, energy, and mind space—and develop your resourcefulness.

* * * *

Mark Clague is a tenured musicologist at the University of Michigan's School of Music, Theatre & Dance, where he also serves as director of Entrepreneurship and Career Services. A treasured mentor, he has helped students land positions with institutes as diverse as Oberlin Conservatory, LA Philharmonic, Google, and the Rock 'n' Roll Hall of Fame.

Taking Measured Risks
by Mark Clague

Risk is an essential part of being. To do something is inherently dangerous. You might fail and (maybe just as threatening to your comfort zone) you might succeed.

Fortunately, artists are inspired by risk. It's our job to embrace it. Artists seek to delight, to surprise, to engage, to enrage—in sum, to give our communities fresh ideas and new perspectives. Saying something is always risky; it's also exciting and always a journey of personal and professional growth.

One logical response is to reduce risk, to be less bold, less ambitious—to try to measure risk and decide if the likelihood of success merits the danger. Yet to measure risk before it is taken is ultimately impossible. Only zero risk can be known. Risk can't be fully controlled. To try to do so is to let risk become the focus, diminishing your possibilities of success.

Risk, instead, is your guide. Risk demands the best that your intelligence and effort can muster. Increase your chances of success by preparing. Risk will galvanize your fears and help you identify the skills, resources, and vision needed to succeed. Work hard to prepare for this success. That said, no amount of preparation can eliminate risk completely.

Instead, expand your target area—your goals—the outcomes (plural) that define your success. Understand that aiming for the pinnacle means falling short much of the time, but that failing to reach the summit is still to ascend far up the mountainside. Learn from the journey. If you're ambitious, you will fail much of the time, but failure is only that if you fail to learn, and if you stop trying to make a difference.

• • • •

What is gained by better understanding the creative process? We must afford ourselves time to follow our curiosities and to be with our thoughts. We must both recognize the "Aha! moment" and also continually reevaluate how our efforts can best advance our goals. If we are to move beyond simply creative thought and into innovation in action, we must do the hard work to bring about meaningful change.

Imagination is something that we must exercise to strengthen and grow if we want to expand this engine of innovation.

• • • •

Moonlight and Chocolate: Finding Inspiration[10]
by Bruce Adolphe

How do you get inspired? This is a common question at composition forums. Performers are asked the same question. We know a performance or a composition is inspired when we hear it, and we want nothing less. For musicians, inspiration must become a way of life—but how do we find it again and again?

Inspiration may come from anywhere: moonlight, mountains, mathematics, a phrase of Mozart, birdsong, a crack of thunder, a starry night, dark chocolate, a stranger's glance. The possibility of inspiration is always out there in the world—and you must be willing and prepared, open and ready.

Take moonlight. It has inspired poets, musicians, and artists for centuries. Even after humans learned that the moon reflects the light of the sun and has none of its own glow, even after astronauts landed on it and stuck a flag in its soil, the moon holds magic for those who seek the feeling and are ready to receive it. Its magic is all about our perception and desire.

Inspiration is the connecting of experience to emotional memory and to imagination. Emotional memories are felt in the body, relived in the moment, experienced anew—fear, delight, joy, passion, sorrow, anger, yearning. When you feel an emotion pulse through your body and your mind suddenly floods with related memories, that is a key moment for imagination and inspiration. Memory and imagination work together.

Working with music students over many years, I developed some exercises that use memory to trigger the imagination and help find that feeling of inspiration. A good way to begin is to start with a memory, any memory at all, and remember it with as much detail as possible. The next step is to let the image evolve "on its own" into something new. Take note of how it feels to allow the image to change without your mind seeming to control it. That is how the imagination works best, and it brings with it the sense of *aha!* that we call *inspiration*.

Years ago, Itzhak Perlman commissioned me to compose a solo violin work for him, and he asked that it be about food. Food? I asked why. He said it was for the fun and joy of it, and that was enough for me. We asked Louise Gikow to write short poems about food for each solo violin movement. Louise and I presented a movement called "Brandy" to Itzhak. Reading through it, Itzhak stopped and said that he doesn't really like brandy and that he would prefer to think of this very lyrical piece as chocolate cake. He immediately began to play the piece with a deliciously sticky chocolate legato. Not only did the notes stick, but the title "Chocolate Cake" stuck, too. Itzhak found chocolate inspiring and brandy not so much. But more important, the technique of the gooey legato that he suddenly found is a perfect example of how performance can be affected by inspiration. There are many kinds of legato a violinist can employ, but a legato inspired by chocolate is bound to be unique, personal, and sound inspired . . . because it is.

But what if *you* are playing a solo sarabande by Bach, where chocolate is not a particularly appropriate image for the technique? Just as Itzhak used the music to lead him to chocolate, which then led to a new idea of how to play the music, try starting with the music itself. Play the sarabande without thinking of technique, but instead allow the music to stimulate your emotional memory; perhaps the music will make you feel sorrow or grief. But you don't want to merely indicate grief in your playing, you want to actually feel it and then allow your memory to reveal its source. From there, you will find that technique is about expression, not something separate. Just as the chocolate inspired a thick kind of bowing, grief may lead you to an expressive use of the bow and vibrato that are more emotionally authentic, more connected to the music and your own life than you may have discovered by practicing the notes over and over, and working on a concept of phrasing that is not your own.

I have found inspiration in all sorts of extra-musical events and ideas, including real-life experiences, concepts in neuroscience, moments in history, visual arts, literature, and other music. When composing the music for the film *Einstein's Light*, I took phrases of violin music by Mozart and Bach that Einstein played and loved, and imagined these phrases floating, bending, shifting, and transforming as if they were part of one of Einstein's remarkable "thought experiments." Imagining Einstein being inspired by the music inspired my own musical thinking. I don't understand the mathematics involved in Einstein's theories, nor can I know what Einstein may have been thinking when he played Mozart or Bach, but the sense of wonder sparked by the *feeling* of the thought experiment was really all I needed to be deeply inspired.

So it is connections that inspire us. The moonlight, the mountains, or the stranger's glance triggers an emotion, which sparks our memory, which ignites our imagination. So to be inspired you must be ready to make those connections; pay attention to your feelings, your inner life, and pay attention to your surroundings. Then, when inspiration "strikes," remember that "technique" should serve the imagination. Practice the techniques of inspiration and imagination, and you will be ready for the real thing.

FIND YOUR MUSE

You can train yourself to be ready for inspiration with exercises that stimulate emotional memory and imagination. Just as you practice your instrument for intonation and technical mastery, you can practice your ability to be emotionally engaged and inspired.

Here is a series of exercises for discovering other ways to play that same Bach sarabande with inspired feeling. In each case, a strong emotional scenario is set up as the environment for your performance and so your imagination is triggered. Before you play the sarabande, imagine each situation shown below:

- You are about to play the sarabande for a group of prisoners who are condemned to death. What do they need from the music? What in the music will speak to them? How would you play for them?
- Pretend now that you know nothing about music and have never played violin, but you are given an enchanted violin that lets you magically play the sarabande when you hold it. You are bewildered as the music unfolds. How does the music sound when you have no control over it? The enchanted violin plays so beautifully, yet you are surprised and delighted by what it does. Let it happen.
- You bring your violin to a hospital where you play for patients every day. Today, the only person listening to you play the sarabande is very depressed and has not said a word for days. There is total silence in the room before you start. Is the patient hearing you? Can you play in such a way as to draw her out of her cocoon? Is it possible that the music you play can bring her relief? How do you play under these circumstances?
- You read a scholarly musicological article that says that Bach clearly intended each phrase of this particular sarabande to be more joyful

than the previous one. You are convinced that this is true. Can you play it that way?
- You are captured by terrorists who immediately notice your violin. They tell you that they will spare your life if you can move them to tears by your playing. You play the same Bach sarabande for them. Should you exaggerate the passion in the music to save your life, or should you trust that your audience will understand it if you perform it as you would in a normal concert setting? Under these circumstances, perhaps you must deeply feel what in the music moves you and thus should move your captors. What is the deep message in this music, and how do you let it speak? Perhaps the less you "do" to the music, the more beautiful it will be. You can only play it once for the terrorists in this exercise, but, of course, in reality you can try this exercise many times.

The point of technique, whether instrumental or compositional, is to serve an inspired imagination. Technique should never display itself but should, at every moment, reveal the spirit of the music. And so an important aspect of our daily practice should be merging technique with inspiration.

What about practicing scales, you ask? Here is an exercise that addresses the problem of playing scales in the same old boring way every day:

- Play a scale as if you hate it.
- Play a scale as if you are a robot with no emotions. This is tricky. Feeling detached or bored is not without emotion. Is it possible to do this?
- Play a scale as if you have just recovered from paralysis of the hands and this is the first time you can play a scale again.
- Play a scale as if you truly believe it is a wonderful piece of music.

SUMMARY

Defining terms central to the mindset of the *revolutionary artist*, learning from multiple perspectives of highly creative musicians who are reinventing our musical world, and decoding the framework that serves as the underpinning of the creative process all bring clarity to what it means to be creative. We are artists, not simply instrumentalists; creators, not just folks who re-create the work of others; and central players in the reinvention of music for the 21st century.

CHAPTER 5

BUILDING A TEAM: COLLABORATION AND NETWORKING

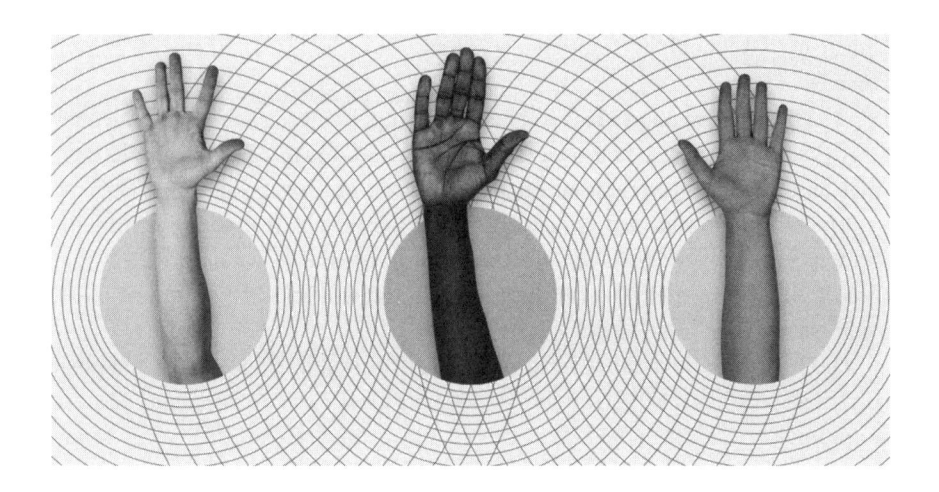

NO MAN IS AN island and few meaningful ideas are simple in the world of change. To succeed, you need a tribe that believes in the ideas pursued, listens to the greater wisdom of the crowd, and taps the unique talents of all collaborators and critical spheres of influence in the greater world.

To deliver technically flawless, artistically compelling performances, musicians invest in the solitude of the practice room. That process can feel like a lifetime. Depending on the balance of solo, chamber, or large ensemble performing in which you participate, it is not unusual to find that the majority of your time is spent in isolation. You will quickly realize that the power of strong collaboration, within both your artistic endeavors and the projects you engage, is critical to your success (and sanity) as an artist.

Understanding the rules of engagement surrounding strong collaborations, hearing the stories from some of the world's leading musicians about how their collaborations unfolded, and learning to avoid the blame game will give you a deeper understanding of what it takes to launch successful collaborations and how you can avoid some of the likely pitfalls.

BRAINSTORMING

Brainstorming is the process through which you draw upon the collective creativity and experience of your crowd. But how do we do this? What are the rules of engagement for brainstorming? What risks are involved?

To maximize creativity in the brainstorming phase specifically, I've culled a few "rules" from my own experience, as well as experts in the field, like Stanford University's d.school and 21CM.org editor and change facilitator Elizabeth Hinckley.

1. All ideas are good ideas in brainstorming. Want to shut down someone's creativity? Criticize the first idea they suggest and you're certain to stifle their voice and that of anyone else in earshot. As Mark McCoy, president of DePauw University, always says, it is not a leader's role to squelch creative energy but, instead, to uncover the "how" in order to bring to life the "wow factor" ideas that come from within their team. In other words, when presented with new ideas, begin with "Wow!" not "How?"

2. Out-of-the-box thinking should be encouraged. I once asked the great jazz trombonist Jiggs Whigham how he kept his ideas fresh over so many years as an improviser, and he replied, "It is simple. I hear the first idea that comes to my mind, and then I play anything but that." My takeaway? Avoid the ordinary. It has already been done, and it clearly didn't make the difference you had intended for it. One of the most out-of-the-box thinkers of the 20th century, Steve Jobs, famously helped craft an Apple commercial with this narration:

> Here's to the crazy ones. The misfits. The rebels. The troublemakers. The round pegs in the square holes. The ones who see things differently. They're not fond of rules, and they have no respect for the status quo. You can quote them, disagree with them, glorify or vilify them. About the only thing you can't do is ignore them. Because they change things. They push the human race forward. And while some may see them as the crazy ones, we see genius. Because the people who are crazy enough to think they can change the world, are the ones who do.

3. Quantity over quality. Generate lots of ideas during brainstorming. The less you focus on whether or not you have the "right" idea, the better. Simply get a load of ideas on the table. There will be plenty of time down the road to vet out the "right" ideas from the "not right at this moment" ideas.

4. Crowdsource toward the best ideas. The reason you formed your team in the first place is that you believe the wisdom of the crowd is exponentially greater than the wisdom of one. (Very wise of you.) So it seems likely the best ideas will come from across your team. Connect, combine, and improve upon the best ideas. This is the life of the entrepreneur, to connect dots that are not seen by others. This is where the greatest opportunities reside.

5. **Create a space that is conducive to collaborative thinking.** Some of the most creative ventures reside in spaces that boast of slides instead of stairs, Ping-Pong tables instead of boardroom tables, and writeable surfaces rather than surface conversations. Why? Because when folks see work as a safe space to play with ideas, be creative, and take risks, things tend to go well.

What suggestions do you have to foster collaborative thinking? Anything we need to avoid?

For me, one of the most successful collaborations in music is the Silk Road Ensemble.[1] Sandeep Das, the group's tabla player, represents the very best of this collective spirit. Tracing back to his debut with Pandit Ravi Shankar and performances at the United Nations General Assembly Hall (2008) and the opening ceremony of the Special Olympic Games in Shanghai (2007), Das's art embodies the openness required for reaching across cultural boundaries.

I recently asked him what he believed defines Silk Road's success, to which he replied, "Respect, trust, and heart. If these three things are involved, collaboration will happen."

THE BLAME GAME

Mark Twain once said, "There are basically two types of people. People who accomplish things, and people who claim to have accomplished things. The first group is less crowded."

If making the world a better place were easy, someone would have already done it, right? So don't be afraid to take chances. What anyone who has strived to do good in the world understands is that failure is going to happen at least some of the time. And if it doesn't, you know you aren't doing profoundly important work. The truth is, success is not always something that we can ensure or control. What you do in the face of failure is where I want to focus our attention.

Think back to a time when you were involved in a project that failed desperately. And this isn't an interview question where you are supposed to "tell me about your greatest failure" and then turn it into your greatest success. I am talking about genuine, unadulterated, epic failure. When your epic failure story unfolded, how did those involved respond? When the pressure was greatest, who took ownership over their own part? And who did not? In other words, who played the blame game?

The blame game is unfortunately much too familiar to many of us. The blame game is what happens when your team takes its focus away from a shared goal and starts blaming those around them for why the project isn't working. Think about it. It's easy: if my plan wasn't good enough to succeed, I can just blame someone else for not holding up her end of the bargain, and now I am in the clear. The best part is that usually you can find someone worthy of blame.

This is not to say that well-run organizations shouldn't care about identifying where problems arise, what went wrong, who needs to make adjustments, and what the best path forward from here is. If you don't fix the problem, it won't go away. But what is also true is that blaming someone doesn't move your agenda forward. It also doesn't help you achieve your goals. Actually, placing blame on someone else takes away agency to put the project back on track. Is it OK to identify problems? Sure. To create solutions? Even better. But falling into the blame game is an endless losing streak that never leads to success.

DePauw University president Mark McCoy also said that coming up with a good reason why you did not accomplish something is not the same thing as accomplishing something. Too often, we spend time and energy talking about why something cannot happen, time that would be better spent redirecting the project toward new goals.

The cold hard truth is that if every time something goes wrong you blame someone else or give up, then the only word on your tombstone will be *failure*. Frankly, I'm shooting for something more. And something tells me you are, too.

LIFE IS GOOD

I remember hearing the story about the two brothers who started Life is Good, the iconic clothing line that is built around the power of optimism embedded within the company name. Traveling from college town to college town, selling T-shirts on the street and hanging out at college parties, the brothers shared one simple goal: "Make a living by creating art."

Living out of a van and surviving on selling T-shirts can't be easy, but here is where their genius lay. After a long day of street sales and soliciting invitations to college parties, they would tape oversized pieces of paper on dorm room walls and draw a few ideas for their next product design, welcoming anyone and everyone at the party to add or comment on the sketch, and connect ideas from one corner of the room to the other. What the Life is Good guys were doing was crowdsourcing the R&D from their customer base. They were drawing upon the collective wisdom of their college-age market and leveraging these insights to develop their next big idea.

Whether it is effective brainstorming, avoiding the blame game, or crowd-sourcing for the best ideas, strong collaboration is essential in order to tap the best from your team. And regardless of whether your team is a pair of siblings launching a business from the road or a close-knit group of musicians wanting to share their art, in order to get the best out of every member of your team you need to create a space where everyone feels comfortable sharing their ideas. That's not as easy as it sounds.

Teams that function well move through problems, not around them. Yes, identify problems. Without doing this you will never have the opportunity to make changes, resolve issues, or forge a successful path. And part of identifying problems is identifying where the breakdown took place. But remain focused on problem-solving, not blame placing. Keep your eye on the prize.

• • • •

Mary Javian is chair of Career Studies and director of Professional Development and Community Engagement at the Curtis Institute, as well as a bassist who frequently performs with the Philadelphia Orchestra. What drives Mary's work? In her words: "To use music to create positive social change in communities."

The Art of Connection
by Mary Javian

Our personal and professional lives rest on a foundation of relationships. The people we surround ourselves with can provide a network of support that carries us through our greatest crises and lifts us up, allowing us to experience a deeper meaning in our life's work.

A career in music, at its best, is a series of opportunities to make connections with people and engage with the world. Ultimately, it is a way of creating meaning in the lives of others. But before we can make meaningful connections through a project, we must first cultivate our own capacity for empathy. Instead of focusing only on our big idea, we need to ask ourselves: What is the community experiencing? How is this endeavor meaningful to our audience, my colleagues, and the field as a whole?

When I graduated from Curtis, I knew that I both wanted to play music and share that music with the world in an impactful way. I formed an advisory council (for what I then called the Curtis Outreach Program) that consisted of passionate arts advocates dedicated to providing underserved communities access to arts. The relationships formed through this sounding board still inform my decision-making, almost 20 years later. I learned that the most successful people know how to find the expertise they need when they don't have the solution to a problem.

My leadership advice? Use the project you are working on to build relationships, both in and out of your field. Test your ideas, always act with empathy, and find meaning in that which is our greatest gift as artists: our ability to connect.

● ● ● ●

SPHERES OF INFLUENCE

It is easy to diminish our ability to make an impact. For one, we all have limited resources. How many times can we (or should we) hit up family members and close friends to support our next big idea? Second, the world is a big place, even as connected as it has become through social media platforms, 24-hour news cycles, and the vast commitment by so many of us to never be farther than arm's reach from our cell phones. So what gives us the audacity to think we can make a difference?

Walt Whitman's words have always buoyed my spirits in good and in challenging times. I turn for inspiration to his poem "O Me! O Life!"

> The question, O me! so sad, recurring—What good amid these, O me, O life?
> Answer.
> That you are here—that life exists and identity,
> That the powerful play goes on, and you may contribute a verse.

"Contributing a verse" does not mean that we must do so alone.

"Spheres of influence" is a simple concept. You know people who know people who, in turn, can connect you to their people. And presumably your expanding network shares some of your value system. It is not a stretch to imagine that if you care deeply about cats, you likely come from a family who had them in the home. Maybe your siblings now have cats in their homes, too. And maybe they have married other cat people along the way. As it works, when chatting with colleagues in the office, you find yourself attracted to those who share your love of cats.

If your artistic mission is to bring music to cats everywhere, believing deeply that every cat deserves the right to experience profoundly beautiful music in its life, then drawing upon your spheres of influence not only connects you to supporters, but also connects them to a cause they believe in and want to find ways to support.

Take a moment and list five spheres where you have influence.

Sometimes it is a bit more complicated than bringing music to cats. But with the entrepreneurial mindset of connecting otherwise disparate groups together to support a shared vision, we can leverage our spheres of influence in powerful ways: like pooling resources, telling your story, funding ideas, and moving your ideas to action. When we create projects where everyone finds value—a win-win world—this exemplifies the very definition of the entrepreneurial endeavor (as opposed to opportunistic: a paradigm in which someone wins at the expense of another).

Let me share a real-world example from a student-guided project that still, to this day, amazes me. In the fall of 2005, within the context of a music business class I was teaching at a regional university, I challenged students to identify a need, gap, or opportunity and then articulate and actualize a creative solution. One collaborative team decided they wanted to work on behalf of New York City jazz artist John Farnsworth. John is a brilliant musician who has enjoyed enormous success within the city, but, like so many other artists, he wanted to extend his reach nationally.

So, understanding that their own skill sets were not going to be enough to bring their idea to life, the students collaborated with a commercial radio station (Smooth Jazz 92.7), a jazz club on New York City's Upper West Side, and some of the most accomplished jazz artists of our day to produce "Live from Smoke"—a radio show that aired weekly to more than a quarter million Central Pennsylvania residents.

What really proved remarkable is how this project did not end simply because the course came to an end. While the planning for these projects occurred during the course, the realization of each one of them came to fruition after the course had been completed, when the students were beyond the reach of the grading system and there were no credits to be gained from the experience.

The students were so engaged in the experience of making a difference that they approached me the following fall with a plan to produce a CD that would capture some of the most exciting moments from the three-show series. *Live from Smoke: Monday Nights with John Farnsworth* was released in 2006 and features among its credits jazz legend Dr. Eddie Henderson; Joe Farnsworth, arguably the greatest living drummer; and former Art Blakey music director and trombonist Frank Lacy.

Amazingly, the students were not yet done wringing all they could from this collaborative experience. Their next project, *The World Is a Classroom: A Social Entrepreneurial Pedagogy for the Digital Age*, is a documentary, not about the project, but rather the educational process used to create it.

The documentary went on to win First Prize for Promotional Videos in the National Broadcast Society's Freedom States Competition. On YouTube, you can still view the film in its 31-minute, full-length version.[2]

So how did a team of music business students connect art, artists, and audiences in such a big way? They led with a dual vision: to grow an artist's career and impact a rural community. They measured their own strengths and weaknesses, capitalized from within, and reached out where help was needed. They found a moving story that resonated with a jazz club owner and a station manager who needed content out of his reach, and then they did the hard work of bringing all of these talents to bear.

Too often it is said, "It's not what you know, but who you know." Based on this experience, I think it is more accurate to say, "'Who knows what you know?"

In the case of "Live from Smoke," the club owner knew that I would guide the project, but he also understood that the students had built a team that could deliver a quality recording—one that reflected the club's commitment to outstanding jazz. The station manager took a chance on us, there's no question about that. But he also became invested in the project, part of the team, and thus within our sphere of influence.

As for the musicians? All of the proceeds of the thousands and thousands of CD sales have gone directly to the artists. This is their win. And what was our win? What we hoped to get out of it all along—a chance to share their story and impact our community. Nothing more. Nothing less.

If we want to run fast, we run alone. If we hope to run far, we run together.

SUMMARY

In this chapter we focused on understanding the rules of engagement surrounding strong collaborations, making overt the relationship between personal responsibility and success, opening our eyes to the power of tapping our own spheres of influence, and learning to avoid the blame game. You should come away with a deeper understanding of what it takes to launch successful collaborations and how to avoid some of the likely pitfalls awaiting each of us.

CHAPTER 6

PROBLEM-SOLVING: DEVELOPING SOLUTIONS THAT WORK FOR YOU

MUSICIANS BEGIN TO WEIGH artistic decisions as soon as they open their case and take out their instrument. In this chapter we discuss the importance of finding the problems we are best equipped to solve, learn the roles that divergent and convergent thinking play in the creative process, and add the "environmental" scan into our ever-growing toolkit of strategies.

PROBLEM-FINDING AND PROBLEM-SOLVING

If curiosity is about problem-finding, then creativity is about problem-solving.

Problem-finding and problem-solving are a set of skills at the core of bringing about meaningful change. As a musician, it is unlikely, no matter how deeply you care, that you will solve the ravenous disease malaria. Why? You likely don't possess the expertise or understand the history of the problem, its causes, the obstacles, what has been tried, and what has failed. You likely don't live within its complexities. You haven't logged your 10,000 hours in this arena. And you don't have the superpowers required to conquer this fateful enemy. What we can do, however, is find the problems we *are* equipped to address. And when we do, amazing things can happen.

Chris, a former music business student of mine, once came to me and asked why our degree program didn't have 24-hour access to a digital recording studio. So I asked him what difference that would make in his and his colleagues' lives, within our program. His eyes lit up and he began rattling off a long list of projects he would pursue, skills he would hone, and challenges he would embrace. More than hearing his words, I witnessed a feeling—the passion behind his message. So, I challenged him to make it happen and offered my support.

At the time, he was taking a class on grant writing. A crucial element of many fundraising campaigns, grant writing, in essence, is problem-finding and problem-solving. Given that Chris needed a grant subject to write about in order to complete the class, he decided to use the digital recording studio idea.

His process looked something like this:

1. **Identify the need.** What we call the "problem statement." The students needed a studio to effectively do their work.
2. **Define a set of clear and measurable goals.** In this case, it was to create a ProTools studio expressly for his colleagues and himself that would be accessible at any time. To accurately identify those goals, he considered:
   - How much funding will I need to pull this project off?
   - How will I measure the project's success?
   - What would it take to maintain the project and even fund for growth?

Now this was just for a class. He handed in his work and got an A for the course, and the semester came to a close. What happened next was when the fun began.

At the start of the next semester, our dean showed up to a class, asking if this student was there. He was. Completely unknown by either Chris or me, the dean announced that the grant had been funded—$20,000. The dean told Chris he was so impressed with his idea he was going to match the funds dollar for dollar. The student now had $40,000 to build his 24-hour-access digital recording studio.

It's here that I want to mention step 3 (and 3½) of problem-finding and problem-solving:

3. **Develop a solution and test it with your audience.** After Chris won his "grant" from the dean, he asked me for help in seeing his idea come to fruition.

Together, we commandeered a room, had the custodian tear out a wall that separated the studio from the now-recording booth, freshened up the look with some paint, brought in some old Oriental rugs to provide acoustical treatment and some cheap but funky IKEA furniture for function and form, and got busy building his ProTools studio. He led the way and I served as a somewhat-kinda-barely-able assistant.

In the fall, the department hired Chris to run the space as its first manager and he began what proved to be a long track record of recording projects. After leaving school he landed an internship with Jive Records and then a position with Atlantic Records. When it was time to name the studio, I chose the Computerized Recording Instructional Studio, using the acronym CRIS to honor Chris's ingenuity and entrepreneurial spirit.

So why did this project succeed? Chris cared deeply about the project and recognized a profound need felt by himself and his fellow students. Chris knew a whole lot about sound recording, the available technology, the limitations of his budget and space, and how to best leverage our team's strengths. He articulated the need in a persuasive manner and had the grit to spend summer evenings after his daytime gig building his dream. The project succeeded because Chris found the problem he was equipped to solve and he brought to that project an honest and pure enthusiasm for doing good. He found the change agent within.

How do we find the problem we, as emerging musicians, are best able to address?

DIVERGENT VS. CONVERGENT THINKING

Given unlimited resources of time, money, energy, and mind space, what would you hope to achieve?

Who would you impact? What needs would you meet, gaps would you fill, and opportunities would you create?

Divergent Thinking

Divergent thinking resides in those early moments during the creative exploration of ideas. Allowing for every possibility and every solution to be on the table, divergent thinking is when we dream wildly. No rules. No limitations. Divergent thinking best occurs when coupled with suspended reality.

It's a little bit like days gone by when your parents sent you out into the backyard or onto the playground for some good-old unstructured play. Left only to your imagination and an abundance of time, you would inevitably create a world you got lost in. This way of thinking is essential to the revolutionary artist. It keeps us open to possibilities without the distraction of obstacles.

The goal of divergent thinking is to generate as many ideas as possible. This sounds easy enough. So what gets in our way? Sometimes we just need to take our blinders off and see the world as it is, in order to see it as we want it to be. Don't believe me? Watch Daniel Simons's Selective Attention Test on YouTube.[1] (Don't continue reading until you do!)

This is the case of the "invisible gorilla," a remarkable insight experiment by psychologists Christopher Chabris and Daniel Simons. If you did not see the gorilla walking through the game of catch, you are not alone: 50 percent of viewers do not. Why? You weren't looking for it, so you didn't see it. Divergent thinking is about opening up our lens to see more possibilities—and, apparently, more gorillas.

Want a few hints on how this best works? There are three games you can play to open up your own divergent thinking, as shared by Stacey Goodman in his Edutopia.com article "Fuel Creativity in the Classroom with Divergent Thinking."[2] In Goodman's words:

> **Collage:** When artfully done, collage brings disparate images together and finds relationships based on aesthetics, absurdity, or spatial arrangements and not their literal meaning or function in the real world. Once the images are decoupled from their literal role, this opens up to nonlinear thinking in general.
>
> **Readymade:** This involves taking ordinary objects and through language, playfully renaming what they are or reimagining how they function. Artist [Marcel] Duchamp's most famous example is taking a urinal, flipping it upside down and calling it *Fountain*. I ask my students to do the same with the ordinary objects around them, and using the material, shape, or alternative functions of the object, they reimagine the object.
>
> **Pareidolia:** A phenomenon of looking at an object and finding semblance of something else that is not really there, much like seeing the shape of a dragon in the clouds, or noticing that a three-prong power outlet looks like a face. I show the students the short animated film *The Deep* by the artist PES, in which ordinary objects are turned into mysterious sea creatures. I then ask them to take photos of examples of pareidolia around them. Students have fun reinterpreting the world.

Even (or especially) those who thrive within this environment of idea generation can get lost playing among the millions of grains of sand in the sandbox. They can fall prey to a never-ending cycle of imagining what could be and never following through to the end on any one idea. Creative thought is a wondrous and joyful thing, but meaning is created only when it takes shape through real-world outcomes.

Convergent Thinking

Divergent thinking must be married to convergent thinking—the act of narrowing in on the idea you plan to pursue. Convergent thinking comes as we sift through the very best ideas generated and begin to narrow our scope toward something actionable.

How we converge on the idea best suited to meet the challenges we hope to address is a complex process, weighing our greatest aspirations against the availability of our most fundamental resources (time, money, energy, and mind space). A delicate mental and emotional tug-of-war ensues as we form an internal feasibility study that pulls against our own passion for moving beyond the ordinary.

Whether penning a new composition, staging grand opera, or performing a pop-up concert, in the end, all creative action and all art has a frame. And creativity is a core competency within the artistic framework. Visual art has a literal frame. Within a musical performance, the performer or conductor creates the frame with that brief moment of focused silence before the opening downbeat. The frame of your art—or better thought of here as your creative ideas—necessarily provides limitations. Limitations that establish boundaries that allow for achievable outcomes. But the real trick is deciding what boundaries are important and what boundaries are simply unnecessary or self-imposed because of our own preconceptions of what is possible—or what we have been told is possible.

Do you thrive as a divergent thinker? Or a convergent thinker? Or are you the rare bird that dreams wildly and acts decisively?

When measuring the impact of the ideas you hope to chase down, create seven questions about the impact the project will have on you, your career, and your audience. Then assign a score for each of them on the scale of 1–5, with five being the highest or most positive impact and one being the lowest or least positive impact, as a way of weighing the cost-benefit ratio of your efforts. Consider questions like:

1. How would you rate the artistic quality of this experience?
2. How will this project grow your career financially?
3. Does this project impact the communities you hope to serve?
4. Does this project help you connect to other musicians and change agents along the way?
5. Will this project position you within your artistic and local community in a way that will serve you professionally and personally moving forward?

6. How passionate are you about the project outcome?
7. Is this project an important stepping stone to something you hope to achieve down the road?

The value gained when tallying your score is directly relational to the quality of your questions, so think through your questions carefully, being certain they reflect what you hope to achieve, both professionally and personally, in launching your project.

Then tally up your score using the following rubric:

- **31–35 = Awesome!** This project leverages the transformative powers of the arts to do good in the world. You're a revolutionary artist!
- **28–30 = Pretty Fabulous.** Your project will make an important impact in the community you are engaging. How might you tweak your idea to get the most out of your efforts?
- **25–27 = Solid Effort.** You have a solid idea that will make a difference. But there is still time to improve what you hope to accomplish. Where aren't you scoring yourself well, and how can you adjust your efforts?
- **24–lower = Unproductive.** This project does not seem to be worth pursuing. You love your art and you want to make a difference. Identifying the right project to do good in the world is an art in and of itself. Don't be discouraged. Get back to the drawing board and become a revolutionary artist.

● ● ● ●

Alain Barker is the founding director of Indiana University's Office of Entrepreneurship and Career Development. His career spans three continents—Africa, Europe, and North America—from which he has gained a broad understanding of cultural, social, and economic issues within the arts.

Situational Awareness
by Alain Barker

Artists and organizations today can thrive in a world in which they combine talent, knowledge, and hard-earned skills with deep situational awareness. This kind of 3-D mindset opens up a range of possibilities that enables an individual, project, or organization to be innovative, adaptive, culturally responsive, and financially sustainable.

Often likened to a pilot's ability to control an aircraft, situational awareness is the perception of environmental elements and events with respect to time or space and the comprehension of their meaning. In the arts, situational awareness can be thought of in numerous ways. Here is an exploration of just a few.

Live Performance: In a world where music runs like water through our cultural veins, what is the function of a live performance? Is it the primary art experience, or has it become the secondary experience behind lifestyle and virtual sound experiences? A growing number of live performances take lifestyle and virtual sound experience into account and have become must-see events.

Interpretation: How much of our interpretation of music style is governed by acknowledged and unspoken habits that have nothing to do with the world in which we currently live? Some of the most exciting performances these days involve new interpretations by musicians who are also familiar with a range of styles that represent their cultural and demographic world.

Audience Development: Is our objective to fill seats in halls with people who "consume" our offerings, or are we now living in a world in which communities co-create events? By committing ourselves to truly engage our community, artists and arts organizations can once again prove valuable.

What might an example of an artistic presentation that embodies each of these look like? Watch the Experiential Orchestra (www.experientialorchestra .com) perform *The Rite of Spring* on YouTube.[3]

These are just a few areas in which a 21st-century musician has to be situationally aware. Which ones can you add?

* * * *

CONDUCTING AN ENVIRONMENTAL SCAN

One last important piece: Know the world around you.

An environmental scan is a strategic way to grasp the big picture before launching your new project, effort, or organization. It's the process of seeking and reviewing information about all of the environmental factors—current and potential—that may impact your project and its goals. By amassing this knowledge, you arm yourself with valuable context. You'll be in a position to make more informed decisions and better adapt as you pursue your project.

In your environmental scan, consider the implications of your geographic location, target demographics, even the political and economic climate. Additionally, you should explore existing efforts that compete, align, or in some way relate to yours. Keep in mind that it's not necessarily about finding "threats" but, more important, opportunities. Perhaps you'll uncover a future collaborator, find a complementary effort under way, or learn a valuable lesson about how projects thrive or fail. This process will help you look inward and think in a new way about what makes your team, inspiration, resources, and skill set unique.

Once you have identified what your project will be, seek information; use all the tools you have available. A great place to start is through conversations or a survey of current stakeholders and networks. Avidly use the internet for research—look for similar missions, people, or organizations that will benefit from your project, press articles, crowdfunding projects, social media pages, websites, and so on. You can also use services like Charity Navigator, the Foundation Directory Online (local and university libraries might subscribe to this paid resource), and GuideStar to assess where funding is coming from for projects similar to yours.

How you compile your learning is up to you! Lists, Excel spreadsheets, notes—all are viable. Benchmarking is one particularly helpful method for comparison purposes. In a table format you can present the aligning projects you've researched and denote various facts that you deem important for each: years in existence, budget size, target audience, and so on. This is an effective way for you to visualize and track the areas in which your effort differs and what advantages or opportunities exist.

The **Toolkit** at the end of this book includes a template for using environmental scans in the planning process. Get planning!

Remember, artists reimagine what is possible, breaking down existing or perceived boundaries. As an artist, you are fully equipped to grapple with complexity, ambiguity, and unlocking your own creative potential. Dream wildly, act decisively. Find the change agent within.

SUMMARY

In this chapter, we learned how problem-finding and problem-solving are inextricably intertwined and rely on two important initial steps: divergent and convergent thinking. In divergent thinking, our goal is to generate as many ideas as possible—for example, how many different ways can I stretch this flute solo to capture this moment effectively? In contrast, convergent thinking is about selecting the best solution—which interpretation makes the most sense in this situation? This is the same process we follow when crafting large-scale projects of our own invention.

To make it a bit more interesting (and richer), we too must seek to better understand the cultural universe in which we operate. To do this, we conduct environmental scans. This allows us to make the greatest impact on our audience, while working synergistically with our partners.

CHAPTER 7

DIVERSITY AND INCLUSIVITY: ABANDONING BIAS AND LISTENING TO VOICES UNLIKE OUR OWN

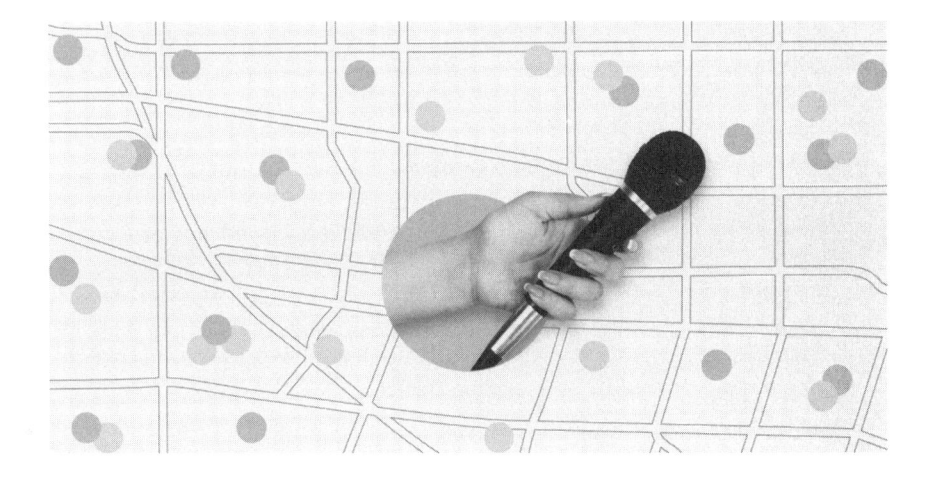

PART OF CHANGING THE world is about listening to the rest of the world. And whether launching a project on your own, with a team, or embedded within a community, listening to voices unlike your own is an essential skill for thriving as a revolutionary artist.

In this chapter, Laura Hlavacek Rabideau discusses the importance of creating an inclusive culture and exploring our own biases and how diversity and inclusion ultimately benefit our lives and society as a whole. The task may be challenging, but, as you'll learn, the rewards are immeasurable.

Driven by the belief that successful organizations are filled with successful people, Laura, in her work as a human resources executive (and informed by her BM in flute performance and MBA from Northwestern) embraces the challenge of creating spaces where all voices are heard and all talents valued.

Diversity and Inclusion
by Laura Hlavacek Rabideau

This discussion might cause you to feel uncomfortable.

We're going to talk about diversity and inclusion. These complicated and sensitive topics are often weighted with the historical impact of racism and discrimination, bias and privilege, the rhetoric of a divisive political climate, and fear of saying the wrong thing. I encourage you to embrace and explore what may feel uncomfortable at first. For it is in those uncomfortable moments that we learn the most. We can, with respect and willingness to listen, have this conversation and see things differently than we have until now.

Ready?

We hear the terms *diversity* and *inclusion* frequently, but we don't often take the time to define them. Diversity, in its simplest form, is all the ways that we differ from each other, including race, ethnicity, gender and gender identity, sexual orientation, age, religion, disability, socioeconomic status, education, and anything else that makes each of us unique. It also includes "cognitive diversity" or different ways of thinking. While we are born with some of these characteristics, others are more a product of our experiences and the choices we make along the way. Inclusion puts diversity into action by fostering an environment of collaboration and understanding, where each individual feels respected and involved. Andrés Tapia, a leading thinker in the field and an influential mentor for me, defines the relationship of these two ideas in this way: "Diversity is the mix, and inclusion is making the mix work."

Another way to think about diversity and inclusion is through your own experiences. Consider a time when you were at your most creative. Perhaps you were extremely engaged in an activity, ensemble, or project, or you were collaborating with others and generating wonderful outcomes as a result. It feels good to think about it, doesn't it? Now think about the opposite experience—a time when you felt shut down, unsure of how to contribute, misunderstood, or, worse, dismissed. What was it about that experience that generated those feelings? Often, the key difference is the degree to which we feel included, accepted, and heard—just as we are. It happens when we feel comfortable enough in our own skin to share our authentic selves, all our talents and experiences, all our innovative ideas—and also when we are truly open to all the talents, experiences, and ideas of others.

An inclusive environment is one that fosters engagement, empowerment, and authenticity. Most importantly, when we access and unleash all of the creativity and talents within each individual—when we use our superpowers—we arrive at a better outcome. Deloitte Australia research shows that inclusive teams outperform their peers by 80 percent in team-based assessments, clearly demonstrating the power of creating a culture where all voices are heard and valued.

Creating an inclusive culture with a diverse mix of people rarely happens by chance. We get in our own way, even with the best of intentions and without knowing it. It happens largely as a function of implicit bias or our tendency to subconsciously act on our assumptions about people different from ourselves. Implicit biases shape our view of the world and influence how we engage with others in all areas of our lives. Bias, a preference for one thing over another, provides the foundation for our beliefs about the world and drives our decision-making. It's critical to understand that bias in this context isn't inherently bad. It's easy to understand a bias or preference, say, for Bach over Stravinsky. The tricky part is when bias refers to an unfair preference or prejudice.

Add "implicit" to the mix and it feels all the more uncomfortable. The word *implicit*, after all, means we have feelings and attitudes beneath our awareness that aren't always identified through self-reflection. Implicit bias helps explain how we sort the mountains of data our brains process each second of the day, as well as why we notice certain things and miss others. It is necessary for our survival, helping us to quickly assess threat or opportunity, to distinguish friend from potential foe.

What if we acknowledge that implicit bias exists and has persistent effects? What if we shine a light on our own bias and consider how it impacts us as colleagues, as artists, and as we engage with the community? If we allow ourselves to become aware of these unconscious preferences, we short-circuit the effect our implicit bias has on our thinking and decisions. I am not suggesting this is an easy task. Everyone has their own lens on the world and their own implicit biases to sort through.

When we decide to explore the influence of implicit bias upon us, it is important to keep in mind that everyone possesses implicit biases. It is simply part of being human. The implicit associations we hold may not align with our stated beliefs or the vision and mission we aim to pursue. We may not even be aware of our implicit beliefs.

The good news is that we have the ability to change our implicit bias. The associations that have formed subconsciously can be gradually unlearned as we become aware and take steps to diminish their impact. Here's how this looks: Research shows that we apply different standards to men and women when making comparisons. One well-known example comes from the world of symphony orchestras. In the 1970s, the top five orchestras in the United States were 95 percent men. By 1997, women had surged from making up 5 percent of the orchestra to 25 percent. This dramatic shift is largely attributed to one key difference in the hiring process—blind auditions. Orchestras began placing the musicians behind a screen, hidden from the audition committee.

When a blind audition is used only for the preliminary round, it has been shown to lead to a 50 percent increase in women reaching the final audition. A simple change greatly reduced the impact of a subconscious bias affecting the final outcome.

Think about the projects you hope to launch over the coming months and years. What hidden beliefs might influence your interactions with your colleagues?

THE INTROSPECTIVE INDIVIDUAL

The first step to changing bias is through introspection. Think about your own beliefs, values, and personal biases. How might these traits come into play as you work to understand cultural differences? Reflect on your feelings about inequity and how to align your conscious, explicit values with your implicit attitudes. Ask yourself hard questions about what influences your decisions about people. Try to notice patterns. Are there similarities in people you spend time with? Whom do you automatically seek out as colleagues or for project partners? Be suspicious of your automatic responses, but remember that they tell you something and that you have the ability to change or modify them.

What patterns have you noticed about how you choose the people around you? And how might that hinder your ability to see a broader perspective?

Armed with this insight, seek experiences that can shift or reverse the patterns of experience in new directions. Open yourself up to new cultures. Engage in open and honest discussion with people who have different experiences in the world and listen with an open mind and heart. Join the new or world music ensemble that has always intimidated or felt foreign to you. Immerse yourself in seeing the world through a different lens, hearing new music and pushing your boundaries.

THE INCLUSIVE TEAM

What makes an inclusive team? Think about the dynamics of a jazz trio. Each member has a unique voice that wants to be heard. But each voice also has to work in relationship to the others. At different times, a member steps into the lead and later shifts to support another voice to share their musical ideas. When it works well, the whole ensemble builds on its members, taking the best from each individual to create something new and unique to that ensemble. And when the members don't listen openly to each other, the crowd heads to the bar to grab another drink.

As you form a team or choose a community of impact, think about the culture you hope to create. What type of interactions and behaviors support an inclusive team environment? Do you, and does your community, truly listen and seek to understand each other's perspectives? Are you able, as a band of collaborators, to talk through difficult topics or share sensitive feedback with compassion and respect? Does each person have equal room to contribute at the table? Do team members build on each other's ideas and make decisions together? Keep these concepts in mind as you create team assessments and share feedback.

• • • •

Mary Pauline Sheridan-Rabideau is double majoring in violin performance and psychology at Furman University in Greenville, South Carolina. A fierce advocate for those at the margins and a strong voice for women's issues, Mary Pauline conducts her life's work at the intersection of making a difference and music. She is Laura and Mark's daughter.

BE THE BOSS
by Mary Pauline Sheridan-Rabideau

Similar to the importance of flour in a cake recipe, ferocity prevails as a crucial ingredient of fruitful leadership. Leading is never easy; however, the task is particularly challenging when a potential leader lives a life plagued by discrimination—a person of the LGBTQ+ community, a person of color, a transgender person, or a woman.

Today, our knowledge and acceptance of who a leader can be is growing; however, to those who still experience the very real discrimination of today's society while aiming to acquire a leadership position, I advise you to internalize the words of a remarkably accomplished woman of our time.

She is known as Beyoncé.

A leader in not only the music industry but also in the business world, this pop sensation illuminates her key to success in stating, "I'm not bossy; I'm the boss." This simple assertion is a motto to lead by. It gives primacy to the goal of cultivating a productive, nurturing, and effective environment. It allows people who are so often told, whether directly or indirectly, that their input is inferior to confidently express their ideas. It evokes a sense of purpose and confidence that is necessary for a leader to possess. And last but not least, it reminds leaders to treat their colleagues with respect.

My advice? Be fierce. Don't be bossy, but be the boss.

IMPACTING COMMUNITY

Part of changing the world is about listening to the rest of the world. The challenge of community engagement holds special considerations to ensure that your idea is welcomed by the community of impact. Working collaboratively with a community requires understanding its members, their shared history, beliefs, and values. To engage with the community requires working collaboratively with its members to first identify need. This is followed by developing ideas, being involved in decision-making, and sharing responsibility.

If you are working with a community that you are also a member of, engaging in an authentic, trusted partnership will be easier. If the community of impact for your project is not your home base, it will be important to be aware of what you don't know. Remember that implicit bias includes cultural assumptions that may not be accurate from the perspective of those in the cultural group.

As you begin to brainstorm about possible projects and communities of impact, remember to not focus only on what you believe the needs of the community are but to engage the community in both defining the need to be met and the process by which to address the need. This requires a real dialogue and active consultation with the community. Bring your curiosity and a willingness to invest in learning about the community of impact from their perspective.

Consider how you will engage with the community you wish to impact. How will you create an environment where all voices are heard and valued?

Explore how these programs and ensembles are working within communities to unleash the power of the arts to drive change:

- The Ritz Chamber Players features African American musicians and composers in a way that builds new audiences in their Jacksonville, Florida, community.[1]
- Project STEP (String Training Education Program) partners with schools, communities, and parents to nurture youth of color in Boston through an intense string training program that has led to careers as professional musicians for dozens of students who may never have considered music to be a viable option.[2]
- The Sphinx Organization, for more than 20 years, has developed talent and provided access to the classical music world for musicians of color.[3]

Want to explore more organizations making a difference while making music? Visit 21CM.org's POP Picks (http://21cm.org/pop-picks/).

● ● ● ●

DIVERSITY IN MUSIC

So what does a musician have to do to become equipped to work in such diverse settings? Or to be more Darwinian about it, what lies within this rare musician that allows him or her to move across genres, cultural barriers, and traditions of the world?

DIVERSITY AND INCLUSIVITY • 79

• • • •

Mike Block

A friend once asked Yo-Yo Ma who he thought was the ideal musician of the 21st century. Without missing a beat, Ma named Mike Block. Recording artist and Silk Road Ensemble cellist, founder of the Global Musician Workshop, and Berklee faculty member, Block exudes artistry that cannot be confined inside a box of any size. Whether collaborating with Bobby McFerrin or will.i.am, Alison Krauss or Lenny Kravitz, his musical agility, considerable improvisational skills, and deep understanding of music from across the globe prevail in presenting spontaneous, high-energy happenings.

Even when watching him perform you realize he is without peer in his approach. An advocate for cellists to take a stand, Mike has invented a cello strap that allows a freedom of movement that the *New York Times* called "Breathless. . . . Half dance, half dare."

I had a chance to catch up with Mike in Greencastle, Indiana, during the Global Musician Workshop—an event that for most is a foreign experience in and of itself. More than 100 students and faculty converge on a rural community in the Midwest, coming from communities across the United States and more than 40 countries, ranging from Iran to South Korea, Syria to New Zealand, and Lebanon to Mali, to engage with cultural traditions unlike their own. Improvisation, learning by ear, and playing in bands alongside instruments as unfamiliar (or familiar, depending on your cultural perspective) as the Indian tabla, Arabic oud, and Korean taepyeongso (traditional oboe family) and saenghwang (ancient wind-blown instrument) are hallmark experiences of participating in this transglobal musical collaboration.

When you meet Mike, you will recognize the joyful sense of wonder he brings to everything he does. He connects as well with people from all walks of life as he does with big ideas and simple truths. With Mike, everything has a sense of optimism, like a first rehearsal, the tuning of an orchestra before the conductor takes to the podium, or the feeling you get when you remove the plastic wrapping off a fresh CD. A world of possibilities awaits. And with this openness and optimism is a readiness to listen to voices unlike your own.

• • • •

BRIDGING THE GAP: A LOOK AT THE SILK ROAD PROJECT'S GLOBAL MUSICIAN WORKSHOP

It's often said that music is a universal language. But language isn't much good unless you're using it to have a conversation. So, how do you start one? For Mike

Block, the answer is to invite musicians from different countries to the same town for one week so that they can spend time learning how to play each other's music.

Block is a cellist, a member of Yo-Yo Ma's Silk Road Project and, more recently, the director of one of Silk Road's newer projects, the Global Musician Workshop. The goal of the Silk Road Project is to bring together musicians from all over the world so that they can collaborate on and teach multicultural music while exploring the intersection of the arts and business. And the Global Musician Workshop is like the Silk Road Ensemble—which contains an ever-changing lineup of some of the world's most renowned instrumentalists—multiplied several times over. It's a weeklong initiative to which musicians of any age from any country can apply. Once they've arrived, they take part in workshops with core members of the Silk Road Ensemble, during which they learn how to play music that originated from places like Mali, Ireland, Korea, Syria, and elsewhere.

As we move further into an increasingly globalized era, how can we use our music to have cross-cultural conversations? 21CM traveled to the Global Musician Workshop to answer this question, to listen to the kind of music these artists were making, and to talk to participants about how their experiences changed them, both as people and musicians. You can hear what they had to say at 21CM.org.[4]

• • • •

Aaron Dworkin, as shared in his opening paragraph of "Collaborating across Diverse Communities," embodies the complexity and richness of diversity. Embracing his own diversity has shaped a career unlike any other. As you read, consider what you uniquely offer the world, as well as how opening your mind to voices unlike your own might reveal a world of tangible possibilities.

Collaborating across Diverse Communities[5]
by Aaron Dworkin

People sometimes ask me why I care so much about diversity and why I have dedicated my life to pursuits that further that end, and I have the easiest response to that question: "I am a black, white, Jewish, Jehovah's Witness, Irish Catholic who plays the violin. I am the definition of diversity. I don't have a choice but to do what I do."

Certainly by any statistical norms, being born a biracial baby in 1970 to an unwed couple in a small village outside of Monticello, New York, and being immediately given up for adoption did not set the stage for the highest expectations in terms of my future capabilities. I was adopted at the age of two weeks by a white Jewish couple in New York City who were professors in neural and behavioral science at Rockefeller University. My adoptive mother was an amateur violinist, and perhaps I wanted, no, needed to connect to her on some level that served as a substitute for not being born to her like my brother and sister. So I began to play the violin.

When I was 10, my family moved from Manhattan to Hershey, Pennsylvania—a drastic social change for me, transitioning from the center of the world's great metropolis to a town that had at the time only one black family in my school. I continued developing on the violin through lessons at the Peabody Preparatory Music Institute in Baltimore, served as concertmaster of the Harrisburg Youth Symphony, and spent my junior and senior years of high school at the Interlochen Arts Academy in Michigan. After Interlochen, I began my tenure as a college student at Penn State, where I was concertmaster of the Penn State Philharmonic, and then went on to complete my bachelor's and master's in music at the University of Michigan.

> **It was not until I was working on my degrees at the University of Michigan that I first learned there were any black composers.**

In all of those musical environments, I was either the only one or one of less than a handful of minorities. It was not until I was working on my degrees at the University of Michigan that I first learned there were any black composers. I literally went into a lesson one day, and my teacher said, "Do you have any interest in playing music by black composers?" I looked at him kind of startled and said, "You mean, black classical composers?"

He kind of smiled and then began to pull volumes of works off of his shelves. This then led to the incredible expansion of music I performed as I focused on the works of black and Latino composers for my undergraduate and graduate recitals. And it led me again to question why no one had told me of William Grant Still, Coleridge-Taylor Perkinson, David Baker, Joseph Boulogne St. George (an Afro-French contemporary of Mozart), or the countless other minority composers whose accomplishments litter the annals of the classical music repertory.

Why had no one told me about George Polgreen Bridgetower, a well-known black violin virtuoso who was good friends with Beethoven and premiered his famous Kreutzer Sonata with him in 1803 in Vienna—and for whom Beethoven wrote the work, which is why you see in Beethoven's original manuscript the inscription, "*Sonata mulattica composta per il mulatto*"?

Why had no one told me that the great Frederick Douglass played the violin or that his grandson, Joseph Douglass, was the first black violinist to tour the United States as a recitalist in the early 1900s?

And so, it was within the context of these questions and immersion in the incredible music that I had recently been exposed to, combined with the lack of any minorities that I would see in the audiences or on stage at classical music concerts, that led me to the founding of the Sphinx Organization. I remember walking into my lesson and telling my teacher, Stephen Shipps, "I've got this idea." Eighteen years later, the institution's mission to address the stark underrepresentation of people of color in classical music has been more successful than I could have ever dreamed when I started it as a University of Michigan undergraduate.

It was also at this time that I began to reflect on all the feedback I received from peers and adults as I was growing up. These comments were often not supportive of understanding the role of minorities in classical music but instead sought to distance me from my own racial heritage. I took up poetry as a means to express what was happening inside my head, eventually authoring a book of poems including the title poem, "They Said I Wasn't Really Black." An excerpt:

Born from white and brown young skins,
I was so diff'rent from the pack.
Adopted by Caucasians at just 2 weeks of age,
They couldn't of known about the other people;
They said I wasn't really Black.

A violinist I was destined for,
Early on I showed them the knack.
It was Mozart for me and Beethoven too,
I never got to memorize Jackson 5 lyrics so;
They said I wasn't really Black.

School bells and cafeteria food,
I sat there with my brown lunch sack.
There was no fried chicken in my zip lock bag,
No confrontation between watermelon and black-eyed peas;
They said I wasn't really Black.

I'd stroll into the rehearsal room
Wishing I was the Daddy-Mack.
I didn't even go to the games, let alone sport the jersey,
Hell, I wasn't even in the band and I wonder why;
They said I wasn't really Black.

I didn't talk the talk and couldn't walk the walk,
Familial prec'dent I did lack.
At first it seemed correct by design,
It took me years 'til I was uncomfortable when;
They said I wasn't really Black.

There were those who made me feel different,
And few who I thought had my back.
I could have taken all the racial slurs
If only it wasn't my friends around when;
They said I wasn't really Black.

    I provide all this background because I believe if we are to overcome the challenges of achieving diversity in the arts, then we must have context in which to present those ideas. And furthermore, I believe there is more at stake than simply ensuring more diversity within the arts. The arts and our performing arts institutions are most vibrant and true when they reflect all of society.

    I am certain that if you are to be relevant with your art, you need to engage those various communities that comprise the mosaic of our society—you must have the ability to engage communities that may have different perspectives, opinions, culture, and even language than your own. Your art can and will transcend these differences, but you must have the preparation and ability to bring that about.

    Just to share one statistic (from the orchestral world, which has some of the best data regarding inclusion among the various disciplines, although I am always advocating for far better work to be done in this space across our field) from the League of American Orchestras' own study: "The vast majority of new audiences over the next decade will be audiences of color, especially Latino audiences." As an artist, do you want to be best prepared to play in those orchestras that are going to be most successful given those realities? Do you want to be best prepared to lead those organizations or even launch your own that will be best positioned to deliver the highest quality artistic content to those audiences? These are the questions you want to ask yourself as you move forward.

    Nigerian author Chimamanda Ngozi Adichie said, "The danger of a single story is not that it is untrue but that it is incomplete." The stories we weave in the performing arts today are incomplete, and I believe it is your responsibility (if you choose to be an artist-citizen of excellence) to deliver more complete stories about the lives we live. And it is my obligation as an educator to prepare students to be relevant to our full society while empowering the disciplines we teach to be relevant to our communities.

What we do know from the lessons of history is that a segmented society, where differences are not celebrated but rather mocked, attacked, dismissed, or not tolerated, is not sustainable for a thriving civil democratic environment. As an artist-leader, you are the bridge that crosses these more shallow man-made barriers. You have the opportunity, influence, and, ultimately, the power to bring human beings together across racial, religious, gender, socioeconomic, and other boundaries. But you must not be passive. You must act.

• • • •

SUMMARY

In chapter 7 we learned that if "diversity is the mix," then "inclusion is making the mix work" (per Andrés Tapia). In addition, we were challenged to look inside ourselves at our own implicit biases, as we begin reimaging how we will engage with others and communities. Aaron Dworkin shared his life story as a diverse musician, Mary Pauline Sheridan-Rabideau gave voice to what it takes to lead as an emerging artist, and we learned a thing or two from one of the most diverse musical experiences anywhere, the Global Musician Workshop. Mostly, we learned the value of listening to voices unlike our own.

CHAPTER 8

THE BUSINESS SIDE: LAYING THE GROUNDWORK FOR A SUCCESSFUL PROJECT

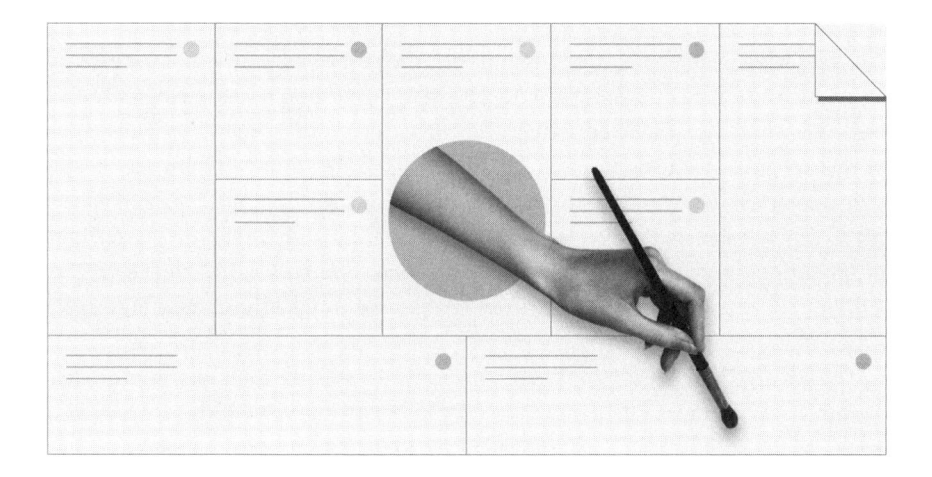

THE CREATIVE PERSON LOVES dreaming—whether it's thinking up entire worlds, imagining new realities, or dreaming up amazing inventions. But there is a difference between dreaming and doing, and to be a revolutionary artist requires both. In this chapter, we discuss how to take big ideas to fruition with a set of tools made just for the job.

THE CASE FOR CRITICAL OPTIMISM

Almost no one boasts of being a pessimist. And that makes sense. Pessimists by definition dwell in a world that we don't want to live in for long, because we can't change it.

In the rare case when pessimists do own their bleak viewpoint, it is often couched in an exaggerated, comedic way that makes it palatable for everyone around them. Case in point: the most beloved of all pessimists, Eeyore the depressed, old gray donkey created by A. A. Milne:

"Good morning, Eeyore," said Pooh.
"Good morning, Pooh Bear," said Eeyore gloomily. "If it is a good morning, which I doubt," said he.
"Why, what's the matter?"
"Nothing, Pooh Bear, nothing. We can't all, and some of us don't. That's all there is to it."
"Can't all what?" said Pooh, rubbing his nose.
"Gaiety. Song-and-dance. Here we go round the mulberry bush."

But, while being an optimist sounds like the best mindset, it is not necessarily an indicator of greater entrepreneurial success. According to Jerry Jao, CEO and cofounder of Retention Science (a leading firm in retention marketing), a balance of realism and optimism pays off: "As a startup founder and CEO, my leadership philosophy is to be 60% realistic and 40% optimistic. My dominant realism allows me to stay humble and make decisions based on facts, rather than on gut feelings or aspirations. However, I also recognize that entrepreneurs don't achieve success without taking risks, and my optimism enables me to take those risks and move forward despite uncertainties."[1]

Winston Churchill famously said, "A pessimist sees the difficulty in every opportunity; an optimist sees the opportunity in every difficulty." If this is true, then a critical optimist sees opportunities and challenges amid the relentless pursuit of making the world a better place. This is the mindset of the change-maker, the music entrepreneur, the revolutionary artist.

It seems the sweet spot at the intersection of pessimism, optimism, and realism is where we want to be. In other words, we should strive to be critical optimists.

Where do you find yourself on the optimistic/pessimistic spectrum? And why?

THE BELIEVING GAME VS. THE DOUBTING GAME

I am often bothered by the John Mayer song "Waiting on the World to Change." The song talks about our experiences in the world as unfair, and how those experiences discourage us from thinking that we can make a difference. Rather than keep trying, we find ourselves simply waiting on others to act.

Such a well-crafted melody accompanied by such a helpless message. What has led to an entire generation feeling so helpless that they lack of agency? And how can we empower emerging artists to lead change in the future they are soon to inherit?

One such way is to illuminate the power of playing the "believing game" rather than the "doubting game."

Peter Elbow, English and writing studies scholar, coined the phrase *believing game* as a way of sharing a perspective on the world. In his words:

> I can define the believing game most easily and clearly by contrasting it with the doubting game. Indeed, the believing game derives from the doubting game.
>
> The doubting game represents thinking most widely honored and taught in our culture. It's sometimes called "critical thinking." It's the disciplined practice of trying to be as skeptical and analytical as possible with every idea we encounter. By trying hard to doubt ideas, we can discover hidden contradictions, bad reasoning, or other weaknesses in them—especially in the case of ideas that seem valid or attractive. We are using doubting as a tool to scrutinize and test.
>
> In contrast, the believing game is the disciplined practice of trying to be as welcoming or accepting as possible to every idea we encounter: not just listening to views different from our own and holding back from arguing with them; not just trying to restate them without bias, but trying to believe them. We are using believing as a tool to scrutinize and test. But instead of scrutinizing fashionable or widely accepted ideas for hidden flaws, the believing game asks us to examine unfashionable or even repellent ideas for hidden virtues. Often we cannot see what's good in someone else's idea (or in our own!) till we work at believing it.
>
> When an idea goes against current assumptions and beliefs, or if it seems alien, dangerous, or poorly formulated, we often cannot see any merit in it.[2]

So for us, the application of Elbow's believing game is to embrace the life-changing experience of artistic expression, the healing powers of music, and our ability to play the lead role in creating our most promising future. It is the belief in the revolutionary artist.

But playing the believing game is not always easy. We live in a cynical world. And the challenges that we face are too large for any one person, one organization, one corporation, or one government to solve. So where do we find inspiration? We find it in those who begin by beginning. Those who accept that not all problems are solvable, but that making a difference, even in part, is part of our calling—a life of means, meaning, and the chance to give back.

We can find inspiration in the work of Musicians for Human Rights[3] to bring beauty to those who have been driven from their homes, torn from their families, and ravaged by war.

And in celebrated violinist and member of the Los Angeles Philharmonic, Vijay Gupta.[4] Gupta is a cofounder of Street Symphony, a nonprofit organization dedicated to bringing live music to the homeless and incarcerated, powered by belief in the redemptive and regenerative powers of music. Through his work, he shows us that you can hone your artistry to the highest level and lead projects devoted to doing good in the world. This is an artist who does not see an ocean of limitations, but a world of opportunities. Gupta leads by sharing the healing powers of his art.

Or people like David Wish, who founded Little Kids Rock, an organization that impacts hundreds of thousands of low-income children.[5] Wish believes that every child deserves the opportunity to experience the confidence and joy of making music. So what did he do? He did something. He took action. But it didn't happen all at once. Wish and his work demonstrates what it takes sometimes to see your dream come true—sheer tenacity and belief in this mission. This is what critical optimism looks and feels like.

Who can you cite that embodies the believing game, and what has been gained through their well-executed optimism?

How do we share our biggest ideas on paper as we transition from creative thinking to creative action? The Business Model Canvas (BMC) is your first opportunity to capture the complexity of your project and begin to articulate the many moving parts that will need to be executed to bring about the change you hope to see in the world. The BMC illuminates the work that lies ahead, and it is a logical step to follow the believing game.

You are now turning the corner on becoming a revolutionary artist.

• • • •

Jeffrey Nytch is director of the Entrepreneurship Center for Music at the University of Colorado–Boulder. He is a leading figure in the arts entrepreneurship movement and someone who has leveraged his entrepreneurial mindset to transform institutions and organizations, as well as in his own creative life as a composer. Jeff brilliantly applies Alexander Osterwalder's Business Model Canvas, originally created in 2008, and translates it into terms that make sense for artistic/creative ventures.

The Business Model Canvas: A Rosetta Stone for Musicians
by Jeff Nytch

One of the most common challenges faced by novice entrepreneurs is trying to identify and understand the many aspects of any business operation. For creatives, the problem is amplified by the fact that it isn't always clear how standard business tools apply to the arts. Here, we'll tackle both of those challenges by examining the Business Model Canvas (https://canvanizer.com/new/business-model-canvas), an open-source tool that visually maps out the various components of a business. The BMC is a powerful tool for two reasons: (1) It not only addresses all key aspects of a business venture but also illustrates how those elements interact with each other; and (2) the Canvas applies to any business model, be it for-profit, not-for-profit, industrial, artistic, physical product, or service.

The Canvas is broken up into three sectors, each with several components: *Market* (consisting of Customers, Channels, and Relationships), *Operations* (Key Activities, Resources, and Partners), and *Financial* (Costs and Income). These sectors revolve around and are shaped by the *Value Proposition*—the center of gravity of the entire Canvas. We'll begin our discussion there.

VALUE PROPOSITION

The Value Proposition (VP) is one of the entrepreneur's most useful tools. It succinctly describes the product in question,[6] its distinctive attributes, who the product is for, and how they benefit. It generally conforms to the following format:

[Name] is a [product entity]. Through its [distinctive attributes] it provides [benefits] to [target market].

When speaking about a common product or type of business, the VP tends to be relatively straightforward. The key, however, is to be as descriptive and accurate as possible: What kind of customers, in particular, support this business? What are the precise benefits they receive?

Here is a sample from a family-owned business in Boulder, Colorado, where I live: "McGuckin Hardware is a Boulder-based home improvement store. Through its knowledgeable staff and exhaustive inventory of hard-to-find items, the company provides expert, specialized service to high-end contractors and discerning homeowners in the greater Boulder area."

The McGuckin statement spells out each component of the VP with great precision—something that is critical if it is to be the guiding force for all other sectors of the Canvas.

- *What is it?*
  A Boulder-based home improvement store
- *What are the distinctive features?*
  Knowledgeable staff and an exhaustive inventory of hard-to-find items
- *What benefits are provided?*
  Expert, specialized service
- *Who reaps these benefits?*
  High-end contractors and discerning homeowners in a particular geographic area

To illustrate how important these details are, consider this weaker, more general version: "McGuckin Hardware is a home improvement store. Through its experienced staff and extensive inventory, it offers excellent customer service to contractors and homeowners."

In this version, details are missing: Where is this venture based? "Experienced" staff doesn't tell me much—experienced in what? Home Depot has an "extensive" inventory, too; how is McGuckin's different? What aspect of its customer service is "excellent"? And lastly, are these benefits for all contractors and homeowners, or is there a particular segment of that market that is drawn to McGuckin over the competition? As you work to craft your Value Proposition, it's important to keep these questions in mind and strive to be as descriptive and accurate as possible.

Let's look at another example, this time from the performing arts: "BDT Stage is a professional dinner theater company in Boulder, Colorado. Through a compelling and diverse lineup of shows, seasoned performers, appetizing food, and an intimate venue, BDT Stage offers first-rate entertainment to families, seniors, lovers of musical theater, and groups from throughout the northern Colorado Front Range region."

Here we immediately see how difficult it is to craft a Value Proposition for an arts group. Articulating the characteristics of an artistic experience can be elusive. Still, each component of a performing arts experience is addressed: the work itself; the performers; the venue; and, since it is a dinner theater, the food. When one is done crafting a Value Proposition, the reader should begin to have a sense of what the product will be like, who will enjoy it, and why.

Lastly, let's look at a VP for an individual artist. These sorts of VPs can be the hardest ones of all to write—partly because describing one's artistic output may be difficult and partly because we tend to be uncomfortable talking about our work in these terms. It's important to recognize, however, that an individual's creative career is as much a business venture as a small business, a not-for-profit organization, or a large corporation. As such, we must grapple with the difficult task of finding words to both describe our work and define our target market.

As an example, I'll share my own VP. Like most musicians, I have more than one area of activity, and therefore more than one VP. This is the one for my work as a composer, and I use this example because it's the hardest part to write—and because I wish to model what talking about our artistic work can look like.

"Jeffrey Nytch is a composer in the 'classical' tradition. Through his highly developed craft, 25 years of professional experience, and a keen eye for innovative collaborations, he brings narrative and expressive vocal, instrumental, and choral music to the musicians/groups who commission him, their audiences, and their community partners."

You'll note that I don't attempt to describe my musical style, per se. This is because to do so would require me to use terminology and lingo that a general reader might not understand—and a VP needs to be understood by anyone reading it. Instead, I try to talk about my music regarding how it impacts the people I'm attempting to reach: collaborations and community partnerships help build audience; "narrative and expressive" music implies a certain degree of accessibility to non-experts in the audience. Listing vocal, instrumental, and choral music shows that I can write for a broad range of instrumental and vocal combinations. Ultimately, I want potential customers to see me as someone who maintains high professional/musical standards, and someone who wants to write music that will help my customers realize their own artistic mission.

If you have ever had an experience with a nonprofit organization, you likely became aware of the importance of vision and mission statements. In fact, you can find them in most companies. The VP is simply a more specific version of "Vision" and "Mission." Take the vision for 21CM: "Revolutionizing the ways people engage through music, we envision a world connected, enriched and transformed by musical experiences."

The VP then asks the entrepreneur to express how, in specific terms, this vision is accomplished through the venture at hand. How does this venture revolutionize the way your customers will embrace and interact with music? What, precisely, is the venture you've chosen to accomplish this? Who are the communities you hope to enrich through your venture, and how will they be transformed through the experience?

Let's look at the VP for an innovative group that reflects the 21CM vision in its programming: "Pittsburgh New Music Ensemble is a professional chamber music ensemble that serves a diverse audience of art lovers in Pittsburgh, Pennsylvania, with compelling, engaging, and immersive performances of contemporary 'classical' music. Its groundbreaking performance paradigm, dubbed 'Theatre of Music,' uses the theatrical tools of lighting, sound design, costuming, spoken word, video, dramatic thread, and cinematic continuity to tell compelling human stories through carefully curated and newly commissioned works of American music."

As you pick apart all of these VPs, you'll see how important each word is. At McGuckin Hardware, the "experienced staff and exhaustive inventory" provide "expert, specialized service." These phrases paint a very clear picture of the kind of place McGuckin is—and the types of customers it caters to ("high-end contractors and discerning homeowners").

For BDT Stage, identifying the company as a professional dinner theater is an important distinction from community theaters. Describing the range of shows it programs communicates the message that, over the course of a season, there will probably be something to appeal to just about everyone.

Mentioning the food quality distinguishes it from a lot of dinner theater, which is not usually known for its cuisine.

For artistic ventures like Pittsburgh New Music Ensemble (PNME) or that of a composer, language becomes even more challenging: You must find words that are descriptive and specific while avoiding any insider lingo that will simply alienate anyone not "in the know." The PNME's Value Proposition is particularly challenging, since the "Theatre of Music" is a unique thing that is not easy to describe. It requires a lot of thought about both the essential nature of the work in question and the best words to describe that work with clarity and conciseness.

GETTING STARTED

To craft a VP, one can follow a series of steps that will aid in the process of finding the right language.

The first step, ironically, involves not worrying about the right language. The best way to start off is with a whiteboard or a big sheet of paper; make columns for What, Features, Benefits, For Whom, and just start putting stuff down for each category. Don't worry about whether the words you put up are the "right ones"—that'll come later. For now, it's important to simply get your mind flowing as you view your venture or artistic product regarding the VP—in terms that, as we've discussed, may feel foreign or out of place in an artistic context.

Next, enlist some friends or colleagues who know your work well. Ask them what you've forgotten from your list. Ask them what words they would use to describe your product. Additional sets of eyes will help give you some perspective on your language before you get too tangled up in wordsmithing.

Once you've spent some time with your long (hopefully) list of words and descriptors, now is the time to begin selecting the words that you think can best capture the most critical information. This is where you'll have to make some choices about what you think the most important things to focus on should be. For instance, the BDT Stage felt it was important to identify the company as a professional one. The way they characterized their audience (families, seniors, lovers of musical theater, and groups) communicates the idea that the repertoire is varied but mainstream. (This is not the place to find avant-garde productions with an Adults Only restriction.) Mentions of the food and the intimacy of the venue are included because they are things about which the target audience cares.

In other words, one has to make some choices when crafting a VP. Sometimes this can be difficult because we want to include everything about our venture or artistic product that is so near and dear to us. The VP forces us to step back and take a slightly more dispassionate approach by asking ourselves, "What do I think is most important to communicate about my venture to the people I hope will value it?" Said another way, the VP isn't for you; it's for anybody with whom you want to share your venture—existing and potential audience, donors, press, talent you're recruiting, and so on.

Two more things about creating a VP. The first is that the more you work on them, the better you get—but they are never easy. So don't get discouraged if the words don't come quickly. Give yourself time to live with the words and concepts for a while; keep coming back to the VP to tweak a phrase or identify a word that's maybe just a bit better than the one (or three!) you came up with first. Take advantage of those outside eyes: ask your friend or colleague, "Do you think this describes me clearly, completely, and concisely? What am I leaving out? How can it be stronger? If you had no idea who I was or what I was about, would this give you a clear picture?" Then, as the final test, actually show it to somebody who has no idea who you are or what you're about, and ask them: "What does this statement tell you? Do you understand what this venture is about, or are you completely mystified?"

The second thing to keep in mind about the VP is that it must be authentic. Writing an "aspirational" VP can be a useful exercise regarding visualizing where you would like your venture to be in, say, 5 or 10 years (that is, as a tool for internal assessment and planning). But the real power of the VP lies in its application to the market/audience for which you are trying to create value. And for that power to be fully unleashed, your statement must be rooted in reality. It must be an accurate and authentic reflection of what you do and why folks should care about it. If it's not, your market will quickly learn that you are not what you claim to be—and that's just about the worst thing imaginable for any business, but especially for one based in the arts.

An accurate and authentic VP is extremely important because it will be the guiding force in addressing all the other sectors of the Business Model Canvas. The entire Canvas exists to help you identify the actions and resources you need to realize your VP in the form of your venture. That's why it's so important to spend the time, care, and reflection required to get it right. Now that we have an understanding of the VP, let's move on to exploring each of the remaining three sectors of the Business Model Canvas.

CUSTOMER SECTOR: CUSTOMER SEGMENTS, CHANNELS, AND RELATIONSHIPS

Since the Value Proposition connects two key elements—the distinctive characteristics of the venture and the customers it serves—we clearly have to understand our clients thoroughly. The Customer Sector of the Canvas does that via three avenues.

Customer Segments defines the customers themselves:
- What are their demographics (age, gender, geographical location, etc.)?
- What is their socioeconomic status?

- Do they have particular, specific interests or characteristics? (A golf equipment store will not likely have nongolfers as a primary customer segment, for example.)
- And lastly, what are their "psychographics"—that is, what are the sensibilities and emotions activated within the patron by your product?

Two things are important to keep in mind as you're defining your customers. The first is that you may have more than one customer segment and that those segments might not always share the same needs. For example, a piano teaching studio most likely includes both young students and their parents; the students want a fun and helpful teacher, while the parents may also want flexible scheduling, an affordable price, and a convenient location for lessons.

Connecting the Customer Segment(s) box to the VP are two fields: Customer Relationships and Channels. **Channels** are the easier of the two to define: channels simply identify the paths by which the product (and information about the product) is delivered to the customer. In our piano studio example, channels would include the lesson itself but also things like e-mail, a monthly newsletter, a Facebook group page, and perhaps things like a Web portal for scheduling and a phone line for direct conversation with students and parents.

Customer Relationships can be a little trickier to articulate, however. This field describes the nature of the relationship between the venture and its customers. For the teaching studio, the character of the relationship is primarily interpersonal: one-on-one, customized, in-person, or via a direct interaction on social media. Sometimes, though, the Customer Relationship is a little harder to characterize. Take Amazon, for example: What's the nature of that relationship? First of all, it's virtual—one never speaks to an actual human being during the totality of the customer experience, from browsing the website to opening the package on your doorstep. Despite the virtual nature of the experience, however, there is still a personalized element: Your account allows you to keep track of your purchases, share a gift list with others, and donate a portion of your purchase to the charity of your choice. Amazon's algorithms identify other related products that you might be interested in—often with uncanny accuracy. So while the piano studio had direct and personalized customer relationships, a site like Amazon has virtual and personalized relationships.

Channels and Relationships are essential to the success of any venture. Identifying the customer segments that your product is for is insufficient to build a loyal customer base. You must also develop the best channels to communicate with them and deliver your product and find the optimal type(s) of interaction to deliver your Value Proposition.

OPERATIONS SECTOR: KEY ACTIVITIES, RESOURCES, AND PARTNERSHIPS

In the Operations Sector, we enter into the nuts and bolts of your venture. It's here that we identify the Key Activities that you (or someone you hire) will have to do to maintain your business. Questions to ask include: How will they consistently and reliably deliver your Value Proposition to customers? What resources are required? Can you utilize partnerships to save money, better reach your customers, or acquire needed resources?

Key Activities embody a sort of "day in the life of your venture." What are all the tasks required of your venture to effectively deliver your product? This list will start with the obvious and become progressively more detailed and elusive as you think about it. For our teaching studio, activities like "teaching lessons" are obvious. But let's drill down into that more deeply: What activities, specifically, are required to teach effectively? You'll need to be aware of the latest method books, pedagogical techniques, and other resources. You may want to visit an annual piano conference or participate in an online forum. If you have studio recitals, what activities do you need to engage in to book the space, publicize the event, and organize logistics? What sorts of marketing do you need to engage in to attract new students? How do you maintain your teaching space? The more you start to delve down into everything that's required to operate your venture, even a relatively simple one such as a teaching studio becomes surprisingly complex. It's important that this step is not rushed, but thought through carefully.

Related to Activities are the **Resources** required. Our piano studio will need concrete resources such as books, a piano, a studio space, and so forth. But there are also intellectual resources: the training and experience of the teacher, for instance. You may also require some outside resources, like a bookkeeper whom you pay $50 a month to help you keep your bills organized.

The **Partnerships** field connects both Activities and Resources to illustrate how important and useful partnerships can be in acquiring resources and supporting activities. A partnership is a mutually beneficial relationship, one that helps you deliver your VP cheaper, more efficiently, and more effectively. Perhaps your piano studio resides in an underutilized church basement, where rent is cheaper than a swankier office suite and the location is better for your students. Perhaps you acquire free marketing services by bartering with a local business and providing free piano lessons to the owner's daughter.

Identifying potential partnerships can play a tremendously important role in the life of a venture because they provide the opportunity to lower costs, and can often improve our customer relationships as well. Moreover, partnerships can open up new sources of previously unreached clients, such as when your presence in the church basement leads to members of the congregation bringing their kids to study with you. For each Key Activity and Resource identified, ask yourself if there is a partnership to create that would address those needs cheaper and more effectively; the more you ponder this, you'll be surprised at the possibilities that will arise.

FINANCIAL SECTOR: INCOME AND COSTS

The last sector on the Canvas is the Financial one—placed at the base of the Canvas, as the element that will support everything above it. This is probably the easiest of the fields to fill—as long as you do your homework and are thorough with your lists. Income and Costs are precisely that: what are the expenses required to deliver your VP, and how much (and from where) will the income be that you gain from that delivery?

A good place to start is with **Costs**, since most of your Key Activities, Resources, and Partnerships will have some cost associated with them. Rent, utilities, supplies, marketing: make sure you comb through your Operations sector carefully, looking for every possible cost associated with them. In doing this, you may also discover that you've overlooked some Activities or Resources that need to be included, so cataloging your Costs can be doubly useful.

Reviewing your **Income** streams can be similarly enlightening. While money earned from teaching is, of course, the primary source of revenue for your piano teaching venture, considering other income streams will force you to consider such questions as: Will you sell your teaching materials at cost? Do you want to charge admission for your studio recitals? Could you offer a discount to customers who pay a whole semester in advance?

In addition to answering these questions in the abstract, you must also load up a spreadsheet and work out actual projections for income and expenses in your first year, second year, and third year. To make these projections as accurate as possible, you must conduct extensive research to ensure your estimates of expenses are on target, that your market will pay what you're projecting to charge, and so forth. Many a business that has done everything right so far still fails at this point because it either underestimates expenses or overestimates income (or both). Make conservative projections and be able to back up your assumptions with cold facts.

In fact, research is important for every stage of the Business Model Canvas. Assumptions and poorly supported projections are the entrepreneur's bane, bringing down many a venture that otherwise had promise. For the Customer Sector, talk to potential customers: get feedback on your idea, ask them how much they'd be willing to pay for it, find out what they would change and what it is they really need and the best way for them to get it. For the Financial and Operations Sectors, use the infinite sources of the Internet to find the best prices on goods and services, maximize your use of partnerships, and be conservative in your income projections. Seek out a mentor who has experience in your field, and see if you can tap into your local entrepreneurial community.

YOUR VENTURE IS A LIVING THING

Now that we've worked our way through the various sectors of the Business Model Canvas and their respective components, there's one more critical way in which the Canvas is useful. You may have already noticed how certain elements of the Canvas are inextricably linked—the relationship between Customer Segments and the Channels you use to reach them, for instance. When we drill down into these relationships more deeply, we begin to see how interconnected our venture really is: Changes in any component can (and usually do) have ripple effects throughout the entire Canvas. Let's look at a few examples to illustrate this.

Imagine for a minute that the community music school you've started resides in a church basement that is unused during the week. The rent is cheap, and it's in the ideal location for your students and their families. This Key Partnership is central to just about every aspect of your venture: It influences the Customer Relationships and Channels you employ, it is hugely important to keeping your finances in the black, and it helps you focus your Key Activities on serving your customers and not worrying about the facility. Now imagine that one day the church's board of directors notifies you that they will not be renewing your lease; they've decided to open a food pantry and homeless shelter and will be needing the space.

Once you've gotten over the initial panic, the Canvas can help you see what you need to change in your venture to keep it viable. It's about more than just finding a new location—it informs the type of location you really need (hopefully another affordable Partnership as opposed to a new Resource you have to pay full price for); it will likely change the dynamics of your Financial Sector. It may also have a big impact on your Customer Segments. Will your new location not work as well for your existing customers? Are there new segments you can now access? All this may mean you'll need to employ a new or different mix of Channels to reach those segments.

You can play this game with all sectors in your Canvas—and it's a good game to play, especially in the planning phase of your venture. It will help you see that no component of the Canvas lives in a vacuum: Each component is connected to and influences all the others, and every component is guided by and must reflect the VP. Having this visual tool helps you work through these connections and keep all the moving parts of your venture working together in harmony.

So is one ever really finished with the Business Model Canvas? Not really. As soon as you've filled in the fields, you may discover a new Customer Segment, refine the use of certain Channels, or experiment with a new kind of Customer Relationship. Costs you hadn't foreseen may present themselves—as might previously unknown streams of Income. You might even realize that your Value Proposition needs to change in some fundamental way, that there is an even better product to pursue or a different and more profitable market to tap into.

In other words, since change is the only constant (in business as well as life), it's best to have a tool to help you manage that change in a comprehensive and holistic way. Therefore, the Business Model Canvas should be a living document, one that evolves and flexes and remakes itself just as your venture does. It's not just a tool for planning your venture; it's a tool you should constantly revisit as you gain experience, learn more about your customers, and identify new opportunities. It's also a tool for gaming out changes you're considering making. For creatives, it's an indispensable resource for understanding, planning, and sustaining their artistic venture.

After you have planned your business operations with the Canvas, you need to consider the process you use to produce the work itself.

• • • •

David Cutler is the author of arguably the most celebrated book in the field of music entrepreneurship—The Savvy Musician: Building a Career, Earning a Living, and Making a Difference. *As a composer, performer, speaker, organizer, educator, and consultant, David has a dizzying calendar of projects under way constantly. Who better to ask about project management?*

Project Management: The Five Ds
by David Cutler

Music entrepreneurs are revered as innovators, bold thinkers, and courageous explorers. But these characteristics alone do not an entrepreneur make. To truly claim the mantle, other ingredients are crucial: detailed strategic planning and an unwavering insistence on getting things done! Below is the process I recommend for bringing complicated large-scale projects to life.

1. DREAM
Far too often when pursuing a project, be it an entrepreneurial venture, financial/artistic/career goal, or anything else that matters, people start by doing whatever comes to mind first. Lacking a clear process or picture of the endgame, they blindly step forward in whichever direction the wind blows, with no compass to guide their actions. Inefficient at best, this approach results in wasted energy and unproductive action. Others start by speculating on the many logistical challenges that may arise along the way, real or imagined. As a result, aspirations become dramatically compromised before even beginning.

I advocate starting with the dream. Grounded ambition is a major plus. If you could wave a magic wand, how would the most successful version of your aspiration look?

2. DESIGN

Dreams are often fuzzy and vague. Phase 2 involves developing the details in writing (as opposed to storing them in your head alone): who, what, when, why, where, how, how much, how long, and so forth.

For example, if you want to write and self-publish a book on practice strategies, guestimate the number of words. Outline major concepts and draft the table of contents. Determine a writing style and other "rules" of the project, as well as the goal number of sales. The design of your dream will undoubtedly change over time when confronted with unanticipated realities, good or bad. But the more clearly articulated your vision at this early point, the more likely you will arrive somewhere desirable.

3. DEFINE

Achieving a huge aspiration can feel overwhelming. When broken into smaller actionable chunks, however, a clear and realistic path to success can be drawn. Armed with a detailed, specific end goal, begin working backward. First, list large-scale activity categories. With the book example above, this includes researching, writing, editing, proofing, indexing, filing, designing, manufacturing, marketing, and distributing. Omitting essential categories adds considerable stress down the road, since you won't think to plan for these aspects.

Then break down actions into increasingly smaller steps. Ultimately, the best descriptions are achievable, specific, and quantifiable—there should be a clear way to assess when and whether each step is completed. For example, "write a 400-word passage on breaking down complex rhythms" is a concrete metric. Defining a series of manageable steps takes time on the front end. But this investment of time ultimately pays off.

4. DATE

Next, schedule when each activity must be completed. The exploding number of user-friendly time/project management apps makes this planning easier than ever. Because it's practically human nature to procrastinate, "deadlines with consequences" are invaluable. Things regularly take longer than anticipated, so leave plenty of cushions throughout.

Determining the sequence of activities can be a challenge. What should you do first? What comes next? It often seems that 20 essential activities compete for attention. Prioritize by urgency and what logically makes sense.

5. DO

Now there's just one thing left—get to work! Consistently make progress toward micro- and macro-goals. Entrepreneurs are renowned for their unflappable tenacity.

Some studies stress that human beings respond well to routines. Regularly working on related activities at comparable times maximizes productivity. Once a line item is completed, proudly cross it off your "to do" list. Beating or meeting deadlines is incredibly gratifying. Keep going until you reach the finish line.

● ● ● ●

SUMMARY

Chapter 8 transitions us from embracing the mindsets of the revolutionary artist to introducing the skill sets needed to move ideas to action. Critical optimism and its foundational challenge of playing the believing game over the doubting game prepares us to be optimistic about our own future and strategic in our thinking. Tools like the Business Model Canvas and project management provide us with the organizational chops to manage our projects, a necessary shift for real-world action.

CHAPTER 9

FROM INSPIRATION TO ACTION: YOUR PROJECT TAKES FLIGHT

SOME PEOPLE SEEM TO successfully move their ideas into the marketplace, while others get stuck. Is there more to being an artist-entrepreneur than simply being creative and having a great idea? In this chapter, we discuss the way forward, with helpful processes to move your ideas to action.

Your venture is taking shape. Your team is assembled. Now it's time to move your ideas to action. And to do so, you're going to need tools to help leverage your position, define your goals, organize your efforts, mobilize your team, and map your way forward.

• • • •

Jonathan Kuuskoski is assistant director of Entrepreneurship and Career Services within the University of Michigan's School of Music, Theatre & Dance. As a pianist, Jonathan has performed across the United States, Canada, the United Kingdom, the Czech Republic, Cyprus, Greece, Norway, and New Zealand, and he is a sought-after clinician and speaker.

Decision-Making in Four Directions: SWOT Analysis

by Jonathan Kuuskoski

Decision-making is a central part of every revolutionary artist's work. Beyond the routine decisions that drive every enterprise at a basic operational level, you will find yourself consistently challenged by opportunities that demand a higher degree of analysis. You'll need to know how to make big decisions like whether you should launch a new product or service, whether (and when) to pursue external partnerships, and which channels will most effectively connect your work to the world. How do you consistently make the best decisions, especially when the stakes are high? We need tools that help us frame our options against our personal goals while also accounting for external forces from the market and beyond.

Of course, you might start with a pro/con analysis, which we all regularly use to make everyday decisions. But the pro/con analysis is not sophisticated enough for an entrepreneur. In its simplicity, it is based heavily on assumptions, often overlooks the dynamic interplay of external forces, and operates in a win/lose world mindset. That's not our game. The outcomes of a major decision are rarely so cut-and-dried.

Enter the SWOT Analysis, a useful tool for decision-making that takes the best advantage of your talents, abilities, and opportunities.[1] Rather than simply comparing positives and negatives, the SWOT Analysis allows you to analyze four factors against each other to help you make informed decisions. Start by listing Strengths and Weaknesses, which are factors internal to your organization. With that information, you move to the external factors—the Opportunities as well as the potential Threats you face. Captured on a matrix, the SWOT places in view the excitement and challenges on the horizon, allowing you to make decisions that will make a difference.

Whether focused on global or local decision-making, this invaluable exercise will help determine whether it is a smart avenue to pursue through the launch of your venture. Once you have the SWOT Analysis, you can choose a course of action that will

- maximize Strengths and Opportunities
- transform/minimize Weaknesses and Threats

Rather than avoiding your negatives, think about what course of action might turn them into positives. You will find that your ability to identify new pathways through tough decisions is crucial to thriving as a revolutionary artist. Why? Because your best career decisions aren't likely to be black or white, and sacrifice is inevitable. The analysis will direct you to multiple potential outcomes for you to explore alternative solutions.

Here is an example of a career decision faced by an aspiring musician, Ophelia Reveur. She needs your help.

Ophelia envisions herself as a chamber musician with a national profile. She imagines a portfolio career where she's performing classical music but also collaborating with a variety of different artists. After hearing about 21CM, she happened upon Anna Bulbrook and her story about transitioning into indie music.[2] Ophelia loves to play, compose, teach both young and old students, and travel. And she is a social animal, so the more collaboration in her life, the better. Her dream career would include regular touring in an innovative chamber group or indie band, collaborations with post-genre performing artists, and educational residencies at both universities and strong pre-college programs. Maybe one day, she thinks, she might even start a summer camp connected to Anna Bulbrook's GIRLSCHOOL that will help empower young people through music-making.

A recent graduate of a Midwest liberal arts college, Ophelia now holds a BM in clarinet performance with a minor in composition. She had a great experience at her alma mater, where she played with a variety of musicians, regularly wrote music for chamber groups, and collaborated with both visual arts and dance students through the annual Collage Concert. Ophelia's also a voracious music listener of all styles. After graduating in May, she decided to stay in her college town in central Indiana. Ophelia keeps busy by teaching part-time at a small studio of young beginners at a local community music center and supplements this with work at a local coffee shop. She has written some chamber works commissioned by friends at school but has not had any "big" premieres by professional groups. Ophelia projects her income for the coming year to be about $20,000 but is hoping to grow it to $40,000 in a few years so she can invest in bigger personal projects. She also volunteers on the advisory board of the local arts council, helping with their website and social media updates.

Ophelia's career plan includes getting into a top master's program near a major US city (New York, Chicago, Boston, and Los Angeles are top choices). To do so, she plans to develop her portfolio over the next two years by (1) expanding teaching experience locally; (2) organizing performances in Chicago, St. Louis, Oklahoma City, and Kansas City; and (3) building a strong reputation in the region as an emerging artist. Before going back to school, she plans to have some of her compositions performed by several established groups in her area, play in at least two of the major cities listed above, and have earned experience teaching students of all ages.

Scenario: Ophelia has just learned about a new national residency program for young artists that will send fellows to a top music institute in Los Angeles for three months to work on a specific creative project. All admitted young artists receive mentorship from a roster of top international artists. Priority will be given to interdisciplinary projects that focus on innovative ways to foster youth music education. Full room and board, one public performance at the institute's well-known gallery, and a stipend of $1,000 are provided for successful candidates. She has just one week to complete and submit the required application materials, including a portfolio and recommendation letters.

Should Ophelia pursue this residency opportunity? To help make that decision, let's use a SWOT Analysis to break down the various factors in play.

INTERNAL FACTORS

Strengths

Questions	Ophelia's Traits
What do you do well? Draw from the results of your Superpowers Assessment.	Ophelia has a strong background working with artists from different media while in college.
What unique resources can you tap?	She knows several peer musicians working in the community who have interests in outreach.
What do others see as your strengths?	Her teaching experience in a community music school provides insight into meeting community needs. She is known for her curiosity in exploring new opportunities in the local community and is respected for taking on leadership responsibilities.
In what situations do you thrive?	She thrives working with others but is most comfortable collaborating with people she knows and trusts. She likes to think of herself as an extroverted introvert.
What personal values served you well during your toughest challenges?	She can be calm under pressure and isn't afraid to speak her mind.

Weaknesses

Questions	Ophelia's Traits
What could you improve?	She has no experience developing or coordinating community arts outreach projects.
Where do you have fewer resources than others?	She does not have a current project in development that would fit the criteria of this residency.
What are others likely to see as weaknesses?	Ophelia is active only at a local level, and just beginning to branch out into the Midwest; she has no connection/exposure to the LA area.
What circumstances challenge you more than all others?	She didn't graduate from a major music program and knows that some people might discount her abilities before they even meet her.
Where do others have advantages over you?	Since her network is regional and not based in LA, she doesn't know whom to contact about whether this is a good fit.

EXTERNAL FACTORS

Opportunities

Questions	Ophelia's Traits
What opportunities are open to you?	This opportunity would provide Ophelia the chance to connect with top international artists.
What trends could you take advantage of?	This type of high-profile achievement is common among top candidates for leading master's programs.
How can you turn your strengths into opportunities?	Since Ophelia knows peer artists interested in developing outreach arts projects and has a strong reputation for taking on leadership roles, this residency opportunity could provide the chance to follow up with peers and see if there is a project brewing locally that would fit the criteria.
What is one unexpected positive outcome of this situation?	She might make a great connection with one of the mentors who could be her "in" to a major master's program.
What is the best-case scenario?	Ophelia establishes relationships that lead to meaningful collaborations with colleagues met during the residency, including tours and recording projects of her own music.

Threats

Questions	Ophelia's Traits
What threats could harm you?	Ophelia will lose income if she attends the residency.
What is your competition doing?	There are potentially much more qualified applicants who are also more established in LA, with direct ties to community partner organizations.
What threats do your weaknesses expose?	Since she has no connection to LA, it is hard to determine what the expectations are there. As this is a brand-new and nationally competitive residency, no data exists on past candidates.
What is one unexpected negative outcome of this situation?	If she gets in but does not thrive in the residency, she might feel like a failure, have lost income, and end up in no better place regarding opportunities for the master's program.
What is the worst-case scenario?	Ophelia loses confidence in her own ability to navigate a successful career, rather than understand that in all of our journeys mistakes are made.

Based on the matrix above, what do you think Ophelia should do? There are some clear potential positives and negatives for choosing to apply for the residency. As you contemplate this question, ask yourself what possible courses of action she could take to change the potential negatives into positives. Are there options beyond accepting the residency that might minimize Weaknesses/Threats by transforming them into Strengths/Opportunities in relation to her career goals?

• • • •

MAKING YOUR GOALS SMART

Consistently honing your ability to see the transformational potential of a circumstance, even a daunting one, is core to the practice of being an entrepreneur. While decision-making should be tied to your long-term goals, keep in mind that artists and arts organizations don't make decisions solely based on amorphous future outcomes. We make most of our decisions in the midst of challenging situations that demand action and have immediate consequences. So the ability to make effective decisions is also tied to the clarity of our perception of how our direct actions affect our short-, medium-, and long-term goals.

We can optimize our decision-making by using SMART goals, which is a framework that helps us break down our large goals into short- and medium-term objectives.[3] Well-defined objectives are steps that, when achieved, map out our pathway to a more promising future. In using them, we train ourselves to honor our progress, which is also helpful in maintaining a positive outlook in the midst of ongoing challenge. A SMART goal is an objective that is Specific, Measurable, Achievable, Relevant, and Time-bound.

Discussion: Let's take a look at Ophelia's situation and help her break down her long-term dream of having a portfolio career collaborating with a diverse group of artists. She already has a general idea of some medium-term goals:

1. Expand her teaching experience locally
2. Organize performances in Chicago, St. Louis, Oklahoma City, and Kansas City
3. Build a strong reputation in the region as an emerging artist

Now let's make them SMART.

What are the specific steps to building a regional reputation? There are many ways you can define that type of success, and Ophelia should be homing in on activities that leverage her skills and address the future work she is aiming for—namely becoming a chamber musician, an in-demand composer, and a respected pedagogue at the collegiate level. She hasn't yet broken into other musical styles. Ophelia needs to take reasonable steps to develop track records in those areas.

To start, Ophelia could establish a presence within a known arts community by regularly attending and supporting local indie music events. Let's be more specific. How much activity should she aim for to develop a presence? Will attending and supporting other artists be enough to establish her local reputation? She could set a specific objective to connect with a few musicians she admires and perform publicly at least once a month in local and regional venues. Having set that, she can move into action steps. What are those venues? Who does she need to contact, and how many of those contacts does she already know? Holding a particular objective in mind also influences our decision.

Likewise, she needs to determine how much she should expand her studio, and to what type of students. If she lacks community engagement experience, she needs to consider including that activity into her portfolio. Making your goals specific forces you to assess how making a decision related to your goals (moving to a new location) changes your options, for better or worse.

Not all goals emerge lacking specificity. Take Ophelia's income goal of $40,000 a year. That's already fairly specific, but she needs a system for measuring her progress. Through which activities should she be aiming to earn her income? Let's say she wants to equally split her income across composing, performing, teaching, and organizing. Now she has a basis for exploring how many commissions she will need to earn $10,000. She'll need to identify the going rate for a commission of varying scopes. A short piano piece will not warrant the same fee as a concerto, but she may be able to write many piano pieces in the time it takes to write a single, larger work.

Wherever possible, aim to bring your specific and measurable criteria together. Measurable goals are those that can move your project in some specific way. In planning for her income, Ophelia should consider how many performances in pursuit of "presence" she would need to give to earn $10,000. Her income goal might influence how many gigs she takes on for free, but if certain performances providing minimal financial compensation offer other value-adds, she may want to leave space in her schedule to do them. Wedding gigs might pay better than a new music concert she organizes herself, but the latter may be crucial to building her connections with local artists. If her efforts pay off and she receives an invitation to sit in with a prominent traveling ensemble, she may want the flexibility to take it on.

So Ophelia may need to diversify her income from several sources. She needs to consider how many lessons to teach, how much she should charge, and what she should be offering in her lessons to justify her price point. In other words, consider which activities may be cash cows, providing a stable base to finance experimental (or more volatile) activities. For example, Ophelia may realize that splitting her income equally across four activities isn't realistic. Perhaps building a stable teaching studio could allow her to earn enough to cover the variability of revenue from her performances.

Those are all quantifiable questions—data-driven information from which you can create schedules, budgets, and bottom-line analyses. Ophelia also needs to consider qualitative criteria—the kind that isn't measured so easily by numbers. Will writing piano pieces or a concerto lead to greater exposure? It's easier to have a piano piece played multiple times, since you just need individual performers to champion the work. On the other hand, a concerto premiered by the right type of ensemble might be a bigger splash. She could track reviews by well-regarded critics and bloggers, which could come out of a premiere, as a way to measure her "presence." Social media tools could help her identify when word-of-mouth buzz picks up about her work as a teacher, performer, or composer. Even a single commission from a leading artist or ensemble could become a launch pad for broader interest, so she needs to consider the connections she's making through her regular performances and the networks those contacts open for her. If she connects with an indie band, there might be entirely untapped income streams, not to mention clout, at her fingertips. And she shouldn't ignore the value of the personal satisfaction and inspiration that her projects are providing on an ongoing basis. These qualitative measures are important because they better describe your trajectory. They provide context for the data points and communicate your understanding of the potential inherent in creative work even at an early stage.

How does Ophelia know which goals to pursue, especially after brainstorming so many options? Objectives should be achievable given your current situation and resources. Again, they represent the step-by-step progress toward a larger, broad goal. Objectives that balloon beyond realism are discouraging, or, at worst, abandoned. They can cultivate a negative mindset and a tendency to sway toward the doubting game.

You may be thinking that framing all your goals in achievable terms might downplay creativity and ambition, but, in fact, it should just be a natural outgrowth of your other SMART criteria. For example, rather than expecting to become "nationally visible" within one year, we've already noted that Ophelia could start by establishing herself regionally. Given her current network, income, and experience, what are some achievable benchmarks for the specific and measurable goals we have discussed? She can get very creative in answering those questions.

If she doesn't have community engagement experience, the idea of building and launching a full-fledged, comprehensive community program in three months might not be possible. But she could imagine a single pilot event, perhaps a week-long, summer day camp inspired by GIRLSCHOOL in collaboration with a community center. Or she could apprentice with an established professional to learn the ropes in that arena. Similarly, if she doesn't have any works written for orchestra, committing three months to writing a 20-minute concerto for a national competition may not be as viable as workshopping portions of it with a local group of musicians who can give her valuable feedback through an iterative process. Ophelia might also gain ambassadors for the work once it is complete.

If hiring a full orchestra is cost-prohibitive, she could use the concept of inchvesting to find a more reasonable solution. Inchvesting is an exercise where you brainstorm a comparable solution that requires 10 percent of the original cost. Maybe a chamber concerto, which requires only 18–20 instead of 80–100 players, is a more viable alternative. What about writing music for an indie group? How might recording it using a university recording studio rather than a commercial one affect her bottom line? The power inherent in using achievable criteria is that they give you permission to acknowledge and value the small steps you need to take to set up bigger successes. They don't stop you from brainstorming creative solutions, and, in fact, you may come to the conclusion that cutting costs in some areas of your work will hurt the end product too much. At least you'll be aware of the alternatives; staying conscious of the strategic reasons underlying your choices results in better decisions. We just don't want Ophelia to ignore the value of an apprenticeship because she has her sights too fixed on the idea of the national spotlight.

Perhaps the most commonly overlooked question in framing objectives is how relevant they are to our long-term dreams. Just because objectives are specific, measurable, and achievable does not ensure they will help you in your pursuit of larger goals. Ophelia needs to consider whether pursuing any of her objectives is worthwhile. How do you know? Consider the ways in which achieving the goal will push her forward in her career. This is where the relevance criterion intersects with your quantitative and qualitative measurements. How is this work aligned with her dream? Is this the right time to pursue this objective?

In deciding whether pursuing the Los Angeles residency is relevant, she could look at the specific opportunities inherent in that choice and figure out whether the skills she would develop, the connections to the people there, and the prestige of the opportunity align with her long-term goals. Ophelia also needs to consider the opportunity cost—the best estimate of whether taking this change on now is of greater benefit than increasing her income and developing her local presence. Is attending the residency relevant for getting into a master's program? Is either the residency or the master's critical to building a national profile as a collaborative artist? If not, remaining static in her current situation may not be the most relevant option, either.

Let's say Ophelia decides not to apply for the residency. If she only expands her teaching studio purely to enhance her reputation, she may be missing out on an opportunity for greater impact in her local community. She should look at alternative opportunities we've discussed above, see how they intersect with her current activities, and prioritize those that are achievable and relevant for the next three months. They can't just be income bearing; these objectives should be deeply rooted in her vision for her future.

Once she has realized her first round of short-term goals, what is the next set of objectives she should move on to for the rest of the year? We all need to set deadlines to make our objectives time bound. More than just creating a sense of urgency, the time-bound criterion will help prioritize your plan and prevent you from pushing aside key steps during stressful, hectic work periods. Knowing that you may well face external factors beyond your control, retaining some flexibility is a good idea. Consider your deadlines as you discuss specific, measurable, and achievable metrics.

Perhaps the next step for Ophelia after her pilot chamber performances is to organize and complete a two-week regional tour. She could also make a list of regional music festivals or venues in those larger cities and aim to take a group there to premiere one of her works. How far out does she need to plan to make this time-bound goal achievable? We need to look at all the steps she needs to take, working backward from a target launch date, to set a reasonable deadline for each of her objectives.

SMART Exercise: Brainstorm at least five new short-term SMART goals for Ophelia (achievable within three to six months), to help her achieve her three medium-term goals. Use the template included in the **Toolkit**.

What is your SMART goal for Ophelia?

Consider how these SMART goals impact your SWOT Analysis of Ophelia's situation. Would you revise your advice to her? Should she reconsider the Los Angeles residency based on these stated objectives? What are her biggest roadblocks at this point? Based on her stated long-term goals, what types of activities should she avoid in order to maximize her ability to realize her SMART goals?

SMART goals can seem daunting. It's challenging to consider all these criteria when you imagine an untested collaborative project. None of these objectives is set in stone. Use them as a compass, rather than as a road map, and build an evaluation of the goals into your regular workflow. If you do, you will create an archive of information that will improve the next round of planning. In that way, SMART goals help us make better decisions and become core to the entrepreneurial process because they provide a framework for testing, evaluating, and revising your idea.

ACTION PLAN

The tools we've discussed in this chapter can help you make better decisions and think differently about what your next steps should be in your pursuit of a more promising future. You've helped Ophelia evaluate internal and external forces to optimize her decision-making and broken down her big dreams into SMART goals. Ophelia is now ready to take action.

An Action Plan is a step-by-step process for realizing your short-term goals. It is relatively simple, yet powerful when informed by your long-term strategic planning. Using an Action Plan helps you organize your work on a day-to-day basis, transforms the stress of decision-making into tasks that will show you incremental progress, and ensures that all collaborators are working on the same page. It's one of our greatest tools for living the believing game.

Action Plan Exercise: Put Ophelia's SMART goal into action with the Action Plan template in the **Toolkit**.

1. List all the steps needed to accomplish the objective.
2. List a brief description of each step, in particular where one action step is informed by another.
3. Indicate who is responsible for each task (team members or external partners).
4. Give a start date and a due date for each task.

How has this process changed your perspective on goal-setting?

Once you have written your Action Plan, you're ready to implement. But we still have one more strategy to consider that's been implied all along. Revolutionary artists don't achieve their big dreams alone. As in any other field, collaboration is an essential element of the entrepreneurial process, and we need to discuss how to leverage the diverse skills of your team to optimize your creative project.

• • • •

Drawing upon her vast experience as a lawyer, not-for-profit executive, and board member, Astrid Baumgardner teaches music entrepreneurship at the Yale School of Music. An active blogger, coach, and consultant, Astrid is a powerful advocate for collaborative leadership.

Collaborative Leadership

by Astrid Baumgardner

You've mapped out the impact you want to make in your community, and now it is time to take action. But already there's fear. What if the work doesn't get done?

To ensure the successful completion of your project, consider leveraging the Collaborative Leadership Model. The Collaborative Leadership Model empowers everyone in your organization to lead their particular aspect of the project. And it makes sense. Each team member has been assigned the role and the tasks they are now responsible for based on their expertise. When every team member can play to their strengths, they work, not just harder, but smarter, and take ownership, feeling motivated to get things done well.

Members of the group also know and appreciate the particular contribution of each team member. Thus, members step up to lead as needed and defer to other members, allowing them to shine in their area of expertise, all of which builds strong relationships and promotes a high degree of respect across the organization. Just think how valuable this is when problems arise and things do not go as planned!

The collaborative leadership structure also fosters group accountability because each team member (1) feels a strong commitment to her fellows and (2) knows how her segment contributes to the overall success of the project.

Therefore, structure your project to take advantage of the individual talents of each team member and allow each person to shine!

* * * *

SUMMARY

To make good decisions about the way forward, you need to know the strengths, weakness, opportunities, and threats facing your organization. A SWOT Analysis is just the right tool to capitalize on the best your team has to offer and minimize the impact of internal and external forces working against you. Being clear, tallying success (and failure), and setting goals that are feasible, relevant, and timely are all outcomes when using SMART goals. You are now in the thick of things, and an Action Plan has never been more crucial to achieving what you have set out to conquer.

We learned that when we map our future and use tools to both understand the conditions in which we work and help prioritize next steps, good things can happen.

Be creative. Be strategic. Be a change agent.

CHAPTER 10

GETTING THE WORD OUT: STORYTELLING, MARKETING, AND COMMUNICATIONS STRATEGY

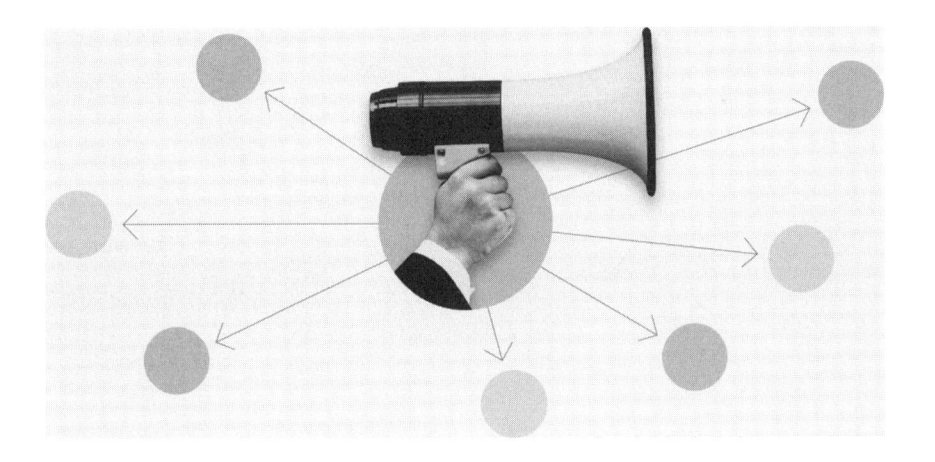

AS AN ENTREPRENEUR BUILDING a business, you are on a hero's journey. To succeed, you must be braver than you've ever been and believe in yourself. You also need customers! In this chapter, we'll focus on the strategy behind selling your entrepreneurial dream, including developing content that tells your story and communicates it effectively to the world.

• • • •

Elizabeth Hinckley is president of DefCult, an organizational development and communications lab. A classically trained musician, Elizabeth worked at the intersection of the arts and communications for more than 20 years, serving as director of public relations for both Atlantic Records and the Los Angeles Philharmonic Association, before launching the arts and culture division at Rogers & Cowan PR. Elizabeth created 21CM.org with DePauw University and served as its founding editor.

Storytelling and Communications Strategy
by Elizabeth Hinckley

BOB'S TALE

Bob Bigg was good at inventing things.

Bob dreamed of changing the world. He wanted to make life easier for people through personalized inventions. But his house was overflowing with prototypes. His wife finally told him, "Either have a garage sale or start a business."

The next day, Bob quit his job at ACME, withdrew his savings, and launched Invent-4-U.

On Invent-4-U's opening day, Bob hired a blimp lit up with his company name and phone number to float over the city and drop fliers for 20 percent off. No one came to redeem the offer. The next day, he ran an ad in the local paper that read, "Invent-4-U is open, 50 percent off." No one came for that one, either.

That night, Bob went to bed but couldn't sleep. "I really think I may not be able to do this," he said aloud. It was then that he heard the rat-a-tat outside. He opened the window just enough to let in what he thought was a firefly. In less than a second, that "firefly" became a young woman with a pixie haircut, delicate wings, and a golden green glow that lit up the room.

Shaking the gold dust from her hair, she said, "I'm Xena, and I've had my eye on you, Bob Bigg. You're a true original. Your ideas are honest and pure, you listen to people's needs, and you help them. So, I want to help you. Tomorrow, you are going to have three visitors. Each will tell you a story and ask you one question. Consider your heart and answer honestly."

Before Bob could ask a question, Xena disappeared.

The next day, Bob went to work, a little worried about his sanity, based on the night before. At 9 AM on the dot, a scrappy young man, no more than 25 years old, walked in. "I'm an innovation engineer, and I'm looking for a job," the man said. "I've already worked in five places and quit them because I didn't think we were making a difference. That's really important to me. So, if I work for you, what change will you try to bring about in the world?"

Bob was taken aback. How did this man even know he was looking for an engineer? He remembered the weird dream he had the night before and thought to himself, "Speak from your heart." He answered, "I believe listening to people, figuring out their problems, and creating personalized inventions to help them will ultimately change the world."

The young man teared up a little, handed Bob his resume, and said, "Hire me."

A few hours later, Bob was leaving for lunch, and a woman walked in. She wore a lavish red dress and expensive-looking jewelry and carried a Pomeranian. Before he could say hello, she blurted out, "I have a unique problem I need help with, and it requires a gifted mind to solve. If I hire you, what can you do for me that countless others have been unable to?"

Bob was so thrilled that a potential client had finally walked through the door, he almost said, "I can do anything!" But he considered Xena's counsel. What did this woman want? "My gift is that I invent bespoke solutions. To tell you what I can do, we first need to have a conversation about what you really need."

Bob was worried he was too cheeky with that last line, but the elegant woman said, "Let's talk."

Four hours later, Bob still had not had lunch. He walked to Jerry's Corner Deli, sat at the counter, and ordered a ham on rye. A few minutes later, a man with a broad-brimmed hat and a checkered suit sat down next to him. The man sighed audibly and said, "I just found out the five companies I invested in are not doing well. Today's CEOs have no vision."

Bob couldn't help but eavesdrop. He desperately needed investors. Feeling like he had nothing to lose, he said to the man, "I run a new start-up, and my vision is to change the world by creating personalized inventions that are so in tune with people's needs they will change lives. I want to reach 20,000 customers by 2020. It's an audacious goal, but I think I can do it. If I have the help of someone like you."

The man looked at Bob and said, "Who are you and what's your company?"

Bob answered, "I'm Bob Bigg, CEO of Invent-4-U."

"Well, Bob Bigg, you sound like a visionary, and I haven't met one in a long time. Let's talk more!"

That night, Bob got into bed feeling positive. He was just about to go to sleep when he heard a rat-a-tat at the window. In under a second, Xena appeared in all her green-glowdom. "How was your day?" she asked.

"Hopeful," Bob said. "I met with a possible employee, client, and funder and they all seem to believe in me. To be honest, I'm not sure what I did."

"You told your story," Xena said. "First, you expressed your heart. Why are you doing this? To bring about change in the world. Next, you explained how you would do this successfully—with your unique gift and a plan and direction others can follow.

"Nice start, Bob. Remember, you are the hero in this tale. To succeed, you must be braver than you've ever been and believe your story. Then, you must 'listen for the need' in others. It may come from your heart, your gift, your vision, or something else."

And, with that, she was off.

Three years before the goal date he gave to the man in the checkered suit, Bob had created 20,000 personalized inventions. His employees, investors, and clients considered him a hero, because he had changed their lives. If you visit Metropolis today, it's easy to find Bob. Just look for the sign with the little green fairy on it.

© DEFCULT 2016

That's the fairy-tale ending every entrepreneur dreams of, even if the reality has more twists and turns. The truth is, Bob experienced many highs and lows in those early years—he changed his fee structure, tweaked his customer base, and fired that inventions engineer.

"Bob's Tale" is an example of parable storytelling. My name is Elizabeth Hinckley, and I run a communications and organizational development lab called DefCult (www.defcult.org). I like to use this method to explain complicated or controversial concepts, and I tell this story when I lead communications strategy workshops for young entrepreneurs.

Parables teach universal truths about various aspects of the human condition. Every element in this story, except Xena, was based on the experiences of entrepreneurs, including me, at the beginning of our respective journeys. You might have paid special attention to the story, not only because you sympathized with Bob, but because you saw a little of yourself in our hero. Good storytelling elicits both sympathy and empathy.

While this chapter title includes "Storytelling," that is only one component of effective communications related to business. In this chapter, we'll focus on the strategy behind selling your entrepreneurial dream to the world, including content, delivery, and external factors.

CONTENT—THE CORE MESSAGE

Let's start with the information you wish to convey to customers about your company and product. After a TED Talk or any speech, research shows that we typically retain about three things. These should, hopefully, also be your core messages.

When I work with young entrepreneurs, much of what I focus on is how to talk about their ideas succinctly, in a way that elicits emotion from the audience. As creators and businesspeople, entrepreneurs like to talk about the *what* and *how* of the product, but customers want to know *why* you are doing it. Your heart. Potential clients also want to learn why they should pick you. What makes you special? Finally, they want to know where you will take them if they buy into your vision.

We introduced you to Simon Sinek's *Start with Why* in chapter 2 and the Business Model Canvas in chapter 8. It's possible to create a Value Proposition (VP) and never ask yourself why it matters to you. It's also possible to proclaim your purpose and never find a way to translate your gifts into a tangible, marketable good or service. But, even when you figure out both, if you don't have the vision mapped out to realize them, it's all for naught.

If every budding entrepreneur (and person) filled in the following and acted on it, in both word and deed, I bet there'd be a lot more business and personal success. The world might improve, too.

The Core Message

I/we believe . . . (heart) . . . will change the world for the better. I/we can actively provide . . . (gift) . . . a unique and wonderful gift to help make this a reality. I/we will know we have fulfilled our vision when I/we see . . . (vision) . . . is achieved.

© DEFCULT 2016

How would you complete this exercise?

If parts of this sound familiar, they are the answers to the three questions Xena asked Bob in the opening story, combined into one sentence I call the Hero Declaration. It is a mantra, strategic direction, and, for the purposes of this chapter, the most important information any audience should remember about you and your organization. By getting in the habit of building your communications strategy from this statement, you will find you can manage your message and ensure consistency across media platforms more easily.

Here's an early version of my Hero's Declaration, a year into the creation of my company, DefCult: "I believe dynamic and unique cultures impact the world for the better. To help make this a reality, I can actively provide my lab facilitations, guidance, and ability to see disparate connections and patterns as unique and wonderful gifts. I will know my vision has been realized when I see increased attendance and passionate audience connections related to these endeavors."

Another way to look at this same material is to consider how social entrepreneurs, and the venture capitalists and foundations that support them, use a concept called Theory of Change to measure project impact. Theory of Change is the empirical basis underlying any social intervention. This concept was developed by Paul Brest, president of the William and Flora Hewlett Foundation. Basically, it includes three components:

- a theory related to changing some aspect of an issue;
- the desired impact or goal to achieve something, agreed upon in advance, that will make a difference; and
- a strategy or logic model as the plan for achieving impact.

You can learn more about the Theory of Change in a 2010 article by Paul Brest in the *Stanford Social Innovation Review*.[1]

CONTENT—A STORY, TOLD WELL

I purposely included a fairy in "Bob's Tale," not only because she serves as a kind of deus ex machina, but also to make the following point: storytelling is an art; communication is a skill. The magic is combining them effectively so your audience falls in love with you. Here are a few suggestions for telling your hero story effectively.

A Hero with a Past: Can you name a story that does not have a protagonist? Even Walter White in *Breaking Bad*, everybody's favorite meth dealer, is an antihero. Like Walter or Bob of Invent-4-U, as an entrepreneur, you are by default the hero in your company's story. You probably have a reason you started this business that relates to something in your past—your origin story; this is a critical piece of information to establish.

Credible Narrators: Hero storytelling only works if the storyteller is believable and a variety of voices gives the illusion of a chorus of fans. Include multiple narrators and storytellers that make the most sense for each mode and medium. An autobiography will be told by you, a feature article will be penned by a journalist, an advertisement will be illustrated by an omniscient or omnipotent voice, and an endorsement will be exclaimed by a customer.

The Tried-and-True Story Arc: To create a believable story for your audience, you need to follow a path the reader will recognize. Also called a story arc, it usually begins with a hero of remarkable talent reckoning with a challenge he/she must overcome. He faces some setbacks along the way, rises to the challenge with heaping amounts of bravery, and ultimately has the win.

Vulnerability and Strength: As humans, we have this funny need for our heroes to show vulnerability and strength, simultaneously or in quick succession.

Tangibility: The most effective stories use the senses to draw you in and keep you invested until the payoff. Rich visuals and descriptive language are a powerful combo in telling the hero's story.

DELIVERY—IDENTIFYING AUDIENCES

Along with the storyteller, the delivery system (or Channels from the Business Model Canvas [BMC]) is made up of communications media and modes of expression.

While we've included "Audiences" (or Customer Segments from the BMC) officially in External Factors (because our customers have free will!), we will discuss them now. Audiences are the most important consideration in developing a communications strategy and are regularly researched throughout the life of a campaign.

"Bob's Tale" is helpful in understanding audience segmentation. He met three people throughout the course of a day. Each represented a different audience: employees (or internal audiences), investors (or donors), and customers. Along with another broader group, the public, that has obvious overlap with the first three, these audiences require different messaging because they respond to different things.

SORTING AUDIENCES

If you have completed the Business Model Canvas for your new endeavor, your Customer Segment (CS) section includes your target audiences and hopefully goes into even more detail about them. To create a communications strategy for your company that is both manageable and affordable, group like audiences together first. You can approach this task using the following sorting mechanism or any means that works for you.

- **Need:** In the Bob story, the employee was looking for a company that he could be proud of, the investor wanted a big-vision thinker, and the customer wanted someone who approached her problem in a unique way. (If you don't know the need, ask the customer!)
- **Relationship to the organization:** Think about a circle. Within the circle are the organization and everyone who works for it. These people have insider information and are motivated by how well the company does, team, position, and so on. Customers, certain investors, and the general public are outside the circle. They may be spoken to differently and receive more marketing-heavy communications.
- **Interests:** Your company probably has various subcategories, or niches, of audiences. You may focus on a small group of individuals who are potential superfans or simply categorize non-music lovers differently than music lovers.
- **Geographic areas:** For companies interested in national or international markets, communications strategies may be changed up according to different cities, languages, or other.

CONDUCTING RESEARCH

Audience research is a very big and important subject. Done well, it can completely transform your communications strategy. Many companies conduct focus groups to understand different demographics and how they connect with your product. But if you are a believer in the power of storytelling, I suggest something called empathy research. Empathy research includes many techniques, but at its core, it's about seeing things through another person's eyes and understanding their story. It also requires shedding preconceptions of what you think you know about your company and Becoming a Beginner Again, as I argued in a 2016 piece on marketing to audiences.[2]

As you get to understand your target audiences better, you will find you want to speak more directly to their concerns and needs. Storytelling is a marvelous way to do just that. Your goal in this research is to figure out what will motivate them to have a relationship with your company, and, by extension, you. By hearing their stories, you enhance yours, too.

DELIVERY—THE MODE AND THE MEDIUM

The system that delivers communications to the public is complex, convoluted, and worthy of a stack of business textbooks unto itself. For storytelling and strategic communications related to your company, here are the highlights.

Modes

Think of modes as different ways to package your Hero's Declaration. A variety of different delivery techniques are used, including the obvious ones that stimulate the senses—video, photograph, illustration, song, text, story, essay, music, and image/text—and not so obvious ones such as storyboard and role play. Design treatments also count, such as fonts and other graphic elements to create different moods and voices.

Modes are divided into three categories: controlled media, uncontrolled media, and in-persons. Each serves a different purpose and has advantages and disadvantages.

Controlled media—This category includes any communications developed by the company. Other names for this include marketing, advertising, engagement, and aspects of public relations. Every company has a controlled media strategy and uses it to ensure their key messages are communicated. Advantages include full company control of your brand and messaging; disadvantages include high cost and a lower level of trust from external audiences compared to uncontrolled media. Each of these serves different roles and provides different results:

- Advertisements: print and video
- Annual report
- Brochure
- Case study
- Catalog
- Company blog

- Company handbook
- Elevator pitch
- Infographics
- Podcasts
- Press releases
- Prospectus
- Social media
- Website
- White paper

Uncontrolled media—This category includes media created by sources external to the organization, including the news media, interest groups, and the general public. Other names for this include journalism, blogging, and posting. Media/Public Relations departments tend to handle uncontrolled media. Note that some can also hang out in the controlled media category. Here is a nonexhaustive list:

- Blogger posts
- Concert reviews
- Documentaries (also controlled)
- Facebook Live broadcasts (also controlled)
- Gossip posts
- Interviews: radio, newspaper, magazine, television
- News items
- News segments
- Opinion/editorial pieces (also controlled)
- Pictorial spreads
- Social media posts (also controlled)

Check out "The Art of the Story—An Artist Video Case Study" by Elizabeth Nonemaker on 21CM.org.[3] It is a great how-to and how-not-to create an artist documentary short.

In-persons—This category includes any activities arranged with engagement in mind. Even though it's called in-person, it can include virtual events as well. Advantages include direct access to the consumer and brand enhancement that is typically well received. Disadvantages include cost, event management challenges, and sometimes difficulty in measuring real impact (particularly if you are participating in an event not exclusive to your company, such as sponsorship of a marathon or charity event).

Media

If modes are about style, media are the mouthpieces. Communications strategists, whether a publicist, marketer, or advertising wizard, make choices about the media they use based on reach (readership, geography, interests), reputation (hip, traditional), and relationships (media contacts, advertising deals, partnerships).

Media include radio, print, television, social media, books, blogs, reports, mail, and, again, events. It feels like new "outlets" are added and subtracted daily.

Each medium handles both controlled and uncontrolled media and has different rules for each. The rules can also differ wildly from outlet to outlet.

EXTERNAL INFLUENCES—ENVIRONMENT AND TIMING

A good story without a receptive environment is like a dazzling diamond tiara lying in the sand on a deserted island. Useless. We've discussed the importance of audience research, now let's talk about taking a scan of your environment (chapter 6) before you launch your communications strategy. In broad strokes, this means understanding not only the audiences you are communicating with but the industry and general public mood. In chapter 9, you conducted a SWOT analysis, which is a helpful tool here, as well. What I'd like to focus on now is timing—creating a communications calendar strategically timed to a launch.

The Communications Calendar

Communications calendar planning is based on two things: media deadlines and the product/event/service launch date. Let's use a typical concert season and assume you have an opening night of September 15 for a concert season that will last until June. Today is November 1, so you have almost 11 months! You want to make a plan that incorporates both controlled and uncontrolled media. The following is a very basic strategy for key tasks you need in your calendar and to-do list, keeping in mind some typical media deadlines. The dates are suggestions and not set in stone.

Concert Season: Communications To-Do List

TASK	DUE FROM LAUNCH DATE
Controlled Media	
Press release	February 15
Gather information	December
Write release	December/January
Get approvals from leadership	February 1
Send to media, specific audiences	February 15
Brochure	**February 15**
Create text and design	December/January
Get approvals from leadership	January 15
Print	February 1

TASK	DUE FROM LAUNCH DATE
Send to mailing lists and others	February 15
Social media campaign	February 15 and continues
Website inclusion	February 15
Advertising (radio, print, television)	February 15 and continues
Uncontrolled Media	
Provide embargoed season release to local daily paper	February 14
Pitch coverage for season opening	May to September 15
Long leads (magazines)	May
Medium leads (radio, TV)	July
Short leads (newspaper, TV, radio)	July to September 15

WHEN EVERYTHING WORKS

The most effective communications strategy combines a great story, message (content), storyteller, audience, mode, and medium (delivery system) and then considers the environment, audience again, and timing (external factors). In business, we tell stories for different reasons. As mentioned earlier, "Bob's Tale" was a parable. It was an effective, "soft pitch" method to teach a lesson, using empathy to capture the reader's attention.

We've discussed various media and platforms that can be used to tell a story. Now, let's look at effective examples in the real world.

Products and Services

ReThink Cyberbullying App on *Shark Tank* (https://youtu.be/FQFTCE3RV1Y)
Mode: Controlled/Uncontrolled Media: Elevator pitch, show-and-tell visuals, Q&A (visual, oral)
Medium: Television reality show/national network
The show *Shark Tank* is an excellent source of elevator pitches as well as Hero Declarations and Stories. ReThink is a good example of a young entrepreneur as the hero, trying to solve a societal issue.

Israel in Egypt with LA Master Chorale (https://youtu.be/23VbK9hqdQk)
Mode: Controlled Media: Documentary with interviews, music, video clips (visual, oral, audio)

Medium: Company website, Facebook, Twitter
A typical choral concert can be challenging to promote. LA Master Chorale has created a documentary-style promo that entices the listener and gives context through storytelling.

Budweiser Ad for Super Bowl: "Born the Hard Way" (https://youtu.be/HtBZvl7dIu4)
Mode: Controlled Media: Video advertisement (visual, audio)
Medium: National television (Super Bowl)
A perfect example of a company using the hero origin story to promote its product and its values, taking advantage of specific timing when viewers are feeling patriotic or nostalgic.

Muslim-Focused Racism (https://www.instagram.com/p/BP076O3la3w/)
Mode: Video illustration using data
Medium: Social media
Mona Chalabi turns hand-drawn illustrations into stories about social issues.

Depression (http://hyperboleandahalf.blogspot.com/2011/10/adventures-in-depression.html)
Mode: Text and illustrations
Medium: Blog
Allie Brosh's colorful, rough-hewn illustrations paint her as the antihero, struggling with issues big and small.

Arts Advocacy (http://21cm.org/magazine/state-of-the-art-form/2016/11/10/arts-entrepreneurs-become-advocates-for-the-c-r-e-a-t-e-act/)
Mode: Editorial using data
Medium: Online music magazine
An example of how data can support editorial.

Arts Education (http://21cm.org/magazine/artist-features/2017/01/04/concert-halls-disrupted-a-talk21-with-stanford-thompson/)
Mode: Speech using data
Medium: Music conference
An example of how to move audiences with the hero's tale in a live format, using the story arc.

Special Issues

Impact Reputation

First People's Center for Education (http://defcult.org/projects/first-peoples-center-for-education/)
Mode: Case study
Medium: Company website
Demonstrates how a company can tell a success story using heroes and data.

Rebuilding/Crisis

ENO [English National Opera] Rebounds with New Leader (https://www.theguardian.com/music/2016/jun/04/english-national-opera-eno-artistic-director-daniel-kramer-interview)
Mode: Interview/feature
Medium: National daily newspaper
A unique example of a struggling organization trying to reinvent itself by bringing in a new hero to start fresh.

Which of these examples resonated with you and why?

Let's circle back to "Bob's Tale" and the reasoning behind its presentation in this chapter. Opening with a story served to both set up a chapter on storytelling and entrepreneurship and capture your attention in, hopefully, a memorable way. The choice to use typewriter font was purposeful. I wanted it to feel like the first draft of a story, with some visual context to pull you in. Throughout the chapter, the story also provided a common language that I, as the narrator, and you, as the audience, could share and build upon.

All communications decisions in business should consider the elements outlined in this chapter, including content, delivery, and environmental factors. In the next section, we'll bring this all together in a plan.

PLANNING EXERCISE: LAUNCHING THE YODELAYHEEHOO! FESTIVAL

In this exercise, you are the communications consultant, hired to develop and implement a communications strategy for the festival.

Scenario: Like composer and festival founder Matt McBane, whom we met in chapter 3, singers Evelyn Jacobs and Tom Frederickson have created a music festival unlike any other, focused on their love of yodeling and German culture.

Like you, they have spent a tremendous amount of time developing their Business Model Canvas into a real plan, have secured funding, and are ready to launch.

Communications Goals: To build awareness for this new event, meet audience goals for travel and tourism partners, and develop the reputation of this fledgling festival and its artistic leaders.

When I start any project, I ask a lot of questions to help formulate my communications strategy. My process looks something like this.

1) **Start with the basic details the public needs to know.**
   - **What:** Yodelayheehoo! is a festival celebrating yodeling culture. This is the inaugural season.
   - **Where:** Bavarian-inspired town of Leavenworth, Washington, in the foothills of North Cascades National Park
   - **When:** Weeklong, starting Saturday, July 14, 2018
   - **Schedule highlights:** Each day will highlight a different yodeling tradition with workshops, a mainstage concert, and related activities.
   - **Tourism:** With Washington's Northern Cascades National Park as a backdrop, this charming festival becomes an international destination for yodeling enthusiasts and lovers of Bavarian and German culture.
2) **Address the most important goal: convincing people to attend this inaugural festival.**
   Our communications strategy is focused on finding them, enticing them, and making the transition from potential customer to customer as easy as possible. Using parts of the Business Model Canvas, the areas to consider include:
   - **Who is most likely to attend (Customer Segments)?** Washington State weekenders, yodeling and music enthusiasts, general tourists
   - **Where do they go for information (Channels)?** Controlled media: travel and yodeling websites, social media. Uncontrolled media: local newspapers, travel magazines, yodeling-specific publications
   - **What are the top reasons to attend (Value Proposition)?** First-ever event of its kind, novel idea, beautiful area of the world, high-end yodeling, great food, lots to do, weekend getaway, yodeling/hiking excursions, concerts.
3) **Craft a Hero Declaration.**
   It might look something like this:
   Yodeling is a natural mood enhancer—everyone who experiences it feels more alive and happy. But few really know much about it. We have launched Yodelayheehoo! to reintroduce yodeling to the public before it

becomes a lost art. As musicians and champion yodelers, we are uniquely qualified to help make this festival a reality. Our short-term vision is a successful inauguration year in Leavenworth. We hope the attention yodeling earns through this festival will start conversations in various communities about its benefits and rightful place in the musical canon, as well as ignite the imagination and interest of future generations to keep it alive.

This statement can be used in its entirety or sliced and diced for inclusion in any controlled media "piece" produced by the festival.

Your Turn

Now, how do we incorporate the Hero's Declaration into our strategy? Through the Controlled Media part of our plan. Due to space limitations, instead of writing out an entire story for the yodeling festival, tackle these two tasks: (a) Try writing the introductory part of your launch press release. This paragraph sets the scene for the media and includes the most pertinent details we learned from our founders in Section 1 of the Planning Exercise. (b) Consider what other controlled media you would create or recommend in your strategic communications plan for this festival. Note which key messages (heart, gift, vision) you would emphasize (or de-emphasize) and what other information you might include.

Let's assume you've sent out both a launch press release to announce the festival's existence and a "season" press release to provide programming. Now it's time to start pitching the festival to the public. This is the Uncontrolled Media part of your plan, and here are your tasks: (a) Look back to the Audiences (Customer Segments) and pick one for whom you want to develop a media pitch list. (b) Create a list of five different media you would pitch and note what elements of Sections 1, 2, and 3 above you would include in your pitch.

Before you develop brochures, launch the website, send out the launch press release, and begin pitching to the media, you need to develop your communications calendar. If opening night of the festival is July 14, what timing would you recommend for these important communications tasks?

You now have created the beginning of a draft communications plan for the Yodelayheehoo! Festival! Bravo. The Communications Calendar To-Do List is an excellent place to continue this exercise for the Yodelayheehoo! Festival, or start to build a plan for your own project.

SUMMARY

As noted, storytelling is an art and communication is a skill, and when combined well, they can do magic. "Bob's Tale" set up the framework for our section on storytelling and introduced us to the Hero's Declaration, a good starting point for communicating both the essence of your company and your vision to the world. The next step is to take that core message, considering which treatment of visuals and text will tell your hero's story most effectively, and follow the hero's story arc to its winning conclusion.

After you have your story, you need an effective way to get it to customers. We delved into the basics of communications strategy, looking at how content, delivery, and external factors work together. If modes (uncontrolled media, controlled media, and in-persons) are the beautifully packaged gift, media (mostly various media outlets) are the charming deliveryman. Choosing the appropriate message, style of presentation, and media channel is a science. To ultimately be successful with your communications strategy and win clients, a strategy combining repetition, consistency, and variety is key, tied to a scan of your current environment and smart timing.

CHAPTER 11

FINDING THE FUNDS: DONATIONS, GRANTS, AND FINANCE MANAGEMENT

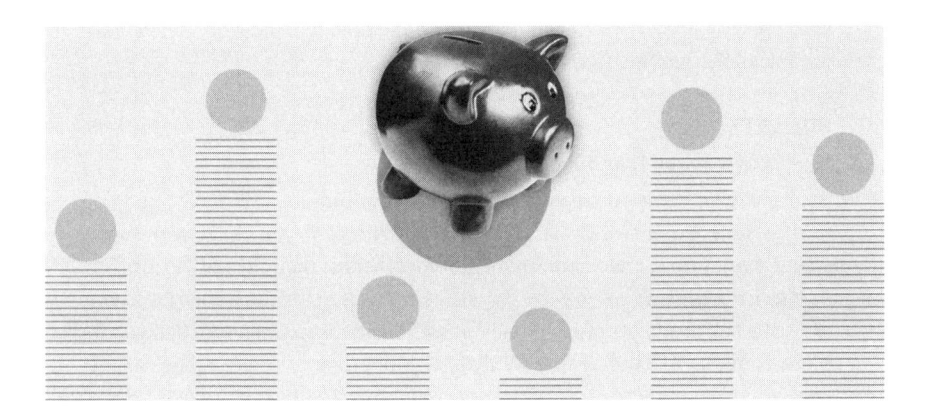

YOU'VE COME UP WITH a great idea for a project or product. You've done your research, reviewed your plan to make it happen, and thought through every detail. Now you need the funds to make it happen. But how? In this chapter, we learn the crucial skills of building a realistic budget and securing funding to realize your idea.

• • • •

Steven Linville is director of operations for DePauw University School of Music and the 21st-Century Musician Initiative, for which he manages a multimillion-dollar budget. An accomplished vocalist and opera and musical theater fanatic, Steven serves as executive producer for Intimate Opera of Indianapolis.

Funding Priceless Ideas
by Steven Linville

These days, there's no lack of knowledge on how to fund a project. A Google search returns about 170,000,000 results on the search "how to write a grant."

Another 302,000,000 results are available for "how to fund a project." So let's narrow it down—"how to fund an arts project" only gives 12,400,000 results. We are making progress!

The truth is, there's no one magical way to fund your project. Some of what you do will be trial and error. Some of it will be luck. But all of it will be hard work.

The following is my guide to funding a project, focusing first on developing a realistic budget and then securing project revenue. This information is not just based on research or earning a degree but also in the hard work and determination it has taken me to fund my personal projects, run various organizations, and feed my musical passion.

BUDGETS

How People Shape Your Budget

Before you sit down to create a budget for your project, make a list of all of the possible expenses. Don't leave out anything—if you think you might spend money on it, include it. Payment for workers or members of the project, money for advertising, and pizza for late-night rehearsals or planning sessions are just a few examples of your many possible expenses. Once your list is complete, compare it to the people involved in your project. Is there a place where you can save money because of the people involved with your project? Let me give you some examples to explain what I mean.

Intimate Opera of Indianapolis (https://www.facebook.com/intimateopera/) is a small, mostly volunteer organization. The institution has functioned both as a stand-alone organization and as a "sponsored project," but never as a 501(c)(3). Each project prepared—in this case, productions of operas, opera scenes, or concerts—is dependent on donations, small grants, and ticket-sale revenue carried over from previous projects.

We save money on projects by developing our skills in areas outside of music. I serve as the artistic director, but I also manage the website, create our publicity materials, and design the lights for our productions. Our executive director often serves as our production stage manager—building props and hunting for costumes. In addition to the administrative work, we both still perform in productions.

Developing these nonmusical skills has given us a cushion in our work. We know that we never need to find money to hire a graphic designer, website designer, or stage manager. However, we have to make sure to balance time and money. While we may be saving money, we each put in extra time.

Whether managing a multimillion-dollar budget for 21CM or producing shows with limited budgets provided by the various theaters and groups with whom I work, the process is the same. I'm given a set amount of money, and I have to make it stretch as far as I can. I choose the staff who I know can take the money I give them and make it go the furthest and still come in slightly under budget. Simply put, I want to be sure that as much as possible of the money spent is seen in the final product—whether a production on stage or a newly launched website.

Building Your Budget

You are now ready to assemble your budget. Remember to assess the return on investment (ROI) and social return on investment (SROI) of every dollar you are spending and to build in a 5–10 percent buffer for those times when your expenses increase or your revenue is less than you expected.

Return on investment is a lens through which you are able to reflect upon your work and the impact it is making. And it is essential when sharing your story with your volunteers, donors, community partners, and more regarding the investment you have made and the benefits it has created. Here's one way you can calculate the return on investment:

$$ROI = Net\ Income\ /\ Cost\ of\ Investment$$

First, tally the total "cost of investment" of your project. Include all of your expenses, including salaries or honorariums, supplies and equipment, rental fees, marketing, licensing fees, and more. Keep track of all of it, so that you have the most accurate figure possible.

Then, determine how much money was brought in through your efforts. Did you receive revenue from ticket pricing? What about a grant? Did a donor, sponsor, or corporation contribute to the project? Then count it. This money coming into the project all counts toward your total revenue. Your net income is determined by subtracting all of your costs from your total revenue.

Finally, use the formula (above) to determine the project's ROI. The higher the percentage, the greater the benefit earned.

ROI has use beyond simply determining the financial well-being of your organization. It also can be used to track the cost/benefit ratio of your educational programming, information essential to determining whether your programming is having the impact originally intended. ROI is useful when crafting marketing strategies. By evaluating the ROI on previous marketing efforts (how much was spent and what resulted), you can reshape your efforts for future campaigns, make decisions about the value of print versus social media efforts, and invest in new technologies to streamline workflow. Measuring the return on investment has applications for every aspect of your work—from staffing to technology, fundraising to friend-raising, knowing, in hard numbers, the efficiency and effectiveness of your efforts is an invaluable tool for revolutionary artists.

But with artists and arts organizations committed to engaging new audiences, making the arts accessible to everyone, and serving the public good as a primary mission, there is more to weigh when determining the (double) bottom line—financial value plus social value.

SROI is a concept essential to telling your story and the value you bring to your community and to the world. SROI weighs intangibles, such as strengthening communities and creating spaces that celebrate the arts, and providing after-school programming for children and continuing education for adult learners. And don't forget the tangible impact the arts have on local economies, such as creating jobs and driving business to local restaurants, hotels, and vendors.

Building a budget is a skill to continuously develop, one that you will come back to often during a project. As you work to increase your revenue, you may secure funding for only parts of your project or your expenses may change. You will have to be prepared to come back and make budgetary edits. Be careful not to get wedded to any expense included in your initial project budget until you are certain you will be able to fund it.

SECURING PROJECT REVENUE

Every project is unique, most often with a portfolio of revenue sources. As mentioned above, Intimate Opera relies on ticket sales, among other resources. Some organizations rely on connecting to outside funding sources, membership fees, board donations, or crowdsourcing. The first step is to determine your sources of revenue.

If you have not yet written a need statement or elevator pitch for your project, now is a good time to do so. This statement will directly feed into various types of funding. Check out "Grant Writing How-To" and "Elevator Pitch How-To" in the **Toolkit**.

Not all sources of funding will be appropriate for all projects. Your project status (independent, sponsored, nonprofit), as well as your focus, will determine how you start your funding research.

Grants

Grants can help fund your project, and they come in all shapes and sizes. The application process is diverse—ranging from short forms to long and in-depth questions. This is when your need statement will prove valuable, and it is often required as part of the proposal.

Steps for Writing Grants
- **Research the granting organization.** What types of projects fall within its focus? Do you know who is on the review board? If so, do any of those reviewers have special interests? Does your project fit those interests or areas of focus? Does your project or organization qualify for funding from this granting agency? If so, go to the next step. If not, start looking for a different granting organization.

- **Read and research the application and process.** This may be the most important step of the grant process. Know the deadlines and the requirements. How much writing will you have to do? How much research? Do you need letters of support? What must be included in the grant? Are there limits to the amount of money requested? What type of budget do you have to submit? Does the grant require matching funds or contributions? Do you have in-kind gifts to report? (Unfamiliar with any of these terms? Browse the Foundation Center's GrantSpace glossary.[1])
- **Make a timeline.** Grant writing takes time and can be exhausting. If you try to write the entire proposal at the last minute, you will miss a step or a critical submission item, which will likely result in your grant not being reviewed.

Start writing and revising. Nobody writes a perfect grant on the first try. It can be challenging to even get words on the page. My advice? Start by starting. Write like you are telling somebody a story about the project. Let them see your excitement, but do not exaggerate. Remember that whatever you say in the grant application will be the expectation for what happens within the project, as well as the standard for the materials submitted at the end of the project. (The **Toolkit** contains a sample grant final report.)

Once you have reviewed your application and have all the required additional materials, it is time to submit. And then wait. If/when you receive funding, do not be surprised if you only receive a portion of the requested amount, gift, or contribution.

If you receive a grant, be sure to acknowledge the granting organization properly. Every organization has different standards. Additionally, be aware that many grants require you to provide detailed feedback about how the money was spent. Before you spend any grant money, find out what you will have to report at the end. What do you need to track? Do you need work samples? What can and cannot be funded? Do you have to submit receipts? Keep detailed records throughout the project process.

Fundraising and Donors

The next core source of revenue is donors. Fundraising from donors takes skill. You have to convince a donor that your project is worth funding. However, you have to invest time in donors to make the donation process comfortable and worthwhile for them, too. Just like you did with grants, research the donor to find interest. Does the donor give money freely or pick and choose causes? How much money can the donor offer you?

You'll have to approach each donor differently—use your elevator pitch, or build a relationship and let the project come up naturally. Some donors will want to know statistics and the need for your project. If you are lucky, a donor will become a lifetime supporter who continues to invest in your project.

Different donors want to see different results. Some only want to see the project succeed. Others want to see some type of recognition. Whatever the expectation, be sure your donors are thanked. A personalized letter is a nice start, but add something specific from the project. For Intimate Opera, that's been free tickets, signed posters, and free T-shirts. To learn more about this, turn to "Thanking Donors How-To" in the **Toolkit**.

Sponsors and Partnerships

Sponsors are similar to donors, but sponsors are typically organizations, rather than individuals, who support the project. Sponsors may support the entire project or just one aspect, such as a concert in a tour or the guest artist in a show.

Each time your project is presented, sponsors should be recognized—verbally, in print, or in another format appropriate for your project. Typically, a company sponsor pays for a logo or product placement in the project.

Partnerships are as important as sponsors and donors. The difference is that partners usually provide a supporting service, rather than financial support. This can be very important when you need to save money but cannot find a good place in your budget to cut funding.

Be aware that *sponsor* and *partner* often are used interchangeably. Regardless of the name you attach, it's important to know that you can get both financial support as well as service support to strengthen your project.

Crowdfunding

Crowdfunding is an excellent way to raise funds for your project while simultaneously spreading the word about what you have to offer. Here are a few things to consider when crowdfunding.

Set a realistic goal. Now that you know the budget for your project, determine how much of that you can realistically raise through crowdfunding.

Choose the right crowdfunding platform. There are a variety of platforms available—Kickstarter, GoFundMe, Indiegogo, Crowdrise, Crowdfunder, and many more. Each of these places different stipulations on crowdfunding. Some sites reward you only if you reach your full fundraising goal. Others will give you any money you raise, regardless of whether you reach your goal. Additionally, every site keeps a different percentage of the revenue. Do your research and determine which platform is best to use for your project.

Make sure you have information to share. Marketing your project is the key to successfully raising funds. You must engage your audience. Most sites require written text. Be sure it is clear and concise, while also inspiring excitement for your project. You may want to include samples of your project or intriguing photos. You will also need to provide a video to tell funders about your project. Make sure the video looks professional, you speak clearly, you provide key information, and you include a final ask for funders to donate.

Have unique rewards for your funders. Many crowdfunding sites allow you to give incentives to donors who meet certain dollar amounts. Make sure these items are unique to your project. For performances, this may include tickets or a VIP reception. (For example, in a recent campaign, Intimate Opera offered "dinner with an opera singer" for the highest donation level.) Additionally, be sure these rewards are something you can afford within your project budget.

Make the first donation yourself. While this may sound odd, it can be very helpful. Many sites allow donations to be anonymous. Nobody wants to be the first person to put money into a project. People want to know that somebody else thinks the project is worthwhile as well. If you make the first donation—even a small one—your other funders will see that there is already interest.

Draw on your spheres of influence. Send individualized e-mails to friends, family, and colleagues who may make donations. These people are the ones most likely to support you. Just like making the first donation yourself, having people you know personally make donations will boost the first stage of the campaign. In large capital campaigns, this is called the "quiet phase." This phase can help your campaign gain momentum at the start.

Set up a social media and advertising campaign timeline. Determine all of the ways in which you plan to spread the word about your crowdfunding campaign. Use sources like Facebook, Twitter, Instagram, and even Snapchat. The methods you use will be determined by the audience(s) you are trying to reach. E-mail campaigns are cheap and can easily reach many potential donors, but they can feel impersonal if not done properly. Prepare this timeline as you are working in your quiet phase. Once you have your advertising plan and have exhausted your donors in the quiet phase, it's time to move into your public phase to spread the word.

Excited to get started? (I thought so.) Turn to "Crowdfunding How-To" in the **Toolkit** to learn more.

Consider print advertising only if your budget allows. Print materials can be expensive, and if you do not have a good mailing list, they can be hard to distribute. You can consider handing out flyers, sending postcards, writing letters, or distributing a press release. However, think about how you respond to these sort of asks. Do you tend to ignore flyers or throw them away? Will others do the same? Remember not to pour more money into print materials than you think you can recoup.

Personal contact always raises more money. People delete generic e-mails and scroll past posts on websites. Keep working your personal connections. You may receive a gift from people you did not expect to participate in the funding. For example, in our Intimate Opera campaign, I contacted a college friend from 10 years prior, not expecting a response. However, I received a kind e-mail to catch up as well as a $100 donation.

Crowdfunding is a flexible and evolving process for every project. Interested in learning more about how crowdfunding can support your efforts? Read on!

Crowdfunding is a revolutionary way for artists to realize their vision and create a community of followers. Two artists, writer Jessica Duchen and composer Dan Visconti, developed successful campaigns in the United Kingdom and United States, respectively. Both offered 21CM.org their different perspectives on what worked best for them and what surprised them about the process.

SMART CROWDFUNDING[2]

JESSICA DUCHEN

I crowdfunded my latest novel. Nobody could be more surprised than I am—because I'd never imagined crowdfunding was for me.

I started writing *Ghost Variations* in 2012. Because it is so different from my previous novels, I sought a new way to take it forward and turned to the groundbreaking publishing house Unbound, which crowdfunds its books. They work out how much the publication will cost to produce, and you have 90 days to raise that amount via its site. Plugged as "the strangest detective story in the history of music," this novel is based on a true incident involving the great Hungarian violinist Jelly d'Arányi, supposed spirit messages, Nazis, and the rediscovery of the Schumann Violin Concerto.

This experience taught me a few things I'd like to pass on to the first-time crowdfunder.

Ensure you have absolute confidence in your project. Only thus can you convince other people of its worth.

Make a promotional video. Unbound recommends this should be no longer than a minute and a half. Argue your case concisely, look friendly, be positive. And try to get yourself properly filmed. I'm afraid I did mine with Apple's Photo Booth application, using my desktop computer's internal camera. It took 27 takes before I had something usable. Everything went wrong. I coughed, my husband barged in, and involving the cat was really not a good idea . . .

Include a sample of your product as a try-before-you-buy. Unbound's campaigns include a few pages of the book.

Offer original and tempting rewards for your pledge levels. For *Ghost Variations*, the basic $15 bought an e-book and a credit at the back. For $28, you became a Super Patron; for $70, you got a special artwork print and access to a playlist to accompany the book. For $17, you could sponsor a character. And for $710, I agreed to give a lecture about Jelly d'Arányi and the Schumann Concerto in your home for you and your friends.

Look out for serendipitous linkups. For instance, it turned out that the Orchestra of the Age of Enlightenment was about to give a rare performance of the Schumann Violin Concerto at the Royal Festival Hall, so I devised a reward that gave patrons a ticket for this plus a drink and discussion with me and fellow supporters afterwards.

Get the word out. On this side of the pond, we're hardwired to scorn "self-publicists" and balk at the notion of becoming one. I suspect it's a British 19th-century class issue. If you are middle or working class, someone will slap you down, ordering you to know your place; and if you are upper class, well, you couldn't *possibly* undertake an activity as low class as trying to *sell* something—unless it's organic jam, for charity, from your country estate. The bottom line is that if we don't push our stuff, nobody else will.

Use and master social media. Along with including information on my long-established blog *JDCMB* and regularly posting about the book's progress on Facebook and Twitter, I created a *Ghost Variations* Facebook page, complete with "sign up" button. Also, I sent e-mails to almost everyone I know.

Facebook proved an excellent tool, though "likes" on the book's page did not always translate into donations. The blog brought a relatively small number of pledges but at higher levels. Twitter drew the same number as the blog but mainly at basic rates. The vast majority of pledges, however, came from people who had received my e-mails. The $28 level proved the most popular; close friends stumped up a bit more if they could, while people I didn't know usually paid the basic "tenner."

Crucially, though, the process proved rewarding in ways I never anticipated. The Royal Festival Hall concert led me to collaborate with the Orchestra of the Age of Enlightenment. I helped in its publicity, which gave me the opportunity to speak about the concerto and my book live on BBC Radio 4. But also, I made new friends: other writers involved in the same process, people who came up to chat at the OAE concert. Generally speaking, the goodwill I encountered gave my morale an extraordinary boost.

Jessica Duchen is a music journalist and author based in London, UK. She writes for the Independent, Opera News, Pianist, *and many other publications. Find out more about her new novel,* Ghost Variations, *at https:// unbound.co.uk/books/ghost-variations.*

DAN VISCONTI

As composer and director of artistic programming for the classical music organization Fifth House Ensemble, my passion is reimagining classical music for a 21st-century audience by presenting concerts in fresh ways. Following our recent visual collaborations with graphic novelists and animators, we decided the next step would be to work with the interactive world of video games: in particular, 2012's Grammy-nominated indie game *Journey*, a pinnacle of what gaming has achieved as a legitimate art form and an experience in which art, music, and motion weave together in an almost operatic level.

To bring the world's first interactive video game concert to life—one in which live musicians react to audience participants as they play through the game in real time—we ran a $5,000 Kickstarter campaign for our *Journey LIVE* concerts. We were thrilled to see the project fully funded in just a couple hours, multiplying this original goal 10 times over during the course of our campaign for a grand total of $52,000.

Below are some tips we learned.

Kickstarter is certainly about crowdfunding, but the platform may be even more useful as a form of marketing and data acquisition. The chance to create and feature a coordinated message, video, and text reaches a lot of people, including many who did not end up becoming backers this time. And one reason Kickstarter was such a useful platform for our project is that the campaign allowed us to figure out where *Journey* fans were. We might have self-produced in the wrong cities and flopped, but running the campaign allowed us to target the right locations for connecting with our audience.

Have a plan to refocus the campaign when it becomes fully funded. Unless one is able to explain how funding an already-funded project will have an impact, there is a risk in losing interest and motivation among potential backers; for our project, an initial goal allowed us to make up the shortfall for a performance in the DC area, yet we managed to raise an additional $47,000 beyond this goal by appealing to fans in cities we had identified and asking for help adding concerts in those cities as well.

Have a variety of perks and price points: tangible swag augmented with free additions that carry real value, like signatures, sketches, lessons with the composer of the game, consultations, even offering to record music on a backer's answering machine (as another successful music campaign wittily proffered). Think of what has low or no cost to you and potentially a lot of sentimental value to a potential backer.

When you make that awesome project video, don't forget to include the "ask." You'd be surprised how many slick-looking Kickstarter videos show off a cool project but never actually make the ask.

Backers will overwhelmingly be people in your own social networks—so begin planning a budget by making a list of friends/family/acquaintances and how much they are likely to donate.

Treat your backers as you would any relationship you want for the long term. Think you're done once the campaign ends? Time to take those backers along to your next project—in our case, future cities and the creation of a *Journey LIVE* social media community and website. Some of these backers might even end up loving one of our future collaborations with a graphic novelist, so connecting them to a "mothership" that's buzzing long after the Kickstarter page goes dark is the way onward to the next project!

Active as a composer, concert curator, and music journalist, **Dan Visconti** *is updating the role of the composer for the 21st century as he creates innovative concert experiences in collaboration with the community. For his ongoing initiatives to address social issues through music by reimagining the arts as a form of cultural and civic service, Visconti was awarded a 2014 TED Fellowship and delivered a TED Talk at the conference's 30th anniversary.*

LAST THOUGHTS ABOUT PROJECT REVENUE

Funders are interested in successful organizations and projects. They are not interested in putting funds into something that needs to be saved or "bailed out." Above all, they are interested in the people who make these projects come to life. They want to invest in people who are passionate and committed to doing good, addressing problems, and making the world a better place. If your project truly does fill a need, funders will be interested in you and your project to help solve a persisting problem.

If you've done all of the work needed and have reached your fundraising goal, congratulations! You're ready to move forward with your project. However, total project funding does not always happen. If you've received partial funding, go back to "Building Your Budget" and work on a modified budget.

As you produce your project, be sure to keep track of expenses, collect W-9 forms when necessary, and keep copies of receipts. You may need these items at tax time or when you report back about grants.

WHAT DOES THIS LOOK LIKE IN REAL LIFE?

Intimate Opera has done a lot of fundraising. As we've started performing new works by living composers, prices have gone up. A recent production of Michael Ching's *Speed Dating Tonight!* is the perfect example. Our costs included rental space, props, musicians, opera rights, technicians, and more. Once we set up our project budget, we realized it was more than we had banked from previous ticket sales. So, we began thinking of ways to cut costs without cutting production value. Relating this to what we've gone over so far in this chapter:

How People Shape the Budget: We asked our accompanist to record tracks to all of the musical numbers so we could use the recordings in rehearsal. This strategy cut our costs for paying an accompanist while allowing us to continue to hold the needed rehearsals.

The executive director also worked at a private-lesson studio space in Indianapolis. Her rental costs for the space were equal to a portion of her lesson fee. Since Intimate Opera was not paying her for lessons, the owner of the space allowed us to hold rehearsals in the studio building for free.

I served as the artistic director and stage director for the production, while also handling all publicity and singing in the show. Our executive director handled the negotiations in addition to serving as the stage manager and singing in the production. Other company members, in addition to performing, chipped in as well.

Building a Partnership: The performance space we wanted to use was more than we could afford. Instead of looking for a different space, we collaborated with the owners and decided we would split the ticket revenue 50/50, rather than us pay them directly for space usage. This meant if Intimate Opera did not sell tickets, we were not out money. However, if we sold lots of tickets, the space would make more money than they would have if we paid their set fee. Both companies were taking a chance. The additional incentive was that the performance space wanted to make that extra revenue, so they pushed hard to advertise our show.

To help offset the possible loss of the performance space—and to ensure the partnership with the performance space would happen—Intimate Opera partnered with a local restaurant to offer dinner before our show, which happened to run on Valentine's Day weekend. This required no additional work for Intimate Opera, and all of the dinner ticket revenue (after the costs for the restaurant) went to the venue.

Finding a Sponsorship: Intimate Opera partnered with three business sponsors. A small donation in exchange for a coupon printed on the back of the show ticket was a win-win. The businesses gained brand awareness and Intimate Opera gained much-needed revenue.

Applying for Grants: Intimate Opera reached out to a local granting agency and was able to secure funding to help offset the costs of the production, thus allowing us to make more profit in the end.

Leveraging Crowdfunding: This was the first time Intimate Opera crowdfunded for an event, and it was very successful. We used Indiegogo, a platform that distributes funds even when you do not reach your goal. While we did not reach the goal we set (which covered the full production), we did receive about 70 percent of that goal.

Between the various sources of revenue and partnerships to minimize risk, Intimate Opera was able to produce a show without fear of financial struggle.

Gary Beckman is director of Entrepreneurial Studies in the Arts at North Carolina State University. He is also the founder (or cofounder) of a lot of what makes up the field of music and arts entrepreneurship, including Artivate: A Journal of Entrepreneurship in the Arts, *the Society for Arts Entrepreneurship Education, the Arts Entrepreneurship Educator's Network, and the field's first essay collection,* Disciplining the Arts: Teaching Entrepreneurship in Context.

HAVE YOU EVER THOUGHT ABOUT WHY YOU CONSUME, NOT PERFORM, MUSIC?

by Gary Beckman

For most, the title question leads to a series of nonspecifics: "It rocks," "I don't know, I just like it," or "It makes me feel good/relaxed/excited." These answers may not sound helpful to emerging music entrepreneurs, but with some applied research, a philosophical foundation for marketing emerges.

If we wanted to transfer these glimpses into the minds of those who embrace music, we might say that some markets are not really thinking about why they consume music or conclude that if they were more "informed" about the *why* of music's role in their lives, then maybe they would make different choices about the music they consume.

Maybe examining this through the lens of some philosophical circles can give us greater insight. Is A(a)rt biological or cultural? Well, it might be both. And both have marketing consequences: You could create marketing language appealing to audiences who consume music for their unknown biological or unexamined cultural predilections, OR to those that consume music for extrinsic or intrinsic biological/cultural "reasons."

In a 2015 article, Gerry Veenstra states, "Breadth of taste [in A(a)rt] is not linked to class. But class filters into specific likes and dislikes."[3] If we couple this with Hans Abbing's discussion of the habitus's importance for artists and markets alike, perhaps this conclusion emerges: Markets consume music for many different reasons, and most of these reasons are not interrogated by consumers . . . but for some reason, they keep consuming music.

Therefore, we might say that music is a powerful "product." For some reason, markets have an insatiable appetite for music—many will pay for it and never seriously interrogate what they are getting in return because, for some reason, they simply need the "product." In my Intro to Marketing course, we called this a captive market. Perhaps, but the musician in me rejects the implications of the term.

Instead, I tell my students that A(a)rt is not a Widget.

To be a leader in music (in any form), I believe we have a responsibility to engage in understanding the A(a)rt form we purport to master/leverage. Whether this means studying aesthetics, researching opinions posited by others, or simply observing music's impact on populations, cogently communicating our understanding of music helps to create a deeper connection between producer and consumer. More important, it sanctions an examination of what it is an audience consumes and why. This, in my mind, creates an informed market more intimately connected to those creating aesthetic experiences.

And this . . . all within the framework of telling your story in ways that move people to action.

• • • •

SUMMARY

Funding your project can be incredibly challenging and at the same time extremely rewarding. In this chapter, we first learned about building a budget; considering the people involved and how they affect your costs or savings; and determining ROI, SROI, and need. Next, we looked at ways to secure funding sources for your project, including grants, donors, sponsors, partnerships, and crowdfunding. Clearly, a budget can be somewhat fluid, particularly in the beginning stages of a project. It is important to reshape your budget and to always remember that even during the struggles, the end result will be worth it.

EPILOGUE

FROM SINGLE PROJECT TO REWARDING CAREER: CONTINUING THE REVOLUTION

LEADERSHIP TAKES MANY FORMS. What it's not is bossy, all-knowing, do-it-alone, my-way-or-the-highway. This epilogue shares the stories of three leaders: one driven by love, one rooted in empathy, and another fueled by the belief that everyone must be afforded the opportunity to live a life through the arts. All are authentic, tenacious, curious, creative, and collaborative. Be the boss.

MacArthur Prize–winning sociologist and Harvard professor Sara Lawrence-Lightfoot has always inspired and comforted me through her writing, giving voice to the healing powers of the arts, even in the darkest moments:

> It is fascinating that the first responses to violence, fear, and despair are often not words, arguments, or analysis. When we feel desperate, words will not do. They do not seem cathartic or productive; they will not carry our complex emotions. The New York City public school teachers from District One who could see the fiery destruction of 9/11 from their classroom windows knew this intuitively. While looking for a way to help their young students rage and grieve, they turned away from the formal curriculum not to words, but to art. They asked their students to draw their fears, paint their pain, dance their anguish, and rap their rage. The raw emotions were channeled into art when words would not do.[1]

Don't underestimate the importance of your work.

* * * *

Deanna Kennett is the education manager of Ensemble Connect, a program of Carnegie Hall, the Juilliard School, and the Weill Music Institute in partnership with the New York City Department of Education. Ensemble Connect is a two-year fellowship program that prepares musicians for careers combining musical excellence with teaching, community engagement, advocacy, entrepreneurship, and leadership.

Inspiration Is a Two-Way Street
by Deanna Kennett

Bringing musical inspiration to populations beyond the world of classical music lovers is now a commonly accepted opportunity and responsibility of being an artist. But what is often overlooked is that inspiration is a two-way street.

My advice to young musicians? Perform for as many different audiences with as many different backgrounds as possible. Not just because you should, but also for the profound opportunity to grow as an artist. In Ensemble Connect, a Carnegie Hall–based fellowship program for postgraduate musicians, we ask our fellows to create and tour interactive concerts for school and community venues. We believe in the importance of giving back to our community and the potential for our fellows to grow musically by connecting with diverse populations.

Understanding how to relate Beethoven to the lives of fourth graders in the far reaches of Brooklyn or inmates in the confines of Rikers Island opens musicians' minds toward a better understanding of music's place in society. And in turn, it changes their interpretation and appreciation of a familiar piece of music and their own role as a performer, forever.

You never know what experiences will spark a lifelong passion. You may be surprised by what opportunities you find when you start looking.

Seek out moments to inspire and take the time to reflect on those that inspired you. That intersection will not only help guide your path but may lead you to find the greatest opportunity for impact.

* * * *

If you were to ask the musicians around you whether music changed their lives in a profound way, I imagine, overwhelmingly, you would hear a chorus of voices singing truth to this assertion. If you were to ask those same friends whether music *saved* their lives, I imagine most would respond with equal conviction. I know I would.

So, if it is true that music can change and indeed save lives, then we as artists, throughout every stage of our career, must share our art form with those who have not yet had an intimate experience with the beauty, power, and mystery of music. Our role as revolutionary artists and arts leaders is to show how the creative energies of the arts can help us imagine new worlds, even when our world is uncertain.

Whether driven by an entrepreneurial spirit or fear that the music they love will lose relevance, or both, what revolutionary leaders know is that "doing the same thing over and over again and expecting different results" is a form of insanity the music world can no longer afford. Today's generation of arts leaders rejects the confines of traditional channels within the profession. They embrace invention, curiosity, creativity, collaboration, and courage. For it is these tools that appropriately equip us to play in the messy, fertile spaces of the artist-entrepreneur.

Inserting themselves at the intersection of art and social justice, today's leaders are redefining audiences and inviting new listeners into the fold by meeting them where they live. They are helping us see the strength in our diversity, providing access to music where it has otherwise been denied. 21CM.org's Sounding Board Series (http://21cm.org/magazine/sounding-board/) has profiled some of these luminaries.

One such leader is Dale Henderson of Bach in the Subways. Henderson takes what was once old and makes it new again through decisive and deliberate action and messaging. He has a deep belief that this timeless music is best shared with new audiences away from the hallowed halls of the concert stage. Henderson favors sharing his music with new audiences amid the traffic of everyday life. Having grown a solo performance in the New York subway system to a global phenomenon in less than a decade, Henderson leads by example—playing music openly, honestly, and in spaces that meet audiences where they live—and by reminding us of the timeless beauty of art music. Listen to Dale Henderson's story, "Bringing Bach to the People," as shared on 21CM.org.[2]

Leaders often ask us to move outside of our comfort zone and experience something new. Mezzo-soprano Laurie Rubin cares deeply about sharing her art and her message that our uniqueness, and even our disabilities, are where we find our most authentic selves and our greatest insights. Blind from birth, Laurie's career as an opera singer has soared, but her real passion lies in delivering antibullying master classes for teens. Laurie Rubin's story was chronicled on 21CM.org in a piece entitled "Embracing Difference: The Mission that Drives Laurie Rubin."[3]

Rubin shares an important message: "When listening to voices unlike our own, what can we learn about becoming more thoughtful, open artists? How can listening to these voices help us become better neighbors within our communities?"

Play On, Philly! leverages music education for social good by modeling leadership in the field of music education and serving the social and cultural needs of at-risk children. Drawing from his personal experiences as a musician, founder and executive director Stanford Thompson wanted to see how the renowned El Sistema program might be reimagined within his hometown of Philadelphia. Explaining the impetus for the project, Thompson asserts, "In the normal flow of our professional lives, we discover talented minority students in need of access to training, a better instrument, or some other form of encouragement and support." He adds, "This is the moment when we must step forward as individuals to resolve specific problems. These collective efforts will augment the music training programs that are already in place. It is a simple matter of caring people taking responsibility." Play On, Philly! tackles racial inequality in classical music head-on. And Stanford Thompson is leading the charge. The fundamental question Stanford Thompson asks is, "Does Music Make You a Better Person?" Listen for his answer on 21CM.org.[4]

Change, as we know, is not simple, or even welcomed, at times. Change is more than realigning priorities; it is about the heavy lift of a cultural shift or safely guiding folks out of their comfort zone and into a new normal of relevance. We are each gifted with the opportunity to lead, traveling paths not yet forged, side-by-side navigating the messy, fertile spaces of the 21st-century musician. In a world rife with challenges, there has never been a greater need for the creative energies of the artist.

In closing, the only leadership advice I have is this: Find ideas you believe in and fight for them every day. For me, that is to reimagine the very definition of education—to prepare the next generation of change agents to make the world a better place. As for the leader I hope to become? Lead in the beginning with vision, and in the end with gratitude. In the middle, be a servant. And stay curious along the way.

Let the revolution begin!

TOOLKIT

GOALS AND OBJECTIVES HOW-TO

Introduction

Any event or activity related to your project should set out to achieve established goals and objectives. Goals and objectives help flesh out the expectations of your activity. A goal is the guiding statement that clarifies the direction and focus of an activity. With your goal(s) identified, you can then develop objectives, which are the steps needed to reach your goal(s).

Step One

Setting goals and objectives is a collaborative exercise. This process aids in strategic planning, allows for evaluation, and creates a performance reference point that can enhance your case for support and build trust among your stakeholders and the public. Team members and directors should brainstorm goals for the program/project/event.

Step Two

Review if the resulting goals are "SMART":

- Specific
- Measurable
- Achievable
- Realistic
- Time-bound

Step Three

Determine if the goals are short term or long term and design objectives based on the timeline of goals.

Step Four

Use your SMART goals to determine "SMART" objectives. Both goals and objectives can be SMART and categorized as short term, intermediate, or long term in scope. Objectives can further be broken into *process objectives*, focusing on related activities, and *outcome objectives*, referencing intended results.

Step Five

Take a moment and identify the specific, measurable, achievable, realistic, and time-bound elements of each.

Step Six

Use an action plan to track the goals and completion of objectives. Reevaluate goals and objectives as you move through your program/project/event to better align achievability.

ORGANIZATIONAL CHART HOW-TO

Introduction

You already know that assembling a curious, creative, and collaborative team is a crucial step on your path to success! An organizational chart is a visual diagram that shows how your team is structured. It identifies member roles and responsibilities and highlights the relationships between different positions.

To organize an effective team, you must consider your own skill sets and passions, as well the expertise, resources, and personalities of those around you. Your goal is to not only engage diverse collaborators, but also smartly determine their appropriate responsibilities. Remember, your team will function best when everyone contributes a skill they value.

Step One

Understand what your endeavor needs to function. Then answer the question, "Who will or can address these needs?" A job description should be crafted for each team member detailing their integral position, specific responsibilities and expectations, and any intended leadership roles or working relationships with the leadership.

Step Two

Communicate your unique team structure and work culture in visual format with an organizational chart. It's common to do this by viewing your team in departments. Depending on your needs, you might have:

- A development department, managing fundraising
- A marketing department, managing promotion and public relations
- An artistic or programmatic department, managing the work output for the public
- A finance department, managing the money and all financial decision-making
- An education department, managing any associated educational components

Step Three

Determine the best structure for your program/project/event, whether it will be a traditional hierarchical organizational chart, a matrix chart, or a flat chart. For a hierarchical chart, delineate the department head within each area and the overarching team leadership overseeing all departments. This format has a top-down pyramid structure, with leadership at the top.

A matrix chart can be used for teams that have more than one manager, and a flat chart is useful for a team without middle management that functions with a top tier of leadership and second tier of workers or team members.

Step Four

Use the organizational chart as a reference point, a snapshot in time. It visually represents the expectations of how the organization will function. It helps everyone clearly understand his or her position in the organization.

OPERATING BUDGET HOW-TO

Introduction

The operating budget, also referred to as the organizational or annual budget, is the financial plan for an organization's fiscal year. Broken up by revenue and expenses and organized by programmatic activity, it is the central financial guide for your team and all activities. But it's also a communication tool: Whatever the majority of the money is being spent on is flagged as a priority by stakeholders.

Step One

To create the operating budget, you must go through a collaborative budgeting process. What fiscal year will be used? Will it be January–December or another span of time? Determine the best budgeting strategy for your program/project/event. The most common budgeting strategy is to begin with known expenses and then fill in with anticipated revenue. The fundraising goal fills in the revenue gap. Some other budgeting strategies to consider are:

- *Budgeting by organization* outcome goals. Here, you would set your outcome goals from the top down in prioritized order. From there, specific, measurable goals should be identified for each intended outcome. Then, the financial impact should be determined or predicted for each.
- A second option is *budgeting by revenue* and expense targets. This approach asks leadership to set targets based on the total revenue and expense goals for the year, build out individual line items, and then make programmatic decisions and goals accordingly.
- A *unit draft budgeting method*, a third strategy, involves starting with draft budgets from each area of your team, which you would then compile. You may have your team members draft an ambitious and a conservative version so you have different scenarios to consider.
- A fourth strategy is *zero-based budgeting*, for when you need or want to create a budget from scratch. This involves analyzing each program or activity you have planned for the year, determining if it is essential to achieving your goal, and building the budget out from there.

Step Two

Review these six steps to any budgeting process:

- Preparing: Evaluate the previous year (if you can) and take into account any external considerations.
- Estimating: Project the expenses and revenue for the year.
- Approving: For a nonprofit, this would fall under the board of directors' governance duties. Otherwise, your team leadership would take this on.
- Implementing: Put your budget and financial plan into action.
- Monitoring: Ongoing tracking of variances between what was budgeted and the actual income or expenses. Budgets are iterative and can change as the program/project/event details change. Budgets are snapshots in time.
- Auditing: This assessment process, formalized for nonprofits, takes place at the close of the fiscal year. It is a great practice to review your own small budget to analyze why changes took place.

Step Three

Put these steps into practice. Start putting numbers down on paper. Identify expenses and possible revenue. What changes need to be made to prevent a loss?

Step Four

Review the budget regularly with the team and make adjustments as needed. Do certain line items need to be reduced because anticipated revenue is not coming in at the level projected? Is more revenue coming in and allowing you to expand certain programs?

Step Five

After the year is complete, compare your first budget to actual expenses and revenue. Use the final budget to inform the following year's projections.

ACTION PLAN HOW-TO

Introduction

Once you have created SMART goals, it's time to make your action plan. This is an even more specific look at your event. Essentially, you're taking the resources and activities identified in your SMART goals and fleshing them out in a task-based timeline.

Step One

Use the resources and activities identified in your SMART goals and the established goals and objectives and insert them into this task-based timeline. An action plan is a map for implementation.

Step Two

Action plan templates are available online and can be customized for any use. Although the format of your action plan might vary depending on how you and your team work together, it should encompass all the identified tasks required to implement your event, along with delegation responsibilities and deadlines. Detail is key!

Step Three

Identify the tasks necessary to reach your goals for your project/program/event. Start by thinking chronologically, but also flag tasks that should be prioritized, integrate key deadlines, and highlight those steps that are dependent on others.

Step Four

Analyze and delegate the tasks. This requires you to give each task a closer look and note who on your team is the appropriate point person. At this point, you may identify a need for volunteers, new resources, or outsourced expertise and can plan accordingly.

Step Five

Give your action plan a once-over by using the SCHEMES mnemonic. SCHEMES stands for:

- Space
- Cash
- Helpers/People
- Equipment
- Materials
- Expertise
- Systems

Use this technique to ensure your plan is comprehensive and not missing anything. Now you are armed with a detailed timeline of what is needed to prepare, implement, and follow up your event.

Step Six

Remember, this is—to a degree—a flexible framework. Things could change and require you to revisit your action plan and make adjustments throughout the process. If you track the adjustments you are making along the way, it will serve as a great learning tool in post-event debriefs and evaluation.

EVENT PLANNING HOW-TO

Introduction

Event planning is a large exercise. This how-to serves as a checklist to help organize your larger plan. This process should be collaborative, including your team, and carried out well in advance of your intended event. Even though the steps are presented in a linear fashion, prioritize each step for your own event timing.

Step One

Determine your event type. Are you creating a cultivation event? A fundraiser? A program or project for the community?

Step Two

Think strategically about the timing of your event. Consider different options to coordinate venue availability and preparation time.

Step Three

Confirm your venue or location. Your venue may impact guest attendance and the type of activities that can be carried out.

Step Four

Create a guest list. Think broadly. You have active participants and donors, but also new prospects, potential collaborators, even press that may be appropriate to also engage with your work.

Step Five

Recruit volunteers. Think about the many ways people can help. Volunteers can help fill the areas of need or expertise to implement your event.

Step Six

Determine pricing for the event for guests. Take into consideration meal costs, venue rental, supplies, decorations, etc. What do similar events in your area charge for admission/tickets?

Step Seven

Secure sponsorships or donors to underwrite a portion of event expenses and help keep costs down. Work to create in-kind partnerships for goods or services. What caterers/restaurants/event supply providers work with other organizations or events similar to yours?

Step Eight

Determine your program. What will happen at the event? What will the flow of the event be? Will there be speakers? Will collateral marketing material or digital video be shared? How about a performance?

Step Nine

Create a follow-up plan. How will you thank guests, volunteers, sponsors, internal team, etc.?

Step Ten

Create an evaluation plan. What are your measures of success? What information are you really interested in learning? How will the collected data inform future events, programming?

Step Eleven

Now that you have planning under way, move forward on implementation of your great event. This gives you the framework you need to continue with your additional planning steps, such as creating a project logic model, action plan, budget, and volunteer recruitment strategy.

VOLUNTEER RECRUITMENT HOW-TO

Introduction

Volunteers are a powerful, not to mention cost-effective, resource! While you may indeed need extra hands behind the scenes to make your next event a success, it's important to take a step back and recognize volunteers as an integral piece within your big picture.

All participants, audience members, collaborators, donors, and stakeholders share one thing in common: they're engaged. Volunteer recruitment is an effective way to not only continually engage individuals but also bring *new* individuals into the fold. Remember, people love to be and feel a part of something!

Step One

Determine if you need volunteers, what jobs they will do, how long they will work, what requirements they need to fulfill, and how you will recognize their involvement. It is easier to recruit volunteers if you have a clear understanding of what they will do and they know exactly what they are signing up for.

Step Two

Research your local Chamber of Commerce and Convention/Visitors Bureau and City Hall to see if they have volunteer sign-up platforms or groups already in place. Depending on your need, keep these three recruitment strategies in mind:

- A "targeted" recruitment approach is a personal ask to a small group of individuals that have a specific skill set or existing background with your work.
- A "broad-based" recruitment approach publicizes the volunteer opportunity to a much wider, even a public, pool of individuals. This approach helps attract a larger quantity and more diverse group of volunteers, though this means greater management and training responsibility on your end.
- A third option is a "concentric circle" strategy. This is when you charge your team and those closest to your work to explore their contacts and networks for potential volunteers.

Step Three

Recruit volunteers. Be sure to capture all of their contact information. Do recruit a few more than what you will need in case of cancellations. There are also a variety of digital tools you may take advantage of, such as VolunteerMatch, VolunteerHub, and LinkedIn. As with any other opportunity to tell your story and motivate support, be sure to communicate how a volunteer will make a difference and note any inherent or added incentives.

Step Four

Communicate, Train, and Thank! Clearly communicate expectations and needs. Provide volunteers with the necessary training to succeed and to ensure a valuable experience for them. Thank them immediately and authentically. Appropriately cultivating the volunteer experience can open pathways to support in other ways. Volunteers are your first donors, they are giving you their most precious resource, their time.

FOLLOW-UP HOW-TO

Introduction

It's advantageous to think about following up within the greater context of your endeavor, beyond the specific activity. It's a key form of stewardship for your current supporters and also a meaningful cultivation strategy for engaging potential supporters.

Step One

Create a follow-up plan. If you are functioning as or working with a nonprofit, some standard follow-up procedures might apply. One example would be for a fundraising benefit in which part of admission covers an expense, like dinner, drinks, or a performance ticket, and the remainder serves as a contribution. Here, your follow-up plan must include a formal acknowledgment letter that notes the tax-deductible amount of each attendee's benefit ticket for tax purposes.

Step Two

Be creative in your follow-up efforts, which should always be planned in advance, executed in a timely manner, and full of gratitude. Your follow-up may come in the form of a personal phone call, an e-mail campaign, a handwritten note, a formal report, or a video.

Step Three

Determine content for your follow-up items. Some tips for content include:

- Again, say, "thank you!"
- Include a way for recipients to provide feedback.
- Share memories—perhaps in the form of pictures, a short video, or a testimonial.
- Make it personal. If you've planned ahead properly to collect contact information, you should make the time to handwrite a thank-you note or add a personalized comment to an acknowledgment letter or e-mail.
- And, lastly, don't miss an opportunity to share what's ahead, like another event, performance, or an exclusive opportunity for this group of supporters.

Step Four

Create a larger line of communication plan. Keep these individuals top of mind for future engagements and solicitations, especially now that they've begun a relationship with your work. Follow-up and cultivation are key to continued relationships and funders.

Step Five

Follow up internally with your team. This is an excellent practice. Hold a debriefing session to hear from your collaborators about what worked, what their experience was, and what should be adjusted or rethought for your next event.

INCOME/EXPENSE HOW-TO

Introduction

The income/expense statement can be called many things: the income statement, budget report, profit and loss statement, statement of financial activities, and so forth. No matter its name, it is a financial statement detailing your revenue and expenses over a specific period of time or for a specific program/project/event.

This is key when it comes to financial planning and management. It can be used for analysis and presentations, assist in decision-making, and serve as a persuasive storytelling document for potential stakeholders. It's also a tracking tool that allows you to measure progress in relation to your greater organizational budget.

Step One

Review digital templates that exist online or easily generate your statement in Excel and customize it for your own program/project/event.

Step Two

If you've already gone through the budgeting process to create an organizational budget, you can copy and paste those same income and expense categories and line items into column A of your new spreadsheet. If not, create your income and expense line items by breaking down your income by source and then your expenses by activity.

Step Three

Create horizontal column headers. These provide context for each line item. You'll want to include a year-to-date column, reflecting the income received and expenses paid in that specific time frame. Columns to track the date money was received or paid, the company or individuals it came from or went to, and what it was allocated for are also standard.

Step Four

To provide even further detail and allow for comparative and planning purposes, you could also have columns referencing:

- The organizational budget figures from your original organizational budget
- The variance, or the difference, between the current income and that projected in the original organizational budget
- The forecast, to show how your organizational budget has been updated

These are sophisticated inclusions and are not necessary for small programs/projects/events.

Step Five

Include a last column for notes and any miscellaneous information.

Step Six

Use this structure to move forward by adding dollar amounts and formulas to make your income/expense statement an efficient working document that can easily be updated and to help track the progression of your program/project/event.

EVALUATION HOW-TO

Introduction

While planning and implementing an event, it's crucial to think about the benefit of an evaluation. Most important is that it is not an afterthought. Rather, an evaluation plan should be incorporated within your event plan from the start, encouraging your team to regularly track performance and seek feedback, and it will ultimately help build your credibility and strengthen your case!

Step One

Design your evaluation plan. There are three main steps for conducting an evaluation:

1. Collecting Data
2. Analyzing Data
3. Evaluating Data

How will you collect data (surveys, interviews, observations)? Who will analyze the data? Who will interpret the findings and create the format for reporting findings?

Step Two

Determine how you will collect data, both existing and new resources. For instance, you might source financial reports, audience statistics, participant comments, grant panel feedback, and more to initially gain an understanding of your current performance and that of your peers. To capture the performance of new activities, you'll likely need to develop data-collecting methods or update the protocols for their use. And you have many options! You might use observations and informal interviews during the event or consider formal follow-up interviews, a review of technologically accessible data like ticket-sale reports, or an assessment tool such as a survey. SurveyMonkey is a free online resource to create surveys for participants. The platform has a bank of certified questions that can help you create a great survey.

Step Three

Craft a thoughtful and clear questionnaire that gathers information about participants' knowledge, behaviors, and experiences surrounding your event. As a best practice, always note the confidentiality of the survey and the value it will add to your work. Let participants know in the text of your survey that their responses are anonymous and you value their feedback. Share your draft survey with peers to be sure you are asking what you think you are asking.

Step Four

Share your evaluation instrument with participants. If you are conducting pre- and post-event surveys, be sure to allow ample time for completion of the pre-event survey.

Step Five

Review and analyze the collected data. If you use SurveyMonkey or another online platform, remember to close the collection tool to prevent additional responses once you begin to analyze. Compile all of your data in a predetermined and consistent manner that allows you to compare and contrast and begin noticing patterns. Did respondents use similar terms to describe your program? Are there common themes or expressions that are conveyed? You'll also want to conduct any statistical tests such as frequencies, percentages, and ratios during this phase.

Step Six

Draw your conclusion from your data. Be sure all pathways to decision-making are documented. How did you arrive at your conclusion? Assess your analyzed data to determine the overall value and outcome of your event based on the analysis. What worked well? What areas could be improved? What surprised you? It is helpful to share your evaluation in report form with your team so that all have access to it for future reference.

FINAL REPORT HOW-TO

Introduction

Most commonly, you will see this term, "final report," used in reference to grants and institutional funding. This is because many funders stipulate that such a report be delivered to them following the completion of your grant-funded activity or event.

A final report is a document through which you share your project activities, successes, challenges, future plans, and actual financials. Sometimes a specific format is required, and other times it can simply take the shape of a short, one-to-three-page letter.

Step One

Research the necessary final report parameters for your grantor and follow the prompts. If no prompts are given, prepare a formal business letter on organization or project letterhead. Developing a final report will allow you to reconcile what you set out to do with how it actually unfolded—financially, programmatically, and logistically. The final report can double as an evaluation tool for your project. It is a way for the funder to evaluate the funded program.

Step Two

In the first paragraph, detail the project time, date, place, and purpose. Give a short overview of the project.

Step Three

In the body of the letter, detail the impact made by the grant funds and how they were used to support your activity. Give details about the project/program/event to help the funder understand what took place. Include information from the evaluations, including attendance, what participants thought of the project/program/event and what challenges or problems you faced. Use a narrative tone to tell the story of the event logically and chronologically. Articulate what you learned and how you would adjust your plans in the future. This is a great place to include quotes from participants that highlight the positive outcomes of the project/program/event.

Step Four

In the final paragraph, acknowledge the importance of the funder's support and formally close the letter.

Step Five

If requested by the funder, provide your actual budget and context or reasoning surrounding the changes from your original budget.

Step Six

Share collateral such as related pictures, programs, or videos. Help to tell the narrative of the program/project/event through visuals.

Step Seven

Triple-check grammar, spelling, and salutation. A final report doesn't have to be limited to institutional funders. Put your creativity to use, and you can easily transform it into an engaging update for your donors and stakeholders! They too deserve to understand your team's success and the impact they, and others, have on your work. You can edit your final report created for one funder into multiple formats to use for other stakeholders.

PRESS RELEASE HOW-TO

Introduction

A press release is your best (and most affordable) tool for communicating your story through the press (newspapers, radio, television news, and more). Be clear, concise, and compelling. And remember, you want to make it as easy as possible for a busy reporter to pick up your story. Here's how you do just that.

Step One

Craft a description of your project that can answer the question, "What is the *news* value in this story?" You must make the case for newsworthiness within your release in order for it to be covered by some sort of news outlet—big or small.

Step Two

Review your description to be sure the following are included:

- *Who?* Who is involved? (keep this limited to key players) Whom does your news affect?
- *What?* What is new or exciting or different? How is your project unique?
- *Why?* Why is this newsworthy?
- *Where?* Where is this happening? Does location add significance?
- *When?* When will it take place? Is the timing significant?
- *How?* How did this project/event/program come to be?

Step Three

Clearly communicate your/your organization's contact information at the top of the news release. This should be followed by a header reading "For Immediate Release," and then the title of your release (your project title).

Step Four

Paragraph one should relay the essence of your news story. Paragraphs two and three communicate further detail and ideally a quote or two about the project. Write your release as a reporter would: keep your sentences factual, use data if you have it, and be succinct. Include a human-interest element. Who is included in the project and why does this project matter?

Step Five

Edit your release to 1–2 pages in length. By providing your contact information at the top, you welcome a journalist to contact you with any questions. Also consider including specific hyperlinks to sources of greater detail, such as a full bio of a collaborator, thereby reducing the need for additional text. Any photos included should be properly credited.

Step Six

Read your press release aloud to yourself. Does it sound interesting? Do you communicate all of the necessary information (double-check your five Ws and How!) Triple-check grammar and spelling.

Step Seven

Research local press and any specialist press that cover projects similar to the one you are writing about. Collect contact information to send releases and build a working media list. Include deadlines; each outlet operates differently, so be mindful of their timing.

Step Eight

Distribute your press release by individual e-mail with the release pasted into the body of the e-mail and included as an attachment. Is your contact information clear and easy to find? Include a short intro to the press release. If appropriate, offer a press ticket to a show or an exclusive interview.

Step Nine

Any photos you share within the release should be properly credited and attached as singular images as well. Do not include large files that are difficult to e-mail.

Step Ten

Follow up with phone calls. Reporters' in-boxes are inundated with press releases. Take the time to follow up and ask if they received the e-mail and give them your elevator pitch.

Step Eleven

Respond to any and all additional information requests in a timely manner. Building media relationships can take time. Be professional and consistent in all of your responses to media outlets to promote a unified message about your project.

ELEVATOR PITCH HOW-TO

Introduction

Sometimes called the elevator speech or elevator statement, the elevator pitch is your go-to verbal spiel. It can be used in a variety of ways, but for our purposes it will serve as a short and memorable verbal summary of your project and its value. In this short span of time you want to:

- Make them care
- Establish credibility
- Encourage a call to action
- Leave them wanting more

Think of this as your sound bite, headline, or teaser.

Step One

Create a pitch no longer than 30–60 seconds (less than 250 words). Review the following questions to help frame your pitch:

What?
- What is your project?
- What problem are you addressing?
- What motivates you to act?
- What is your innovative solution?
- What is your unique value proposition?
- What is your competitive advantage?

Who?
- Whom will you serve?
- Who are your collaborators/partners?

How?
- How are you creating change?
- How is your project funded?
- How can others help make an impact?

Step Two

Read through your pitch. Does it clearly articulate the importance of your project? Does it clearly identify who is involved and why? Does it include a specific ask or call to action?

Step Three

Practice, practice, practice. The elevator pitch should sound natural but energetic. You will be able to clearly communicate the importance of your project and persuade others to join you to increase impact in your community.

POSTCARD/FLYER HOW-TO

Introduction

Postcards and flyers are "guerilla marketing" techniques that help you connect with individuals directly and indirectly. Both materials can be directly mailed to specific people, handed out publicly, or shared with local organizations for distribution to their respective client bases.

Step One

Whether you tackle this marketing strategy in-house or decide to outsource to a designer or other knowledgeable collaborator, consistency is important. All marketing materials should have a clear brand or "feel." The postcard/flyer should incorporate imagery, font, colors, and language used elsewhere in your marketing materials (website, blog, social media, letterhead, advertisements, etc.) The postcard/flyer is part of the family of marketing materials for your organization/project/program/event. Consistency is paramount.

Step Two

Create/review direct-mail address records and drop-off locations/places for distribution. Postcards/flyers can be directly mailed to specific people, handed out publicly, or shared with local organizations for distribution to their respective client bases.

Step Three

Draft a distribution plan. How many will you mail, hand out, drop off? How much time do you need to produce, print, and mail? Think about deadlines in relation to timing of event.

Step Four

Create a postcard/flyer design that clearly presents a call to action. Include:

- Date/Time/Place of event/program/project
- Eye-catching imagery (photo, design, etc.)

- Easy-to-read font
- Color scheme that aligns with your project/event/program
- Clear and concise written content (fragments are OK)
- Persuasive action language such as: "Join us," "Call now," "Sign up today"
- Impact/benefit
- Provide relevant contact information and an easy URL for more information

Step Five

Review your postcard/flyer to ensure your design is delivering one, deliberate message. Triple-check spelling and information accuracy.

Step Six

Determine printing strategy: in-house, through a local printer shop, or online. Keep in mind, this is a digital printing job (not offset printing, which is typically for huge print orders). The more you print, the cheaper the price per piece, so it's often better to slightly overestimate the quantity.

Step Seven

Print and distribute.

DATA/INFOGRAPHIC HOW-TO

Introduction

You are in the process of learning the powerful skill of idea-driven storytelling. It is to your benefit to integrate specific detail and data into this conceptual and emotionally powered mode of communication.

Think about it: In today's digital age, information is instantaneously accessible and initiatives of all kinds are held to new levels of accountability and transparency. These realities inform your work, your initiative, and how you can masterfully communicate it. By incorporating data, you can underscore the poignant takeaways for your audience.

Simply put, data:

- Shares impact in a concise way
- Is understood by a widespread audience
- Is memorable

Step One

Determine what information/data you want to share that is relevant to your project/event/program. How can sharing this data help to create a compelling message? Research relevant national-trend data to use in place of missing specific data to help communicate the need for your project.

Step Two

Use clear visuals and easy-to-read text. An infographic should allow the reader to glance quickly and gain an understanding.

Your infographic should:

- Show the data
- Encourage thought
- Avoid distorting the data
- Present data in a finite space

- Make large data sets comprehensible
- Encourage visual comparison
- Share an overview and reveal detail
- Serve a clear purpose: description, exploration, explanation, reasoning, etc.
- Be tied to any statistical or verbal descriptions of data

Step Three

Edit for grammar and spelling. Be consistent with tense. Use compelling data; don't collect or share data that have no bearing on the project/program/event.

Step Four

Share your infographic with funders, partners, and other stakeholders to communicate the need for your program or the outcomes of your project. Check out the many free online tools to help create your infographic.

PREZI HOW-TO

Introduction

Prezi is digital presentation software that emerged in 2009 as a user-friendly resource and tool for creating 21st-century, high-quality presentations. This platform allows you to bring to one space compelling written, verbal, and visual elements to tell your story to those who can support your work.

Step One

Determine if you require a paid, increased membership level or if the free, public account will suffice. The beauty of Prezi is access—for both the creator and the audience. Your presentation, similar to any other digital asset, will be searchable, viewable online, downloadable, and shareable in e-mail, on websites, and across social media. Prezi is a more flexible alternative to PowerPoint.

Step Two

Craft a creative and thoughtful delivery for your story. You are no longer limited to just your words, as in an elevator pitch, or solely video, as with a video profile. You can incorporate text, audio, video, hyperlinks, sound tracks, and so much more. Don't forget to use the animation and transition elements to underscore the relationships and the main points that you want your audience to walk away contemplating.

Step Three

The possibilities are truly endless as you develop your message in this active digital landscape. After familiarizing yourself with the software, you might also find it helpful to create a presentation or two for internal information sharing, onboarding of new collaborators, team updates, and the like.

Step Four

Review Prezi's extensive knowledge base, where you can find the answer to almost any question you can dream up while creating your first presentation.

Step Five

Work to create your Prezi presentation as a sharable tool to communicate information regarding your project/program/event. Double-check grammar, word choice, and spelling.

SOCIAL MEDIA CAMPAIGN HOW-TO

Introduction

A social media campaign is an outlined parameter for your integrated marketing strategy across a variety of social media platforms. As an extension of your other promotional efforts, this is a space where you have the flexibility to be very creative, responsive, and targeted in your messaging.

Step One

Draft a detailed campaign plan that specifies your goals. What are your goals?

- Do you want to increase your social media followers?
- Do you want to create general buzz or awareness?
- Do you want to increase project or hashtag mentions?
- Do you want to encourage digital sharing and participation?

Step Two

Do some research during this phase about social media capabilities other than those with which you may be personally familiar. For instance, how can you create a successful, well-promoted Facebook event? Have you considered a "Twitter Opera" and recruiting additional volunteers to help increase the buzz surrounding a particular event or activity?

Within your plan, specify the social networks you'll be using and strategize your approach for each. Your plan should include parameters for posts in terms of language, tone, length, and timing. Remember, every outlet has its own personality and norms, so what works on Facebook may not be the best approach on Twitter. In fact, you might find it best to limit your campaign to specific outlets that are more likely to connect you with your target audience. In addition, it's a great idea to create a uniform hashtag, title, and/or tagline to be used consistently when referencing your project.

Step Three

Determine who will be your point person for your social media campaign and create a schedule of posts, including the space for regular interaction and real-time posting and responding. It is important to directly engage with people in real time, making participants feel included and valued.

Step Four

Measure and analyze success throughout your social media campaign. What times of day or types of post attract greater activity? Use this data to inform your campaign moving forward.

Step Five

Remember to post often, keep it social, tell important stories of the project/program/event, and offer opportunities for engagement.

Step Six

Always post with correct grammar and spelling. Use original photography. Present your program/project/event honestly.

VIDEO PROFILE HOW-TO

Introduction

Video profiles have become a common communication tool and can take on many different forms. What we're focusing on today is the video profile that serves as a visual elevator pitch. Just like a verbal elevator pitch, you are setting out to making a compelling and concise pitch about your work.

The beauty of the video version is that you have the power of words *and* imagery at play. You can deliver a memorable message that is easily shareable across countless digital platforms, greatly expanding your potential audience base!

Step One

Craft a clear and concise message that communicates your idea effectively. Review and follow the outline for verbal elevator pitches. Be sure to include how someone watching can contact you for more information about your idea.

Step Two

Practice your message until you can say it with ease, speaking naturally and comfortably, in a conversational tone. Practice in front of a mirror to be sure your facial expressions match your desired tone of delivery.

Step Three

Choose an outfit for your video that aligns with the formality of your audience. Who will watch and respond to your video? Do you need to dress in business attire, or is a casual outfit suitable?

Step Four

Find a quiet, well-lit space that allows the video viewer to focus on you and your message. Great lighting is important. Experiment with different rooms/spaces.

Step Five

Use technology that you are familiar with to record the video. You want the video to highlight confidence in yourself and your idea. Be sure your video can be shared with ease. Consider creating your own YouTube channel.

Step Six

Review your video, listening for unnatural breaks in speech; watch for facial expressions that detract from the message. Share the video with a few peers. What did they hear? What did they notice? Rerecord, if necessary, to be sure your message is being communicated effectively.

Step Seven

Your video profile is ready to be shared.

WEBSITE/BLOG HOW-TO

Introduction

It's no secret that websites have become a necessary communication, branding, and promotional tool. If well thought out, your website can take your endeavor to the next level and introduce a new layer of audience engagement to your work.

Step One

Determine the type of digital presence you want.

- Is a website or blog necessary to build upon social media and e-mail communication?
- In what ways will your project/program/event benefit from a finite, centralized crowdfunding campaign web page?
- Are there resources in your organization/team to create regular content?
- Is it necessary to have your own website, or can you add a page to a collaborator or partner site?

Step Two

If you determine a website/blog is necessary, research the available free content management systems for ease of use and provision of tools. Keep in mind your audience's needs. All free content management systems come with easy-to-use templates.

Step Three

Register a domain name. Be sure the name chosen clearly identifies your website. Sign up for a web hosting account. Weebly does offer free options for hosting.

Step Four

Upload content and images for initial launch. Set a schedule for updating content. Proofread for grammar and spelling.

Step Five

Share the site/blog with peers for feedback. Does the site/blog help possible funders/partners understand your program/project/event in a more robust way?

Step Six

Share the completed site, update it, promote it, and drive traffic to it.

SPONSORSHIP HOW-TO

Introduction

Recruiting a sponsor, much like any other supporter, centers on relationship building. A sponsor may be an individual or a company. A sponsor's support may include a donation, in-kind goods or services, or volunteers. Most often you would seek sponsorship support surrounding a particular event, activity, or project.

Step One

Determine what kind of support you need and what kind of sponsor is best positioned to make the investment.

Step Two

Build your master list. Include vendors, leaders, and companies with whom you already have a connection. These existing relationships could make all the difference! You should also research potential sponsors outside of your network.

Step Three

Look for companies or community leaders with interests and business activity that align with your endeavor or the community you are serving. Sponsor lists are posted on event web pages and in event programs. Find events/projects similar to yours and check out their sponsor lists.

Step Four

In your sponsorship letter and package, your goal is to compel the potential sponsor to participate in your endeavor. Remember, yes, it is a solicitation, but it's also a marketing "sales" document. Think creatively about what type of support you need, what the sponsor will receive, and how you can make that request in a persuasive way. Be sure to consider what the value will be for the sponsor in this partnership. You might have to craft different messages for different potential sponsors.

Step Five

Prepare your sponsorship letter on your group's letterhead and be sure to include all of your contact information. The first paragraph should provide brief context about the organization, what the organization does, and what your request is. The second paragraph should describe the need being met or the problem being addressed. The third paragraph should further highlight the benefits for the sponsor, ranging from public recognition to tangible reward.

Step Six

To complete your sponsorship package, design an "at-a-glance," one-page document that outlines the sponsor-giving options and associated benefits. If you design this document strategically, you can have it simultaneously serve as a response form for the sponsor as well! Review sponsor recognition and benefits for detail and creativity. Will the benefits appeal to the funder? How do you know? For instance, volunteer support could warrant a listing of the sponsor and volunteers by name in your program. However, a $5,000 gift might come with a program and website listing, verbal acknowledgment in a speech at the event, and inclusion of the sponsor logo on all communication materials surrounding your project for the year.

Step Seven

Send out sponsorship packets to all potential funders. Use e-mail and postal mail to reach as many potential sponsors as possible. Keep track of what is sent out.

Step Eight

Follow up the letters to sponsors with a phone call. Double-check that they received the letter and offer to answer any questions about the program/project/event they might have.

Step Nine

Record what works for future use. Track the sponsors that responded and what appealed to them.

Step Ten

After the program/project/event, be sure to appropriately thank your funders and supporters.

FUNDRAISING GOAL HOW-TO

Introduction

All fundraising initiatives hinge on a fundraising goal, whether that goal is made known to the public (like in a crowdfunding campaign) or not. Behind the scenes, this goal is most often arrived at through a budgeting process that outlines your project's financial plan. It delineates what and who it will take to complete your project from start to finish along with the associated expenses. Any projected income (earned or contributed) that is already expected to help cover these expenses will also be included. The remaining income needed to balance the budget evolves as the fundraising goal.

Step One

Review your project/program/event budget. The fundraising goal is the amount needed to cover the deficit in income. Be sure to include in-kind opportunities as part of your fundraising goal.

Step Two

Identify sources of contributed income available to you. Sources of contributed income are:

- Foundations
- Corporations
- Government agencies (arts council, city, state, or national grants)
- Individuals (individual donations and bequests, typically highest percentage)

Step Three

Keep a frequently updated record of what sponsors are confirmed and how far you are to your goal. Do you stop at your goal if you have time to fundraise more? Of course not! Additional funds can help to increase your impact through your project/program/event.

Step Four

Your fundraising goal may change as the budget becomes more concise. Be sure to work closely with your budgeting team to be sure goals are met but also to help increase impact if additional funds are committed.

Step Five

With your fundraising goal determined and well planned, you can map out your fundraising strategy to achieve it. Get creative and be open to thinking of different scenarios that could result in your fundraising success!

ENVIRONMENTAL SCAN HOW-TO

Introduction

An environmental scan is a strategic way to grasp the big picture before launching your new project, effort, or organization. It's the process of seeking and reviewing information about all of the environmental factors (current and potential) that may impact your project and its goals. By amassing this knowledge, you arm yourself with valuable context. You'll be in a position to make more informed decisions and better adapt as you pursue your project. This visual tool will help to identify needs, gaps, and opportunities in your community.

Step One

Determine the geographic location that will be scanned.

Step Two

Create an inventory list of all institutions, service providers, and existing efforts in your immediate community that offer arts-based programming and service.

- What institutions are present?
- Whom do they serve?
- What programs provide overlapping or duplicated service?

Step Three

On a sheet of paper, use shapes like circles and squares to begin to visually map offerings in your community.

- Denote different institutions or organizations.
- Identify and list programs offered.
- Identify and list audience served.
- Identify and list cost for each program.
- Overlap or connect programs or offerings that are similar.
- Use color to code organizations or institutions that offer similar programs.
- Be sure to include organizations outside of the arts that also provide arts programming.

Step Four

Identify gaps in service and programming. What programs/projects/events are not being offered? Who is not being served?

Step Five

Utilize this information as the starting point to help determine what possible projects/programs/events you could offer.

CASE FOR SUPPORT HOW-TO

Introduction

From this central document, you will craft diverse fundraising communications to use as tools to inform those helping you garner support for your project. It is a foundation piece that can be transformed into grants, direct mail appeals, crowd-funding campaigns, and so on. The more time and thought you put into your case for support, the easier it is to use.

Step One

Start to create your document with the following headings:

- Introduction
- Organizational history
- Statement of need
- Connection of fundraising objectives to the organization
- Summary of future goals
- Leadership
- Gifts and benefits (mostly individuals)
- Financial information
- Conclusion

Step Two

Work to create clear and descriptive paragraphs for each section, leaving the introduction to work on last. You will need to work with your storytelling and ideas to action teams to gather all of the information necessary to complete the document.

Step Three

You might not be able to fill in all of the items fully, but be creative in how you do attend to each section. Your organization might not have a five-year history, but it does have an origin story. Most often, you'll find that the statement of need is your secret weapon. This is where you get to the heart of your case, answer the question "Why?" and explain the profound impact your initiative will have. This is your opportunity to present not only the evidence that supports the necessity of your project, but also that which establishes you and your team as capable, creative, and tenacious leaders.

Step Four

Consider these things as you continue to craft your case for support:

- Use inclusive and donor-centric language.
- Create a sense of urgency.
- Suggest a chance of loss.
- Tap into your donor's emotions.

Step Five

Be sure to tailor this document into different formats for different audiences. Be aware of tone and language. Triple-check grammar and word choice before sending the document out.

Step Six

Track who the case for support was sent to and what resulted.

CROWDFUNDING HOW-TO

Introduction

Crowdfunding is precisely what its name suggests: raising funds from a crowd. It has earned widespread appeal within our digital age as a successful means of galvanizing support from many smaller-level donors. Today, countless crowdfunding websites exist, providing a framework for creatives like us to innovate and invite others to share in our journey.

Step One

Select a digital platform. Research associated fees, requirements, parameters, options, and for how long the campaign can run.

Step Two

Tell your compelling story. All platforms have a general template to follow. Put in the time to make a concise, high-quality video message that highlights your project's value in a dynamic and powerful manner. Your goal is to capture the attention of a broad audience and persuade them to join you in supporting your project/program/event.

Step Three

Share the draft campaign with peers to be sure you are communicating the need clearly and passionately moving viewers to the role of supporter. Be sure all grammar, spelling, and word choice in written text is correct.

Step Four

Share your campaign online through social media channels. Ask close friends and current supporters to share your campaign with their networks as well. Be active every day online to promote and share about your campaign. You can also promote in person and via letter to drive traffic to the online campaign.

DIGITAL APPEAL HOW-TO

Introduction

We all know that e-mail is an efficient, cost-effective form of communication, and it has in turn become a powerful fundraising medium as well.

A digital appeal allows you to reach an impressive audience in a concise, visually engaging, and action-oriented manner. For the recipient, these appeals mark a convenient way to give; for some, it makes the difference between giving or not.

The key to your digital appeal's success is effective placement in your larger fundraising strategy. For instance, sharing your appeal across your social media platforms, in a blog, e-newsletter, or on your website enables repeat messaging and exponential access.

Step One

Determine how you will share your appeal for support across multiple platforms including:

- E-mail
- Social Media (Facebook, Twitter, Instagram, LinkedIn, etc.)
- Blog
- E-newsletter
- Website

Because the digital world thrives on interactive behavior, you can also better target your content, answer questions in real time, and thank supporters almost instantaneously.

Step Two

Create content to e-mail to your list of individual prospects.

- Use a catchy subject line.
- Keep the body of the appeal captivating and concise.
- Incorporate user-friendly online giving options.
- Place your ask as close to the beginning of the message as possible.

- Use photos, videos, testimonials, etc., to leverage engaging text.
- Integrate a clear and repeated call to action.
- Use the "two clicks or less" rule to get to the online contribution page.
- No online contribution page? Use a digital pledge form.
- Be sure all contact information of the donor is captured.

Step Three

Review and edit. Double-check the salutation, grammar, spelling, and word choice. This is one chance to make a great impression. Do not allow poor editing to stand in the way of your digital appeal.

Step Four

Follow up with a second version of the appeal. Give the prospect a reason to read it again and remember to drive traffic to the online campaign.

Step Five

Be sure to thank your donors!

DIRECT MAIL HOW-TO

Introduction

This type of appeal is a tried-and-true fundraising activity that remains successful even in the digital age. It is, however, often supplemented with a digital appeal, which can serve as follow-up reminder or a means of targeting a new subset or different subsets of prospects . . . or all of the above!

Step One

Determine your timeline. A direct mail appeal does require some initial time and expense, plus stamps.

Step Two

You need to compile your recipient list with addresses and prepare, print, and mail your appeal. Be sure to check that addresses are correct!

Step Three

Assemble the standard appeal package, including:

- A one-page letter
- A reply card with instructions on the various ways to give
- A reply envelope (slightly smaller than your appeal package envelope)
- Appeal package envelope

Step Four

The heart of a direct mail appeal is the letter. You must communicate your story and persuade an individual to invest on a single sheet of paper. Provide some general context about your project; make your case for why it is meaningful and how a gift will make a difference; and, most importantly, *ask for support!* Ask for a specific dollar amount based on your knowledge of a specific individual, their wealth capacity, and their affinity for your project.

Step Five

Use the appeal to direct people to a digital crowdfunding campaign, mimic the crowdfunding culture by specifying a fundraising goal in your letter, or encourage support by presenting a matching gift opportunity.

Some general rules:

- Involve your reader by using the words "you," "your," "we," and "us."
- Leave plenty of white space on the page; be clear and concise.
- Be effusive with your thanks.
- Directly ask for support; be specific.

PEER-TO-PEER FUNDRAISING HOW-TO

Introduction

Peer-to-peer fundraising leverages a ripple-effect fundraising strategy in which your networks empower their networks to raise funds on your behalf. In this approach, your role shifts from directly asking for support to asking and making a case for your network to leverage its own influence.

Step One

Identify those who:

- Have a deep affinity for your project
- Are generously volunteering their time, effort, and maybe even money to help your effort
- Have a clear understanding of your goals, method, and impact
- Have a continuing involvement throughout the project

Step Two

Provide these supporters with clear messaging, great marketing materials, and your available time to help support their efforts.

Step Three

Give them permission to convey their genuine experience and connection—this is powerful; this is persuasion. Encourage them to connect with donors outside your immediate sphere of influence.

Step Four

Encourage this group of supporters to help:

- Multiply the impact of limited resources
- Formalize the power of "word of mouth" communication
- Utilize in-person and digital forms of communication to boost fundraising

Step Five

As awareness surrounding your project increases, your peer-to-peer fundraisers' ripple effect grows. Be sure to support your peer-to-peer fundraisers as they share your project and communicate its worth; keep in mind that their audience will be largely those who already know and trust their opinion—a major perk. Write thank-you letters and use phone calls to let them know the large impact they are having on the project/program/event's success.

Step Six

Track whom your peer-to-peer fundraisers contact and who contributes toward the project/ program/event. As your team/organization moves forward, these new supporters can also become peer-to-peer fundraisers.

INDIVIDUAL PROSPECT RESEARCH HOW-TO

Introduction

Individuals hold great potential as volunteers, advocates, audiences, guests, sources of knowledge, collaborators, connectors, and—of course—as financial backers. It's no secret that the more engaged someone is with your effort, the more inclined that person is to give.

This is why you always start with those closest to you and your project when seeking individual support. Next, you'd look for one degree of separation via the personal contacts of your core individual base. But given your fundraising goal and plans for growth however, it is probable that you will still need to find, attract, and cultivate more individuals and their support.

Step One

Create a spreadsheet (prospect profile) to keep track of your supporters. Create spaces for name, contact info, basic context about the individual including how he or she is connected to you or the program/project/event. Start with those closest to you and your project. Add friends and family of those closest to you. You will still need to find, attract, and cultivate more individuals.

Step Two

Find supporters outside your direct sphere of influence.

- Review fellow arts organization donor lists in programs and on websites.
- Review social media and LinkedIn information.
- Source public information about individuals from business journals, newspapers, magazines, philanthropic directories, annual reports, and so on.
- Use Google to find out who sponsors what in your community.
- Databases such as WealthEngine, DonorSearch, NOZA, Zillow, and LexisNexis are also useful but can come with a fee.

Step Three

Assess your growing knowledge about an individual in the context of "the three Cs:"

- Capacity—What can you discern about this person's financial capacity and ability to give?
- Commitment—What's this person's understanding of and interest in your project?
- Connection—How is this person associated with your project; what or who is the link?

Step Four

Review your newly created database and begin to plan how you will reach out to these possible project/program/event funders. Triple-check to be sure all names are spelled correctly and that appropriate titles are used in all correspondence (Mr., Mrs., Ms., Dr., etc.).

INSTITUTIONAL PROSPECT RESEARCH HOW-TO

Introduction

Finding and soliciting funds from a foundation, corporation, or government agency is a multistep process. It begins with a ready project in place, followed by institutional research. Institutional research helps you identify funding opportunities and prioritize where your project may best align and therefore be the most competitive. To be successful, be sure to familiarize yourself with application requirements and review processes, create a grant calendar, and make an initial inquiry, if necessary. A formal application typically follows.

Step One

Create a spreadsheet to keep track of available institutional prospects. Include columns for name and contact information as well as for grant deadlines, application links, and grant program officer names.

Step Two

If you find a grant with a deadline you can meet, review the grant to determine parameters, requirements, etc. Often, you must be a 501(c)(3) to be considered for the grant.

Step Three

To apply for funds from a grantor like an arts council, foundation, or agency you must:

- Have a project planned and ready to execute
- Understand the institution's funding guidelines
- Be sure your project falls within their funding guidelines
- Understand the funding application requirements and review process, such as whether they require a letter of intent (LOI), an online application, or a mailed/e-mailed/faxed form
- Be sure your project can meet the requirements and deadlines
- Familiarize yourself with past grant awards to understand funding priorities

Step Four

Be sure you have enough time before your project begins to complete the application, have it reviewed by the agency/institution, and be awarded. Most grants do not offer funding for projects already in progress.

Step Five

Check out these databases—free and fee-based—to round out your research:

- Foundation Center Directory Online (often public libraries have a license for this)
- FoundationSearch America
- Guidestar
- GrantStation
- Chronicle Guide to Grants
- American City Business Journals
- Hoovers
- Yahoo! Finance
- LexisNexis
- The Catalog of Federal Domestic Assistance
- The Federal Register

Step Six

Subscribe to newsletters from a variety of government agencies and foundations, along with the Foundation Center's *Philanthropy News Digest* to receive regular updates of funding opportunities in your in-box.

MATCHING GIFTS HOW-TO

Introduction

Matching gifts can be hugely impactful. While 1:1 matches (where $1 dollar matches $1) are the most common, there are other kinds as well. A typical matching-gift scenario is the corporate match. This is when an employer matches an employee's gift to a nonprofit at a specified level. It's a win–win–win. The donor leverages their gift at no extra cost, the company contributes to a worthy cause while supporting its employee base, and the nonprofit reaps the financial benefits.

Step One

Determine if a matching-gift strategy is useful for your project/program/event. A matching-gift strategy relies on an existing supporter, leader, or key advocate of your effort that is willing to create an incentive for other gifts.

Step Two

Determine what kind of incentive the key supporter will offer. Perhaps they want to match every dollar raised in a specific time frame. Or they might want to give a predetermined gift amount that will become available to the organization after other fundraising benchmarks are met. Some individuals will make their gift upfront, giving permission for it to be framed as a matching gift to create a new incentive.

Step Three

Leverage this donor's generosity in your solicitation materials. This fundraising approach creates credibility and a sense of urgency for supporting your program/project/event. Use digital and traditional tools to get the word out that your program/project/event has a matching-gift opportunity.

Step Four

Follow up with all donors with appropriate thank-you letters and outcome reporting.

GRANT STEWARDSHIP HOW-TO

Introduction

So, you've just received the good news: Your grant proposal has been awarded. Congrats! Now what?

One of the first things to do is prepare an acknowledgment letter thanking the funder for the award and their commitment to your project. As with any supporter, you want to be timely in your thanks and ensure this new stakeholder knows just how instrumental they are. You may draft a simple letter of thanks, or at times—for instance, with government grants—you will have a more formal acknowledgment or signed contract to submit.

Step One

Know the requirements for grant acknowledgment if the grant comes from a formal institution/organization. Otherwise, an acknowledgment letter is appropriate. Be sure the letter is:

- Timely
- Grammatically correct and includes an accurate description of project
- Highlights the importance of funder to project

Your case for support or appeal letter can serve as a model for your acknowledgment letter. Instead of communicating what you will do, you communicate what you did and what was successful. Be sure to also include what you learned in servicing the need/addressing the problem and how your learning will impact how you further address the problem.

Step Two

Donor recognition goes beyond an acknowledgment letter or grant agreement. Donor recognition is outlined in appeals, be sure to follow up and give what was offered. Always double-check how funders would like their name and logo displayed. Common ways to recognize donors through name and logo follow:

- Website
- Programs
- Flyers
- E-mail campaign
- Brochures
- Social media

Step Three

The donor acknowledgment process is not a single transaction. Continue to cultivate the relationship to ensure repeated engagement with future projects/programs/events. You can engage the donor/funder in multiple ways including:

- Other event or project invitations
- E-mail updates of milestones
- Include them in stories and celebrations of success
- Double-check final reporting requirements
- Be aware of next funding cycle deadlines

Step Four

Track all donor communications to be sure you are communicating equitably with all donors and not accidentally overlooking anyone.

GRANT WRITING HOW-TO

Introduction

So, you're hoping to submit a grant proposal, but aren't sure where to start. No worries. Although most proposal requirements drastically vary from one funder to the next, typically all grants have prompts to answer. This how-to section assists with the standard letter grant that foundations and some other funders require. Most grants that come in a template or have prompts to address also require answers similar to the following format.

Step One

Craft the need statement, identifying the need or problem you hope to address. Describe how you intend to help. Offer the impact you hope to create. Identify possible collaborators and how you can work together. Describe how this request fits into the total project.

Step Two

Outline project goals and objectives. List desired outputs (what will physically happen; e.g., students will hear a concert). List desired outcomes (what change will occur that can be measured; e.g., students will increase knowledge about composer X).

Step Three

Describe the methodology behind the program/project/event creation. Give specific details about how the project emerged and how your project will unfold. Walk the reader through every part of what the audience will experience. Share the qualifications of those responsible for execution of the program/project/event. Describe how your plan in the short term holds implications for the long term.

Step Four

Describe your evaluation plan. Describe how you will use surveys or interviews to track changes in learning, attitudes, and behavior of the audience. Describe how you will collect stories from the audience. What did they like? What did they experience? Describe how you will use this information to better strategize and adapt your plan in the future.

Step Five

Write the executive summary. It is important to write this portion last, allowing for the best summary of the project. Give an overview of the main points of your proposal. Be sure it sparks curiosity and entices audience to learn more.

Step Six

Check all grammar, spelling, and word choice. Be sure to meet the funder deadline for submission. Grants are not accepted late.

RETURN ON INVESTMENT HOW-TO

Introduction

Return on Investment, or ROI, is a measurement tool that evaluates an investment's efficiency.

To calculate it, use this formula:

$$\text{Gain from Investment} \div \text{Cost of Investment} = ROI$$

Step One

Determine the cost of your program/project/event. Determine the gross gain from your program/project/event (revenue). You can use the formula above to determine ROI.

Step Two

ROI can be used to track:

- Programming
- Marketing
- Fundraising activities
- Economic impact

This is great data to inform future programming, projects, and events. The higher the ROI, the greater the success. Tracking ROI can also help to create budgets for projects moving forward.

Step Three

Nonprofit organizations can articulate a project's dynamic value proposition and make the case for support all the more compelling. This is where the social return on investment, or SROI, can make a difference. This measurement captures a double bottom line of social value and financial value.

The SROI formula is:

(Tangible + Intangible Value to the Community) ÷ *Total Resource Investment = SROI*

Step Four

You will analyze the outcomes of your work and translate the "intangible value" into financial terms. Think through measurable indicators of your outcomes, including test scores, attendance, digital activity numbers, and so on. Be sure to use the same units throughout your calculation.

Step Five

Be consistent with how you track SROI. This is valuable data to share, but you must be able to provide logical and consistent measures to support the outcome. With this data in your toolbox, you can research proxies and begin to put a dollar value on each indicator of each outcome. You can also use any external factors that may have impacted your results (a new law, nationwide trend, natural disaster) to help quantify.

THANKING DONORS HOW-TO

Introduction

Remember, fundraising hinges on relationship building! Recognition should underscore every phase of your engagement with both individuals and institutions—from cultivation, to solicitation, to ongoing stewardship. You can also get creative in how you say, share, and show your thanks for the meaningful contributions making your work possible.

Step One

Be sure all donors have been tracked throughout the program/project/event. Use this record to also be sure all donors have been thanked accordingly. Create a spreadsheet with first/last name, salutation, address, and zip if you don't already have one.

Step Two

Create the acknowledgment letter. Include the following:

- The amount, mode, and date of the contribution, and
- A statement confirming that no goods or services were exchanged and the gift is tax deductible to the full extent allowed by law.
- Sometimes, however, a gift may include both a contribution and payment for a good or service. For instance, if I buy a $500 ticket to your gala event, which covers my ticket to your show with a "fair market value" of $50, my tax-deductible contribution to you is $450. Here, it's imperative to indicate the full amount of my contribution and further specify my tax-deductible portion in my acknowledgment. For those of you exploring crowdfunding campaigns with or for a nonprofit, any costs related to your rewards would have to be similarly taken into account.

Step Three

Double-check your letter for appropriate salutation, grammar, and word choice.

Step Four

Review your letter. Does it sound respectful, grateful, and honest? Does it briefly describe the positive outcomes from the program/project/event? Does it encourage your donor to remain engaged in other ways?

Step Five

Continue to thank and cultivate your donors through other ways, including:

- Phone calls
- Handwritten notes
- Event invites
- Naming opportunities
- Public recognition in a speech, website, or program recognition
- Updating with details about their impact on the organization/audience served

Step Six

Thank-yous should be mailed as soon as possible following the event/project/program. Use programs like MailMerge to speed up the process. Always try to use a real ink signature on the thank-you letter, even if the letter itself is a form letter.

NOTES

CHAPTER 1

1. Originally published at http://21cm.org/magazine/sounding-board/2015/11/01/entrepreneurship-and-the-artist-revolutionary/
2. http://21cm.org/magazine/state-of-the-art-form/2015/04/01/developing-the-entrepreneurial-musician-at-fresh-inc/
3. http://21cm.org/pop-picks/2015/11/01/ensemble-acjw/
4. http://21cm.org/artist/decoda/
5. http://21cm.org/pop-picks/2015/11/01/musicambia/
6. http://21cm.org/magazine/sounding-board/2015/05/10/silkroad-develops-global-musicians/
7. http://21cm.org/pop-picks/
8. Originally published at http://21cm.org/magazine/state-of-the-art-form/2015/01/13/what-is-a-21st-century-musician/
9. https://www.music.umd.edu/special_programs/national_orchestral_institute2007/conductors/ross
10. https://www.youtube.com/watch?v=782GpSv9pTM
11. https://www.youtube.com/watch?v=jGSctM_8K_E
12. You can watch those performances at https://www.youtube.com/watch?v=n4tJKh__fak and https://www.youtube.com/watch?v=PFh7LAFel4w
13. https://csosoundsandstories.org/category/music-now/
14. http://www.laradownes.com/web/page.aspx?title=The+Artist+Sessions
15. http://www.artsjournal.com/sandow/2013/05/from-lara-downes-walking-the-walk.html
16. http://www.artsjournal.com/sandow/2013/07/from-lara-downes-success-and-surprises.html
17. https://www.youtube.com/watch?v=NkcBbY7q3gw
18. https://www.youtube.com/watch?v=B0WehsRnJPA
19. https://www.youtube.com/watch?v=IjiaRgynfdk
20. http://www.artsjournal.com/sandow/2014/02/from-lara-downes-billie-holiday-and-me.html
21. http://21cm.org/magazine/why-practice/2015/08/11/david-taylor-embracing-the-joy-of-the-struggle/
22. Listen to the full interview with David Cutler here: http://21cm.org/21cm-u/learning/book-club/2016/02/04/the-savvy-music-teacher/

CHAPTER 2

1. http://21cm.org/artist/project-trio/
2. http://21cm.org/artist/fifth-house-ensemble/
3. http://21cm.org/21cm-u/laboratory/audience-development/2015/02/19/the-harvest-concert/
4. http://21cm.org/artist/baladino/
5. http://21cm.org/artist/decoda/
6. https://www.washingtonpost.com/opinions/with-a-song-in-prisoners-hearts/2015/04/24/ca20118e-eabd-11e4-9767-6276fc9b0ada_story.html
7. http://21cm.org/magazine/artist-features/2016/06/09/a-conversation-with-decoda-and-red-tail-ring/
8. http://21cm.org/magazine/artist-features/2017/01/04/a-conversation-with-brad-wells/
9. http://21cm.org/artist/caroline-shaw/
10. Originally published at http://21cm.org/pop-picks/2015/11/01/musicambia/
11. https://www.ted.com/talks/simon_sinek_how_great_leaders_inspire_action

CHAPTER 3

1. http://21cm.org/author/sarah-robinson/
2. http://21cm.org/magazine/artist-features/2016/11/10/how-i-stopped-asking-permission-to-have-a-career-in-music-a-talk21-with-sarah-robinson/
3. Originally published at http://21cm.org/magazine/sounding-board/2016/10/06/harnessing-your-superpowers/
4. http://21cm.org/magazine/sounding-board/2016/10/06/harnessing-your-superpowers/
5. Originally published at http://21cm.org/magazine/sounding-board/2015/07/06/a-composers-take-on-building-a-festival/

CHAPTER 4

1. http://21cm.org/magazine/sounding-board/2016/02/05/the-art-and-science-of-it/
2. http://21cm.org/21cm-u/learning/book-club/2016/11/10/the-minds-ear/
3. http://www.gugak.go.kr/site/homepage/menu/viewMenu?menuid=002001004004
4. http://21cm.org/artist/fifth-house-ensemble/
5. Mihaly Csikszentmihalyi, *Creativity: Flow and the Psychology of Discovery and Invention* (New York: HarperCollins, 1996).
6. http://21cm.org/magazine/why-practice/2015/08/11/david-taylor-embracing-the-joy-of-the-struggle/
7. https://www.youtube.com/watch?v=Lo18F5ObPng

8. https://www.youtube.com/watch?v=qWG2dsXV5HI
9. https://www.ted.com/talks/mihaly_csikszentmihalyi_on_flow
10. Originally published at http://21cm.org/magazine/sounding-board/2016/10/06/moonlight-and-chocolate-finding-inspiration/

CHAPTER 5

1. http://21cm.org/magazine/sounding-board/2015/05/10/silkroad-develops-global-musicians/
2. https://www.youtube.com/watch?v=mifJWgPVHS0 (Part 1), https://www.youtube.com/watch?v=OC4cLEr6ads (Part 2), https://www.youtube.com/watch?v=jGAxAq5nPtc (Part 3), and https://www.youtube.com/watch?v=autav_gz0uo&t=11s (Part 4)

CHAPTER 6

1. https://www.youtube.com/watch?v=vJG698U2Mvo
2. Stacey Goodman, "Fuel Creativity in the Classroom with Divergent Thinking," *Edutopia: George Lucas Educational Foundation*, August 12, 2015, retrieved from https://www.edutopia.org/blog/fueling-creativity-through-divergent-thinking-classroom-stacey-goodman.
3. https://www.youtube.com/watch?v=VuT1Wr6J4R0

CHAPTER 7

1. http://21cm.org/pop-picks/2017/01/04/ritz-chamber-players/
2. http://21cm.org/pop-picks/2017/01/04/project-step/
3. http://21cm.org/pop-picks/2017/01/04/sphinx-organization/
4. http://21cm.org/magazine/artist-features/2016/08/04/bridging-the-gap-a-look-at-the-silk-road-projects-global-musician-workshop/
5. Originally published at http://21cm.org/magazine/sounding-board/2017/01/04/collaborating-across-diverse-communities/

CHAPTER 8

1. Jerry Jao, "Optimism vs. Realism: Which Breeds More Entrepreneurial Success?" *Forbes*, December 4, 2013, retrieved from https://www.forbes.com/sites/jerryjao/2013/12/04/optimism-vs-realism-which-breeds-more-entrepreneurial-success/#4f5f45555126.

2. Peter Elbow, "The Believing Game: Methodological Believing," *English Department Faculty Publication Series* 5, University of Massachusetts–Amherst (January 2008), retrieved from http://scholarworks.umass.edu/eng_faculty_pubs/5.
3. http://21cm.org/pop-picks/2016/10/06/musicians-for-human-rights/
4. http://21cm.org/pop-picks/2016/04/07/vijay-gupta/
5. http://21cm.org/pop-picks/2016/02/05/david-wish/
6. For the purposes of this chapter, I use *product* to refer to both physical objects and services. A product is simply something for which there is a market and refers equally to mass-produced, utilitarian things, unique works of artistic expression, and everything in between.

CHAPTER 9

1. Originated by Albert S. Humphrey in the 1960s, SWOT analysis continues to be used widely today. Mindtools.com is an excellent resource for learning more about SWOT and other career development tools, including free worksheets. Templates used in this chapter are based on those from http://www.mindtools.com/pages/article/newTMC_05.htm.
2. http://21cm.org/magazine/sounding-board/2016/05/05/an-indie-rocker-shows-her-classical-roots/
3. George T. Doran, "There's a S.M.A.R.T. Way to Write Management's Goals and Objectives," *Management Review* 70, no. 11 (1981): 35–36, retrieved from http://community.mis.temple.edu/mis0855002fall2015/files/2015/10/S.M.A.R.T-Way-Management-Review.pdf.

CHAPTER 10

1. Paul Brest, "The Power of Theories of Change," *Stanford Social Innovation Review* Spring 2010, 47–51, retrieved from https://worldfellows.yale.edu/sites/default/files/files/Power%20of%20Theories%20of%20Change.pdf
2. http://21cm.org/magazine/state-of-the-art-form/2016/07/07/to-re-invent-the-audience-experience-become-a-beginner-again/
3. http://21cm.org/21cm-u/learning/in-the-field/2016/04/07/the-art-of-the-story-an-artist-video-case-study/

CHAPTER 11

1. http://grantspace.org/tools/knowledge-base/funding-research/definitions-and-clarification/glossaries
2. Originally published at http://21cm.org/magazine/state-of-the-art-form/2016/03/10/smart-crowdfunding/
3. Gerry Veenstra. "Class Position and Musical Tastes: A Sing-Off between the Cultural Omnivorism and Bourdieusian Homology Frameworks," *Canadian Review of Sociology* 52, no. 2 (2015): 134–59.

EPILOGUE

1. Sara Lawrence-Lightfoot, *The Third Chapter: Passion, Risk, and Adventure in the 25 Years after 50* (New York: Farrar, Straus and Giroux, 2009).
2. http://21cm.org/magazine/artist-features/2017/03/09/bringing-bach-to-the-people/
3. http://21cm.org/magazine/artist-features/2017/06/01/embracing-difference-the-mission-that-drives-laurie-rubin/
4. http://21cm.org/magazine/sounding-board/2017/07/05/does-music-make-you-a-better-person/

INDEX

Abbing, Hans, 146
Acknowledgment letter, 216–217
Action steps
   Action Plan How-To, 159–160
   Evaluation How-To, 169–170
   Follow-up How-To, 165–166
   planning for, 111–112
   SWOT analysis and, 102–106
Adichie, Chimamanda Ngozi, 83
Adolphe, Bruce, 45, 52–55
Adventure (Laforet), *19,* 20
Aha! moment, 49
Amazon, 94
Anderson, Greg, 6, *6*
Art entrepreneurship
   about, 1–5
   art defined, 10–11
   business of art, 85–86, 98–100
   careers in art, xv, 14–15
   importance of art, 147, 148–149
   time for creativity, 49
   See also 21CM
"The Art of the Story" (Nonemaker), 124
Arts Advocacy story, 127
"The Art (+ Science) of 'It'", 44
"The ask," 143
   See also Fundraising
"As Slow as Possible" organ playing (Cage), 18, *18*
Audiences
   developing, 71
   identifying, 121

   needs of, 122
   sorting, 121–122
Awakening Your Brain (Rosenfeld), 35

Bach in the Subways, 149
Backers of projects. *See* Donors; Partnerships; Sponsors
Barker, Alain, 70–71
Bates, Mason, *8,* 8–9, 24–25
Baumgardner, Astrid, 112–113
BDT Stage, 90, 91–92
Beckman, Gary, 145–146
Becoming a Beginner Again argument, 122
Believing game, 12, 86–88
Benchmarking, 72
Bias, 75–76
   See also Diversity and inclusion
Blame game, 59–60
Blind auditions, 75–76
Block, Mike, 25, 79, 80
Blogs, 188–189
BMC. *See* Business Model Canvas (BMC)
Bob's Tale
   analyzing, 121–122
   hero in, 121
   as parable storytelling, 126
   reasoning behind, 128
   story of, 116–119
Brainstorming, 58–59, 78, 109–110
Breaking Bad example, 120–121
Brest, Paul, 120

Broad-based volunteer recruitment, 163
Budgets
    creating, 135–136
    modifying, 143
    Operating Budget How-To, 157–158
    people shaping, 134–135
    See also Crowdfunding; Fundraising; Income and expenses
Budweiser advertisement, 127
Business Model Canvas (BMC)
    Channels, 94, 121
    communication strategies using, 129
    Customers, 93–94, 121–122
    Financial Sector, 96
    getting started with, 92–93
    interconnections within, 97–98
    Operations sector, 95–96
    purpose of, 88
    See also Value Proposition (VP)
Business of artists
    critical optimism and, 85–86
    entrepreneurship, 1–5
    project management, 98–100
    See also Careers

Cage, John, 18, *18,* 20
Calendars, 130
Careers
    creating, 14
    opportunities in, xv, 14–15
Carlsbad Music Festival, 37–42, *39, 40*
Case for Support How-To, 196–197
Chabris, Christopher, 68
Change
    challenges of, 150
    as constant, 97–98
    leadership and, 26, 86–88
    Theory of Change, 120
Channels of BMC, 94, 121
Chicago Symphony (CSO), 13
Chocolate cake as inspiration, 53
Churchill, Winston, 86

Clague, Mark, 51–52
Collaboration
    about, 1–5
    benefits, 12
    Collaborative Leadership Model, 112–113
    creating a career using, 14
    diversity and inclusion for, 79–84
    in evaluation of insights, 49–50
    of jazz artists, 63–64
    See also Community; Red Tail Ring; Relationships
Collage (game), 68
Communication strategies
    about, 37, 131
    calendars, 125–126
    Communications To-Do List, 130
    components of, 126
    Evaluation How-To, 169–170
    Final Report How-To, 171–172
    Follow-up How-To, 165–166
    planning exercise for Yodelayheehoo! Festival, 128–130
    Press Release How-To, 173–175
    Video Profile How-To, 186–187
    Website/Blog How-To, 188–189
Community
    about, 37
    Carlsbad Music Festival as, 37–42, *39, 40*
    diversity and inclusion in, 80–84
    engagement with, 71, 77–78
    See also Collaboration; Relationships
Concentric circle volunteer recruitment, 163
Consumption of music, 145–146
Content of message, 119–121
Controlled media, 123, 130
Convergent thinking, 69–70
Costs of projects. *See* Budgets; Income and expenses
Creativity
    about, 1–5

INDEX • 227

Adolphe on, 45, 52–55
creating a career using, 14
defining, 43–44, 45–47
fostering, 44
framework for, 48–51
preparation for, 48–49
as purposeful, 12
risk-taking in, 51–52
time for, 49, 139
See also Ideas
Creativity (Csikszentmihalyi), 48–51
Credible narrators, 121
Critical optimism, 85–86
Critical thinking, 87
Crowdfunding
about, 138–140
Case for Support How-To, 196–197
Crowdfunding How-To, 198
Duchen on, 140–141
Intimate Opera and, 145
tips on, 142–143
Visconti on, 142–143
Crowdsourcing, 58–59, 60
Csikszentmihalyi, Mihaly, 48–51
CSO (Chicago Symphony), 13
Curiosity
about, 1–5
benefits of, 12, 29
Cage as example of, 18, *18,* 20
careers and, 14
courage needed with, 25
creativity beginning with, 48
Degas on, 17
Laforet as example of, *19,* 19–20
leadership and, 26
locating your genius and, 28
making time for, 24–25
today's revolutionaries and, 20–23
"Why" question and, 26–27
wonder, 36
Curtis Institute, 61–62
Customer relationships, 94

Customer Sector, 93–94
Customer Segments, 121–122
Cutler, David, 14, 49, 98–100

Das, Sandeep, 24–25, 59
Data
Data/Infographic How-To, 180–181
Evaluation How-To, 169–170
information gathering, 72
Prezi How-To, 182–183
Social Media Campaign How-To, 184–185
Deadlines
communication calendar, 125–126
creativity needing time, 49, 139
fundraising campaign timeline, 139
in project management, 99
Decision-making and SMART goals, 106–111
Decoda ensemble, 3, 21–23, 27
DefCult, 115–122, 119, 120
Defining process of project management, 99
Degas, Edgar, 17
Delivery system in storytelling, 121, 126
DePauw University School of Music, 133
Depression story, 127
Design process, 99
Digital Appeal How-To, 199–200
Digital recording studio idea, 66–67
Direct Mail How-To, 201–202
Divergent thinking, 67–69
Diversity and inclusion
collaboration with, 79–84
inclusive teams, 76–77
introspective individuals, 76
music and, 78–79
Rabideau on, 73–77
Sheridan-Rabideau on, 77
"Doing" stage of project management, 99–100

Donors
    about, 137–138
    Case for Support How-To, 196–197
    Event Planning How-To, 161–162
    incentives for, 139, 140–141, 142
    recognition of, 138, 210–211
    Thanking Donors How-To, 216–217
    See also Fundraising
Doser, James, 10–11
Doubting game, 86–88
Downes, Lara, 9, 9
Drapkin, Michael, 1–2
Dream process, 98–99
Duchen, Jessica, 140–141
Dworkin, Aaron, 80–84

Einstein's Light (film), 53–54
Elaboration of insights, 50–51
Elashvili, Anna, 27
Elbow, Peter, 12, 87
Elevator pitches
    about, 126, 136, 137, 186
    Elevator Pitch How-To, 176–177
Email appeals, 199–200
Emotional memory, 52–55
Empathy research, 122
ENO (English National Opera) story, 128
Ensemble Concert, 148
Entrepreneurship, 1–5
Entrepreneurship Center for Music at the University of Colorado-Bolder, 88
Environmental scans
    about, 71–72
    Environmental Scan How-To, 194–195
Evaluation How-To, 169–170
Evaluation of insights, 49–50
Event Planning How-To, 161–162
Exams, truth about, 30–32
Exercises for inspiration, 54–55
Expenses. See Budgets; Fundraising; Income and expenses

External factors
    in storytelling, 126
    in SWOT analysis, 102, 105–106

Failure, 33–35, 51–52, 59–60
Farnsworth, John, 63–64
Fifth House Ensemble, 21, 47, 142–143
Final Report How-To, 171–172
Financial Sector of Business Model Canvas, 96
Flow theory, 51
Flyers, 178–179
Follow-up How-To, 165–166
Foreign traditions, 44
Foundation Center's GrantSpace, 137
4'33" (Cage), 18
Frames for creative ideas, 69–70
Frederickson, Tom, 128
Fundraising
    backers' interests, 143
    Case for Support How-To, 196–197
    consumption of music and, 145–146
    Digital Appeal How-To, 199–200
    Direct Mail How-To, 201–202
    Final Report How-To, 171–172
    Fundraising Goal How-To, 192–193
    Individual Prospect Research How-To, 205–206
    Institutional Prospect Research How-To, 207–208
    Intimate Opera example, 144–145
    Linville on, 133–139
    Matching Gifts How-To, 209
    Peer-to-Peer Fundraising How-To, 203–204
    quiet phase of, 139
    Return on Investment How-To, 214–215
    See also Budgets; Crowdfunding; Donors; Grants; Sponsors; Volunteers
Future Doors project, 28

Gamin, 47
Genius, 28
Ghost Variations (Duchen), 140–141
Gikow, Louise, 53
Gladwell, Malcolm, 48
Global Musician Workshop, 25, 79, 80
Goals
    Fundraising Goal How-To, 192–193
    Goals and Objectives How-To, 153–154
    SMART goals, 106–111
Goodman, Stacey, 68
Goodyear, Stewart, 7, *7*
Grants
    about, 66, 136–137, 145
    Case for Support How-To, 196–197
    feedback on, 137
    Final Report How-To, 171–172
    Grant Stewardship How-To, 210–211
    Grant Writing How-To, 212–213
    Institutional Prospect Research How-To, 207–208
Green, Judson, xvi
Guerrilla marketing techniques, 178–179
Gupta, Vijay, 87–88

Harding, Tayloe, 25–26
Henderson, Dale, 149
Hero Declaration
    about, 120
    crafting, 129–130
    examples, 120, 126
    mode as delivery technique, 123–124
    purpose of, 131
Hero stories, 120–121, 126–128
Hewlett Foundation, 120
Hinckley, Elizabeth, 44, 58, 115–122

ICadenza, 35–37
Ideas
    driving stories, 13
    imagination as superpower, 36
    incubation of, 49
    inspiration, 52–55, 148
    measuring impact of, 69–70
    preparation for creativity, 48–49
    skill sets for, 13
    See also Creativity
Impact Reputation story, 128
Implicit bias, 75–76
Incarcerated individuals, 3, 21, 27
Inchvesting exercise, 109–110
Inclusive team, 76–77
    See also Diversity and inclusion
Income and expenses
    expenses, 134–136, 143
    Financial Sector of BMC, 96
    Fundraising Goal How-To, 192–193
    goals, 107–108
    Income/Expense How-To, 167–168
    streams of income, 96
    See also Budgets; Fundraising
Incubation of ideas, 49
Individual artists, 90–91, 92
Individual Prospect Research How-To, 205–206
Information gathering. *See* Data
Innovation, 47
In-person media, 124
Insights, 49–51
Inspiration, 52–55, 148
    See also Creativity; Ideas
Institutional Prospect Research How-To, 207–208
Interests of audiences, 122
Internal factors in SWOT analysis, 102, 104–105
Internet research, 72
Interpretation of music style, 71
Intimate Opera campaign, 134–135, 139, 144–145
Introspective individuals, 76
"Invisible gorilla" test, 68
Isolation, 57

Jacobs, Evelyn, 128
Jao, Jerry, 86
Javian, Mary, 61–62
Jazz collaborations, 63–64
Job descriptions, 155
Jobs, Steve, 58

Kennett, Deanna, 148
Key activities of venture, 95–96
Kickstarter campaigns, 142–143
Kuuskoski, Jonathan, 101–106

Laforet, Vincent, *19*, 19–20
Lake Powell Aerial 02 (Laforet), *19*
LA Master Chorale, 126–127
Launch press release, 130
Lawrence-Lightfoot, Sara, 147
Leadership
    advice on, 150
    being the boss, 77
    change and, 26, 86–88
    Collaborative Leadership Model, 112–113
    Henderson on, 149
    Kennett on, 148
    Lawrence-Lightfoot on, 147
    Rubin on, 149
    understanding Art forms, 146
Life is Good example, 60–61
Linville, Steven, 133–139
Little Kids Rock, 88
"Live from Smoke" (radio show), 63–64
Live performances, 71

Ma, Yo-Yo, 4–5, 24–25, 79
Mail appeals
    Digital Appeal How-To, 199–200
    Direct Mail How-To, 201–202
Matching Gifts How-To, 209
Mayer, John, 86
McBane, Matt, 37–42, *39, 40*, 128
McCoy, Mark, 58

McGuckin Hardware statement, 89–90, 92
Media
    as mouthpiece, 124
    press releases and, 130
    for storytelling, 126–128
    uncontrolled, 124, 130
    See also Social media
Messages, 119–121
Milne, A. A., 85–86
The Mind's Ear (Adolphe), 45
Mindsets, 12
Mission, xv–xvi, 91
Modes
    as delivery technique for Hero's Declaration, 123–124
    for storytelling, 126–128
Moonlight, 52–55
Musicambia, 3, 27
Musicians for Human Rights, 87
Muslim-Focused Racism story, 127

National Association of Schools of Music (NASM), 24
National Gugak Center, 47
Needs of audiences, 122
Need statements, 136
Networking. *See* Collaboration; Relationships
Nonemaker, Elizabeth, 124
Nytch, Jeff, 88–98

Objectives. *See* Goals; SMART goals
"O Me! O Life!" (poem), 62
Operating Budget How-To, 157–158
Operations sector, 95–96
Opportunities, 71–72, 102, 105
Optimism, 12, 36, 85–86
Opus Orange, *40*
Organ^2/ASLSP (Cage), 18
Organization, budgeting by, 157
Organizational Chart How-To, 155–156

Osterwalder, Alexander, 88
Outliers (Gladwell), 48
Out-of-the-box thinking, 58

Parable storytelling, 116–119
Pareidolia (game), 68
Partnerships, 95–96, 138, 144
Peer-to-Peer Fundraising How-To, 203–204
Perlman, Itzhak, 53
Persistence, 12
  See also Tenacity
Pessimism, 85
Piano teaching studio example, 94–95
Pittsburgh New Music Ensemble (PNME), 91
Planning process
  environmental scans, 71–72, 194–195
  as preparation for creativity, 48–49
  for Yodelayheehoo! Festival, 128–130
Play On, Philly!, 150
PNME (Pittsburgh New Music Ensemble), 91
Pop-Up Philly project, 28
Postcard/Flyer How-To, 178–179
Premo, Evan, 22–23
Premo, Laurel, 22–23
Press releases
  for launches, 130
  Press Release How-To, 173–175
Prezi How-To, 182–183
Print advertisements, 139
Prison system, 3, 21, 27
Problem-solving strategies
  Barker on, 70–71
  convergent thinking, 69–70
  divergent thinking, 67–69
  environmental scans, 71–72, 194–195
  problem-finding and, 65–67
  situational awareness, 70–71
Pro/con analysis, 102
Project management, 98–100

Project STEP (String Training Education Program), 78
PROJECT Trio, 20, 50
Promotional videos, 140
Purposeful creativity, 12

Quiet phase of fundraising campaigns, 139

Rabideau, Laura Hlavacek, 73–77
Rabideau, Mark, 13–14, 22–23, 46
  See also 21CM
Readymade (game), 68
Rebuilding/Crisis story, 128
Recognition of donors, 138
Red Tail Ring, 22–23
Relationships
  connections through, 61–62, 97
  with customers in BMC, 94
  fundraising and, 139
  partnerships as, 95–96
  sorting audiences by, 122
  See also Collaboration; Community; Donors; Team building
Relevance of goals, 110
  See also SMART goals
Research stage, 96
Resources, 95–96
Retention Science, 86
Return on investment (ROI)
  about, 135–136
  Return on Investment How-To, 214–215
Revenue
  about, 136
  budgeting by, 157
  grants, 136–137
  partnerships, 138
  sponsors, 138
  See also Budgets; Fundraising
Reveur, Ophelia (example), 103–106, 107–111

Risks, 51–52
Ritz Chamber Players, 78
Robinson, Sarah, 33–35
Roe, Elizabeth, 6, *6*
ROI. *See* Return on investment (ROI)
Roomful of Teeth ensemble, 24
Rosenfeld, Jennifer, 35–37
Ross, James, *7*, 7–8
Rubin, Laurie, 149

Sandow, Greg, 5–9
Sarabande exercises, 54–55
The Savvy Musician (Cutler), 98
SCHEMES mnemonic, 160
Schram, Nathan, 3, 4, 27
Schumann Violin Concerto, 140
Selective Attention Test (YouTube video), 68
Seymour, Peter, 4, 20–21, 50
Shark Tank, 126
Shaw, Caroline, 24
Sheridan-Rabideau, Mary Pauline, 77
Short-term goals, 110
Silk Road Ensemble, 24–25, 59, 79–80
Simons, Daniel, 68
Sinek, Simon, 26–27, 119
Situational awareness, 70–71
Skill sets, 12, 13
SMART goals
  about, 106–111, 153–154
  Action Plan How-To, 159–160
Snoza, Melissa, 3, 47
Social media
  about, 139, 141
  Digital Appeal How-To, 199–200
  Social Media Campaign How-To, 184–185
Social return on investment (SROI)
  about, 135–136
  Return on Investment How-To, 214–215
Son de San Diego, *39*

Sphinx Organization, 78
Sponsors
  about, 138, 144
  Case for Support How-To, 196–197
  Event Planning How-To, 161–162
  Sponsorship How-To, 190–191
  See also Budgets; Fundraising
SROI. *See* Social return on investment (SROI)
Start with Why (Sinek), 26–27, 119
Stone, Jayme, 4
Story arc, 121
Storytelling
  analysis of parable, 119–122
  Bob's Tale, 116–119
  external influences, 125
  hero stories, 120–121, 126–128
  speaking to needs, 122
  See also Hero Declaration
Street Symphony, 87–88
Strength of heroes, 121
Strengths in SWOT analysis, 102, 104
Stretches for creativity, 48–49
Success definitions, 35
Superpowers, 35–37
Supporters. *See* Audiences; Donors; Fundraising; Partnerships; Sponsors; Volunteers
SurveyMonkey, 169–170
SWOT analysis, 102–106
Szent-Györgyi, Albert, 28

Tangibility of hero stories, 121
Tapia, André, 74
Targeted volunteer recruitment, 163
Taylor, David, 14, 48
Team building
  blame game and, 59–60
  brainstorming, 58–59
  Collaborative Leadership Model, 112–113
  importance of, 57

INDEX

Javian on, 61–62
Life is Good example, 60–61
relationships and, 61–62
spheres of influence and, 62–64
See also Collaboration
Tenacity
   benefits of, 42
   careers needing, 14
   Carlsbad Music Festival example, 37–42, *39, 40*
   as superpower, 35–37
   truth about tests and, 30–32
10,000 Hours rule, 48
Tests, truth about, 30–32
"Thank yous"
   Follow-up How-To, 165–166
   letters to donors, 138
   Thanking Donors How-To, 216–217
Theory of Change, 120
"They Said I Wasn't Really Black" (poem), 82–83
Thompson, Stanford L., 33–35, 150
Threats in SWOT analysis, 102, 106
Timelines. *See* Deadlines
Twain, Mark, 59
21CM
   artist documentary tips, 124
   Book Club, 45
   creation of, 115
   crowdfunding perspectives, 140–143
   differences in approach of, xvi
   POP Picks, 78
   Sounding Board Series, 149
   superpower assessments, 37
   traveling to Global Musician Workshop, 80
   21CMposium, 34–35, 47
   vision, 91
   website, 20
21st century musician definitions, 5–9
21st-Century Musician Initiative, 133

Uncontrolled media, 124, 130
Unit draft budgeting method, 157

Value Proposition (VP)
   colleagues' input on, 92–93
   crafting, 89–93
   customer sector and, 93–94
   mistakes arising from, 119
   operations sector and, 95–96
Veenstra, Gerry, 146
Video game concert, 142–143
Video Profile How-To, 186–187
Village Music Walk, 39–41
Visconti, Dan, 142–143
Vision, xv–xvi, 91
Volunteers
   about, 28–29
   Event Planning How-To, 161–162
   Volunteer Recruitment How-To, 163–164
   See also Donors; Fundraising
VP. *See* Value Proposition (VP)
Vulnerability of heroes, 121

Weaknesses in SWOT analysis, 102, 105
Website/Blog How-To, 188–189
Whigham, Jiggs, 58
Whitman, Walt, 62
"Why" question, 26–27
Wikipedia definitions, 46
William and Flora Hewlett Foundation, 120
Wish, David, 88
Wonder, 36
   See also Curiosity
Wu Man, 39, *39*

Yodelayheehoo! Festival, 128–130
YouTube video on selective attention, 68

Zero-based budgeting, 157

ABOUT THE AUTHOR

Dr. Mark Rabideau is a cultural entrepreneur whose focus is re-imagining how we must prepare musicians to thrive within today's shifting marketplace and cultural landscape.

Mark's own entrepreneurial spirit has generated projects ranging from producing and hosting *Live from Smoke* (a radio show from NYC's upper-westside), founding and serving as Executive and Artistic Director for *Artists Now* (a non-profit arts organization), producing *Worlds End* (an original work with the American Repertory Ballet), and publishing and editing *21CM.org*, a monthly journal devoted to the future of music. He is the author of *The 21CM Introduction to Music Entrepreneurship*, a hybrid-flipped classroom online text for preparing the next generation of music entrepreneurs.

Mark regards his bravest moments as a performer as those spent playing with "the world's most dangerous orchestra" (the Juárez Symphony Orchestra in Juárez, Mexico); his most cherished moments happened while commissioning, performing, and recording new chamber music with his quartet, CTQ.

Mark is the Director of the 21st Century Musician Initiative. His only hobby is collecting curious, creative people to add to his life. Mark has a wife he adores and three beautifully talented children.